T0347304

Patent Policy

Intellectual property rights have become increasingly important for our modern economies in recent years. Although the entire patent system has a profound effect on the decision of firms of whether to conduct research and at which volume, patent law is the heart of the entire patent system. Therefore, this book focusses on the economic effects of certain provisions in patent law by using economic models dedicated to patent policy.

The first part of the book presents a brief overview over the history of patent systems and introduces the main components of modern patent systems. A short introduction of the principal provisions of United States patent law constitutes the centre of the subsequent analysis as it serves as a link between law and economics. The second part presents core economic models for central provisions, collecting the most fundamental results in a national framework in the field of literature. Part three is concerned with selected provisions of patent law in an international framework. It provides valuable insights into the situation of developing countries which are the chief recipients of technology transfers.

Patent Policy will be of interest to researchers interested in the field of modelling patent policy. It can be also used as supplementary text in courses in industrial organization, innovation economics, and law and economics.

Pia Weiss is currently a Lecturer in Industrial Economics at the Nottingham University Business School, Nottingham, UK.

The Economics of Legal Relationships

Sponsored by Michigan State University College of Law

Statement of scope

The Economics of Legal Relationships is a book series dedicated to publishing original scholarly contributions that systematically analyze legal-economic issues. As with other book series, each one can take a variety of forms:

- Each book may be comprised of a collection of original articles devoted to a single theme, edited by a guest volume editor.
- A book may be a collection of refereed articles derived from the Series Editor's "call for papers" on a particular legal-economic topic.
- An individual (or coauthors) may wish to author an entire book.

Each book is published in hardback, approximately 250–300 pages in length and is dedicated to:

- Formulate and/or critique alternative theories of law and economics – including – the new law and economics, the economics of property rights, institutionalist law and economics, neoinstitutionalist economics, public choice theory, social norms and law and economics.
- Analyze a variety of public policy issues related to the interface between judicial decisions and/or statutory law and the economy.
- Explore the economic impact of political and legal changes brought on by new technologies and/or environmental concerns.
- Examine the broad array of legal/economic issues surrounding the deregulation – reregulation phenomena.
- Analyze the systematic effects of legal change on incentives and economic performance.

Call for authors/volume editors/topics

An individual who is interested in either authoring an entire volume or editing a future volume of **The Economics of Legal Relationships** should submit a 3–5 page prospectus to either series editor. Each prospectus must include: (1) the prospective title of the volume; (2) a brief description of the organizing theme of the volume whether single-authored or edited; (3) an identification of the line of literature from which the proposed topic emanates, and (4) either a table of contents or, if edited, a list of potential contributors along with tentative titles of their contributions. Please note that the series editors only accept individual manuscripts for publication consideration in response to a specific "Call for Papers."

Send the prospectus directly to a series editor:

Professor Nicholas Mercuro
321 Michigan State University College of Law
East Lansing, MI 48824
PHONE: (517) 432-6978
FAX: (517) 432-6801
e-mail: mercuro@law.msu.edu

Professor Michael D. Kaplowitz
Michigan State University
Department of Community, Agriculture,
Recreation and Resource Studies
East Lansing, MI 48824
PHONE: (517) 355-0101
e-mail: kaplowit@msu.edu

The Economics of Legal Relationships
Edited by Nicholas Mercuro and Michael D. Kaplowitz, Michigan State University

Compensation for Regulatory Takings
Thomas J. Miceli and Kathleen Segerson

Dispute Resolution
Bridging the settlement gap
Edited by David A. Anderson

The Law and Economics of Development
Edited by Edgardo Buscaglia, William Ratliff and Robert Cooter

Fundamental Interrelationships Between Government and Property
Edited by Nicholas Mercuro and Warren J. Samuels

Property Rights, Economics, and the Environment
Edited by Michael Kaplowitz

Law and Economics in Civil Law Countries
Edited by Thierry Kirat and Bruno Deffains

* The first three volumes listed above are published by and available from Elsevier

Patent Policy

Legal–economic effects in a national
and international framework

Pia Weiss

LONDON AND NEW YORK

First published 2010
by Routledge
2 Park Square, Milton Park, Abingdon, Oxon, OX14 4RN

Simultaneously published in the USA and Canada
by Routledge
711 Third Avenue, New York, NY 10017, USA

Routledge is an imprint of the Taylor & Francis Group, an informa business

Typeset in Times New Roman by Glyph International Ltd.

British Library Cataloguing in Publication Data
A catalogue record for this book is available from the British Library

Library of Congress Cataloging in Publication Data
Weiss, Pia, 1969–
Patent policy : legal-economic effects in a national and international framework / Pia Weiss.
    p. cm.
Includes bibliographical references and index.
1. Patent laws and legislation–Economic aspects. 2. Technological innovations. 3. Technology transfer. I. Title.
K1505.W45 2010
346.04'86–dc22

                                                          2009042245

ISBN13: 978-0-415-48105-2 (hbk)
ISBN13: 978-0-203-85318-4 (ebk)

To my father

Contents

Figures

Tables

Abbreviations

$[a,b]$	closed interval
(a,b)	open interval
$\{a,b\}$	set
$\mathbb{R}_+$	set of positive real numbers
$\mathbb{R}_0$	set of non-negative real numbers
a_i^l	aggregated research effort of $n_i - 1$ firms
α	appropriability measure
b	patent breadth
β	efficiency parameter
$c(\cdot)$	production cost function
$C(\cdot)$	research cost function
d	index for the Markov-state
$d(\cdot)$	instantaneous deadweight loss
δ	deadweight loss relative to monopoly profits
E	expectation operator
$F[u_k]$	cumulative distribution function for the improvement size of an invention
$f[u_k]$	corresponding density function to $F[u_k]$
g_i	particular path of history until i
G_i	set of histories that lead to g_i at i
h	research effort
H_i	industry research effort
$\mathfrak{h}$	hazard rate for firms
i, l	country index
j	firm index
k	patent race index
$k(t)$	renewal fees
K	patent fees
λ_i	innovation efficiency of country i firms
$\bar{\lambda}_i$	some cut-off level of the innovation efficiency of country i firms
n_i	number of firms in country i
p	price
$\pi_{ji}(z)$	general, state-dependent instantaneous (flow) profit
π^c	instantaneous (flow) profit under competition

π^m	instantaneous (flow) profit for a monopoly
ψ	maximum of the non-obviouness standards
$Q(\cdot)$	demand function
q_i	market demand; market share
r	exogenous interest rate
$r(\cdot)$	best response function
$R(\cdot)$	aggregated best response function
ρ	minimum of the non-obviousness standards
s	non-obviousness standard
σ	consumers' surplus relative to monopoly profits
T	patent term
θ	probability that a given inventions satisfies the non-obviousness standard
u_k	improvement size of the kth invention upon the preceding one
U_k	cumulated quality
$V_{ji}(z)$	general, state-dependent value function
$w(z)$	instantaneous welfare
$\mathfrak{w}$	hazard rate for the society
$W_i(z)$	general, state-dependent welfare function
x	disutility parameter
y	patent scope
$Z[\cdot]$	distribution of the history
z	*state* of a Markov chain
z^C	state challenger of the Markov chain
z^I	state incumbent of the Markov chain

1　General introduction

Patent rights seem to be a policy instrument that provokes great controversy. Proponents claim that, although not perfect in design, patent systems facilitate innovation, stimulate economic growth and therefore raise social welfare. Opponents point out that patent systems create an entry barrier for small innovative firms, are used as an anti-competitive device and bar access to modern technologies for poor countries; thus, patent systems reduce social welfare. Discussions about the advantages and disadvantages have accompanied the entire history of patent systems and will certainly continue.

Over the decades, a vast body of theoretical and empirical literature on patent systems, patent instruments and related issues, such as innovation and licensing, has been accumulated. The focus of the literature has shifted. Formerly, an answer to the *grand question* of whether or not patent systems as a whole should be relied on to foster innovations has been sought. Nowadays, only few scholars study alternative mechanisms to encourage new and (socially) useful inventions. Instead, ways are explored that are likely to improve the effectiveness and the efficiency of *existing* patent systems.

The shift in the principal object of inquiry is not so much a proof of failure to answer the *grand question*; rather, it bears witness to the fact that patent systems have become extremely complex instruments, and that we know surprisingly little about how they work.

A number of policy instruments have been studied, but mostly without reference to an international framework. This is remarkable especially because the import of technology or the role of national patent laws as a trade barrier were important factors in establishing and shaping patent systems. The most recent example is the Agreement of Trade Related Aspects of Intellectual Property (TRIPs Agreement) which creates a minimum standard for the protection of intellectual property with which every member of the World Trade Organization (WTO) has to comply. Some of the developing countries might only have ratified the TRIPs Agreement because they expected it to have a positive effect on their economic development. Although there is empirical evidence for this supposition, there are also studies that cast serious doubt on this hypothesis.

To shed some light on the circumstances under which developing countries may benefit from a certain patent regime is reason enough to examine the effects of patent instruments again. Yet, even for industrialized countries, the exercise may yield new insights as to how the performance of existing patent systems can be improved in an increasingly globalized world economy.

The present work does not attempt to provide an exhaustive treatise of patent instruments and their effects. Innovation activities are one of the most important aspects of economic life. Patent systems aim at increasing welfare by increasing or decreasing the incentives to create innovations. It has been demonstrated that the market structure does affect innovation activities and that a successful invention potentially changes the market structure in a given industry. Consequently, in answering the question of how to design a patent system, related issues such as competition policy and especially prevailing anti-trust regulations should be taken into account. Although certainly interesting and instructive, these aspects are beyond the scope of the present work.

Even if attention is restricted to the instruments of patent systems, the endeavour proves to be too ambitious. The patent system not only consists of the patent law. Some provisions are deliberately formulated in rather general terms so that the patent law becomes a flexible tool that is able to cope with present and future developments. Therefore, the patent office and the courts have considerable discretion. The guidelines of the patent offices or the case law developed by the courts are the result of the attempt to use this discretion in a systematic manner. Social tendencies, such as the anti-trust movement in the 1920s and 1930s in the United States, have certainly influenced patent guidelines and the case law. Again, a thorough investigation into the performance of any patent system has to take these factors into account. Since these *informal* sets of rules and customs are country specific, they have to be neglected when the general mechanisms of certain patent instruments are to be studied.

The present work, then, exclusively focusses on a few provisions and patent instruments that may well be regarded as the core of patent law: the patent requirements, patent length and the scope of a patent. It is demonstrated how changes in these policy instruments affect social welfare. In this way, conclusions on the circumstances under which a certain level or combination of the patent instruments proves to be optimal can be drawn.

The national framework

Patent law is restricted to a nation's territory, so it is natural to commence the examination of the effects of patent policy instruments in a framework of a closed economy. Indeed, most of the existing literature on patent policy relies on a model economy without international relations. The attention to a closed economy is well chosen, especially because the intricacies and the interplay of policy instruments require further study.

Consequently, patent instruments in a national framework constitute a principal part of the present work. Here, the effects of single and combinations of policy instruments can be studied in a richer setting. In addition, the results provide a useful benchmark against which results obtained from an international framework can be evaluated.

The international framework

Although patent law is bounded by a country's border, it may have international consequences. Foreigners may apply for and be granted domestic patents. In case the underlying invention is turned into a marketable product which is produced in or imported into the domestic country, profits flow into the foreign country. Consequently, the design of the national patent system does not only affect domestic but also foreign welfare.

These cross–border profit flows may reach remarkable levels. Within the group of industrialized countries, flows into and out of a given country may have a similar magnitude. In this case, one might argue, using an international framework as the object of inquiry is not really necessary. Even if this argument were to hold true, the situation is completely different for developing countries. Almost by definition, firms in developing countries have only a limited capability of undertaking research and, therefore, of creating patentable inventions. As a consequence, the resulting net profit flows out of a developing country may well reach a level where they have to be considered when the efficiency of the patent system is to be improved.

The structure of the book

The work is divided into three parts. The first provides general information on patent systems. The second is dedicated to effects of patent policy instruments in a closed economy, whereas the third introduces two policy instruments in an open economy.

The first part commences with an overview of the history of patent systems and different attempts to justify intellectual property rights in the form of patents. It is demonstrated that patent systems are an extremely flexible policy tool. Indeed, this characteristic might be crucial in explaining why patents nowadays dominate alternative incentive mechanisms such as prizes or awards. Subsequently, a short introduction into patent law is given.

The second part presents models that focus on one patent instrument each. In particular, patent length, patent scope and breadth as well as the non–obviousness standard are considered. The questions to be answered, however, remain the same: (1) Given that the number of policy instruments is limited, how should the patent system be designed and, (2) which factors affect the optimal design.

Traditionally, policy recommendations for developing countries or specific technology fields or industries are made on the basis of the results obtained in Part II. Usually, the results are adapted so as to take deviating country character-istics into account. However, it seems undisputed that identical economies should use the same design for their patent system. In Part III, the policy instrument of *patentable subject matters* and the non-obvious standard are used to demonstrate that the external effects generated by inventions are strong enough so that national patent laws can correct the associated incentive structure only to a limited degree. As a consequence, even identical countries may benefit from internationally heterogeneous patent systems.

Part I

Patent systems and patent law

2   Introduction

The first part gives a short overview of the general aspects of the patent system. Because the patent system as such is not the prime focus of the book, it is important to understand how the different parts interact in the whole patent system. It is only then that the results derived from theoretical models introduced in the second and the third parts can be meaningfully translated into realistic policy recommendations.

Chapter 3 briefly relates the history of the patent system from two different perspectives. First, a general overview of the evolution of the patent system is given. This not only shows us which events shaped the system. It reveals also its strengths and weaknesses, and it reminds us why certain provisions have been introduced. This knowledge is especially useful when evaluating the relative performance of the patent system. This chapter also pays special attention to international patent treaties that form the background for the third part of this book. Currently, three treaties exist, which are open for every country to join. Each of them have different aims.

Chapter 4 introduces the two most influential schools of thought that have frequently been used to justify the existence of patent systems as well as their design. Economist are trained to adhere to a utilitarian point of view where welfare is the universally accepted standard according to which all changes in the whole economic system are measured. Utilitarianism has exerted less influence in other areas of social sciences where non-utilitarian schools of thought are more influential. Introducing the natural rights theory as a justification for patent systems in addition to the utilitarian patent theories helps to understand a lawyer's perspective towards intellectual property rights.

Chapter 5 aims at familiarizing economists with the main legal issues of patent systems. This is accomplished by tracing an invention through the whole system, i.e. from filing the application to a judge's ruling in infringement or validity cases.

Subsequently, attention is drawn to patent law and its economic effects, the principal subject of the book. The main provisions governing various aspects of a patent are treated as legal policy instruments, i.e. the main channels through which the quality of inventions eligible for patents as well as the strength of the conferred rights can be adjusted. Finally, a demonstration of how these legal policy instruments are modelled in economics is provided.

3 A short history of the patent system

Our modern patent systems are the result of a long evolution. Here, we recount the history of patents very briefly, mainly to demonstrate two important points. Firstly, the patent system has been changing more or less continuously over the centuries. Each of the more marked adjustments reflects responses to advances in known technology fields, the creation of new technology fields or broader developments in society. Patent systems have mastered each of these challenges. They certainly are not working efficiently, but judged from a purely historical point of view, they perform reasonably well.

Secondly, prizes and awards have been used together with privileges to exclusively trade in certain goods and services or under special conditions. Privileges can be seen as the predecessors of patents as a reward system. The patent system prevailed, whereas prizes and awards are rarely used today. The reason for the unequal development of the different policy instruments can be seen in their ability to cope with imperfect information and uncertainty. Clearly, both hypotheses are interrelated and are taken up in the next chapter.

The second part of this section is dedicated to the three most important international treaties that every country may join.[1] For each of them, the circumstances are described which lead to the negotiation table. Subsequently, the main achievements and most salient features of the treaties are explained. This second part of the chapter is important for the third part of this book that models international aspects of patent policy.

3.1 A general overview

The idea of patents is quite old. Early traces reach as far back as to the fourteenth century, and the patent system seems still to be far from optimal as the numerous demands for a patent reform in various countries prove.[2] It is far beyond the scope of this work to attempt to give a comprehensive overview of the history of patents. Instead, only certain aspects are presented that set the background against which the models in the subsequent chapters are developed.

The section starts with the early history of patents and mostly describes developments in England. Subsequently, the history of the patent system in the United States (US) is introduced because the remainder of this work mainly refers to the US system. Finally, the most important international treaties are discussed.

3.1.1 The first patents

Hippodamus of Miletus (498 BC–408 BC) apparently proposed a reward system to foster innovations, including legal innovations. Aristotle (384 BC–322 BC) criticized the idea in his *Politics* (Merges and Duffy 2002: 1). Despite the fact that the concept of a reward system was obviously known in Ancient Greece, the first patents can only be traced to the Renaissance. Given the eighteen hundred years that elapsed until the first patents were granted, it is natural to ask why a patent system did not develop earlier in the history of Western civilization.

The nature of a patent

The answer lies in the very nature of a patent. Firstly, a patent is a document that bestows upon the owner certain rights which 'guarantee' supra-normal profits.[3] Secondly, the patent system and therefore also patents themselves are part of the institutional framework of our societies. As such, it shares the properties and characteristics of all institutions. In particular, an institution never adapts without friction to changes in society. Instead, a certain degree of tension between the altered environment and the old institutions has to be built up before the latter finally adjusts. Owing to the inherent inertia, the reasons for the appearance of the patent system must lie in certain developments in the Middle Ages that eventually turned a well-adjusted institution into an obstacle: the guilds.

3.1.2 The guilds in the Middle Ages

In the Middle Ages, guilds became very strong in Europe. Guilds were an important institution and they performed a number of tasks. They settled disputes among members and often maintained a minimum quality standard. Guilds also protected the common trade interests of their members. Their regulations were quite rigid: setting up one's own business in a particular trade was only possible for members.[4] In addition, an invention could be used by any guild member without compensating the inventor (Bernhardt and Kraßer 1986: 41).

This custom highlights the medieval concept of a class society. Persons are first and foremost members of their class. Their rights and obligations were defined by the position of their class in a social hierarchy. Guilds were an integral part of the medieval social system and its rules and regulations balanced rights and duties for each member.

At the dawn of the Renaissance, the rigid class structures loosened. More and more, persons perceived themselves as individuals and not as members of a particular class. Contrary to the times when guilds were first formed, the advantage for the owner of an invention seemed no longer to be the reasonable price for the protection guilds offered. This shift in perspective was also driven by advances in the legal system. Thus, at the end of the Middle Ages, guilds became an obstacle to innovation.

The antecedent of a patent system

The privilege system was at least originally introduced to counterbalance the increased power of the guilds that now stifled competition and entrepreneurship. Privileges conferred the right to practise the trade for which it was granted by the King or the Sovereign. In England, the first *letter of patent* was signed in 1311 (Bainbridge 2002: 311) (see also Table 3.1).

According to today's standards, only a minority of privileges were issued for true inventions. Often, they were granted for introducing a trade or technology that was well-known and practised abroad into the country (Bernhardt and Kraßer 1986: 41). In contrast to later years, privileges were not only bestowed on citizens, but also on foreigners provided they settled in the country that issued the privilege. Although a person could *apply* for a privilege, a formalized set of rules according to which they were granted did not exist, and a person had no enforceable right to it (Bernhardt and Kraßer 1986: 42).

The Venetian Senate's Act

The *Venetian Senate's 1474 Act* is the first recorded attempt to introduce an administered patent system. All essential features of a modern patent system were present: patent requirements were specified, a definition of the rights that were conferred was given, patent prosecution and patent enforcement as well as remedies to be applied in case of a violation of rights were put forth (Merges and Duffy 2002: 4).

It is subject to debate whether the Venetian Senate's Act is a historical curiosity without any practical importance even at the time or whether it influenced neighbour states and trade partners. Bernhardt and Kraßer (1986: 45) argue that the well-established privilege system remained the principal instrument to protect inventions and new trades in Venice. In contrast, Penrose (1951: 2) points out that nearly a hundred of these *special* privileges have been granted between 1475 and 1500. Merges and Duffy (2002: 4) even suggest that the idea of a systematic legal protection for inventions was spread by Italian craftsmen who travelled across Europe and was finally brought to England.

Developments in England

In the first part of the reign of Queen Elizabeth I, letters of patent were often used as a means to attract foreign artisans and, thus, to import technological knowledge (Merges and Duffy 2002: 5). By the end of her reign, the privilege system had been reduced to a fully fledged monopoly system. Although never strong, the link between a privilege and some aspect of usefulness or novelty of the subject matter was abandoned altogether. Instead, privileges were bestowed on courtiers or other persons that were in the sovereign's favour.[5] Partly, *letters of patent* were granted in order to raise revenues for the Crown, which was perpetually short of money (Bainbridge 2002: 312).

These developments became detrimental for commerce and eventually led to the *1623 Statute of Monopolies* in England. This Statute explicitly outlawed all monopolies except the ones granted for true inventions. The Statute of Monopolies recognized a utility requirement, but a written description was not necessary to obtain a *letter of patent*. However, by the early eighteenth century, the written description requirement was an acknowledge standard (Bainbridge 2002: 312); yet the system remained registry based.

With the beginning of the Industrial Revolution, the notion as to the nature of an inventor's contribution to society that justified monopoly rights changed. Formerly, it was the new manufacture or new art itself, and it was at least in the beginning common practice that the inventor had to demonstrate the operability of his invention. Now, the focus shifted towards new and useful information so that the written description requirement became even more important and was more rigorously applied (Merges and Duffy 2002: 6).

3.1.3 The development in the United States

The British colonies in North America

England brought the concept of a patent system to its American territories.[6] The power to shape laws lay with the colonies that were formed. Consequently, the patent system was not unified across the colonies and conflicts regarding ownership and priority inevitably arose. There were several instances in which a patent was issued for the same invention to different persons in different states. Naturally, the patent owner in one state would sue the patent owner residing in another state when the latter tried to sell his products in the former one's state.

The 1790 Patent Statute

By the time the British colonies declared their independence, the problems of an ununified patent system had become obvious. It is, therefore, not surprising that patent law became federal law in the newly born American nation. According to Article I, Section 8 of the Constitution, the Congress is given the right and the obligation

> to promote the Progress of Science and useful Arts, by securing for limited Times to Authors and Inventors the exclusive Right to their respective Writings and Discoveries.
>
> (Merges and Duffy 2002: 7)

The first patent statute was introduced in 1790, and the first patent was issued in the same year.

Patent rights were granted for new and useful inventions. The novelty requirement stipulated that the device or process in question must not have been used or known in the US at the time of registration (cf *infra*). Similar to the Venetian Senate's Act, a formal patent examination did not take place; inventors registered their inventions at the patent office. Whether or not the invention did fulfil patent requirements at the time of registration was investigated by courts only if someone challenged a patent.

The nineteenth century

In the nineteenth century, two major changes were introduced. The registry-based system was exchanged for an examination system and the non-obviousness criterion was developed.

At the first glance, it is not obvious that starting to determine whether an invention satisfies the patent requirement before granting patent rights was the optimal response to the increase in patent registrations that was driving the Industrial Revolution. Indeed, receiving a patent in a registry-based system requires minimal resources. Patent rights can be enjoyed almost immediately even with a vastly increased number of patent registrations. However, expensive and prolonged lawsuits over infringement cases and allegedly invalid patents increased immensely. When registering, a patentee could never be certain that the patent would be upheld in court when challenged. Worse, the patent could not be contested for years, thereby prolonging the uncertainty. In a registry-based system, a marked raise in registrations will increase uncertainty, make patents in general less valuable and, therefore, undermine the effectiveness of the whole patent system. Thus, introducing a formal patent examination system in 1936 created more certainty for the rightful patentees and reduced the workload of the courts.

The increasing number of patent applications revealed another shortcoming of the early modern patent system. Inventions must be new and useful, but novelty in itself does not measure the degree of technological progress the invention does achieve. As such, the novelty requirement is insufficient to ensure that, amongst the vast number of applications, only *large* inventions were granted patents. Thus, the non-obviousness standard (cf *infra*) was developed requiring inventions to be non-trivial. From the mid-nineteenth century on, the non-obviousness standard was used by courts, but it was only codified in the 1952 revision.

Early twentieth century

In the early twentieth century, the mode of doing research in our modern form was born.[7] Increasingly, an invention was no longer the result of one individual's efforts. Instead, it was the output of a research department established by large firms to protect and secure the market dominance they had previously achieved.[8] They started to build in some cases considerable patent portfolios.

In the 1920s and 1930s, the public reacted to this ongoing development with mistrust and an anti-trust movement formed. It was felt that large companies built those patent portfolios to stifle competition. Patents were no longer seen as society's just reward for generating useful inventions and knowledge.

After World War II

After World War II, the 1952 Patent Act reinforced most of the fundamental principles laid out in the 1790 Patent Statute and its 1836 Revision. However, the anti-patent sentiments that originated in the 1920s and 1930s continued during the 1960s and 1970s.[9] They resulted in a low probability with which patents were upheld in court.

Before the *Court of Appeals for the Federal Circuit* (CAFC) was founded in 1982, patent cases were heard before one of the district courts. Their rulings differed widely, and often parties tried to bring a claim before a district court that had a history of ruling in the parties interest in similar cases.[10] At the same time, it was feared that the US industry was losing competitiveness against Japanese firms. Thus, partly to overcome diverging rulings of the district courts, but mainly to strengthen patents and the patent system as whole, the CAFC was established. Right from the beginning, the CAFC was more inclined to affirm the validity of a patent (Merges *et al.* 2003: 111).

The 1990s

In 1995, the US government signed the treaty on *Trade Related Aspects of Intellectual Property* (TRIPs Agreement) and implemented it immediately. As a consequence, the US patent law had to be amended in some respects to bring it into accordance with the TRIPs regulations (Merges *et al.* 2003: 296). In particular, the patent term is now 20 years from the application date as opposed to 17 years from the issuing date. Patent rights were extended to include the exclusive rights of selling and importing goods associated with a product or process patent. In addition, US patent applications those subject matter is also covered by foreign applications are now published.

3.2 International patent treaties

3.2.1 The Paris Convention

The consequences of different patent systems

In the second half of the nineteenth century, patent laws had been implemented in many countries.[11] They differed widely in almost all respects, and some provisions had a particularly strong impact on international relations as the following two examples show.

Most countries required the patentee to *work* the patent within a certain time, i.e. usually within less than a year. If the subject matter was a process, it must be used after this time. If the patent was granted for a product, production must have started in the issuing country within this time span. In case the patent owner did not comply with this provision, authorities had the power to revoke the patent. Thus, it was regularly impossible to retain patent protection *and* import products covered by a patent into the issuing country.

By the mid-nineteenth century, novelty had become a standard patent requirement. Consequently, an invention was only eligible for patent protection if it has previously not been known or used (cf *infra*). Novelty was destroyed by a number of circumstances. Among other instances, an invention was regarded to be not new if it had been described in a foreign patent application or had previously been presented as e.g. a prototype at an exhibition.

The inception

Before this background, it is hardly surprising that the International Exhibition in Vienna in 1873 was the occasion that brought about the first international patent treaty. Austria was one of those countries that regarded the novelty requirement to be forfeited if prototypes were shown at an exhibition. The American delegation was aware of the fact that all applications made after the Vienna Exhibition for a subject matter used for a prototype would be declined. Consequently, they pressed Austria to adapt the patent law accordingly. Although Austria did not bow to the pressure of the US, they passed a special law expressly protecting the exhibited inventions.

The negotiation process

In fact, it took several conferences and the establishment of a permanent committee to reach an agreement. The first conference was held in Vienna directly after the International Exhibition. Although the unofficial meeting took place when anti-patent sentiments were still strong in Europe, the resolutions of the conference were decidedly pro-patent. In addition, a committee that organized the next unofficial conference was formed.

In 1878, the second unofficial conference took place in Paris. The ambitious goal was to install an International Patent Union which would replace national patent laws by a uniform international patent for all members. However, it soon became clear that opinions on patent policy differed to such a degree that its high aims had to be exchanged for a feasible approach of harmonizing certain aspects of patent laws.

Partly because the conference was unofficial and partly because consent could still not be reached on a number of issues, a permanent committee was formed. It took on the arduous task of drafting the legal text and organizing the first official meeting on which the draft was to be discussed. This conference took place in Paris in 1880. Here, the draft was officially adopted, yet some alterations were necessary. The Paris Convention was finally approved and signed in 1883.

The achievements

Among the most important achievements of the Paris Convention are the *national treatment* of foreigners, priority and the independence of patents.

According to the provision of *national treatment*, foreign and domestic inventors have to be treated equally. The importance of this provision lies in the fact that it did not rest on reciprocity: any country that offered patent protection had to confer exclusive rights on e.g. Dutch inventors. Yet, their own citizens could not obtain Dutch patents since the Netherlands had abandoned their patent system at that time. Hence, the participants agreed to a provision which meant that outflows of profits due to patent protection for foreigners did not meet inflows of profits from that particular country. This was certainly a tremendous step at the time.

The priority rule provides for a certain period, usually twelve months from the filing date of the first patent application, in which novelty of the invention cannot be forfeited by actions of third parties. In particular, this means that a patent application in one country cannot obstruct the novelty for an application in another country because they are treated as if they were all filed at the same, prior date. In addition, every other person is barred from applying for the same invention in a country within this specified period of time.

The provision on the independence of patents means that invalidation or revocation of a patent in one country does not entail the same effect for patents of the same invention in other countries.

Administration

As to 2009, the Paris Convention has 173 members. The most recent member is Thailand which joined in August 2008. The Paris Convention has been revised six times. Currently, the Stockholm revision of 1967 in the amended form of 1979 is in force. The Convention is administered by the World Intellectual Property Organization (WIPO) in Geneva.

3.2.2 The TRIPs Agreement

The problem

By the early 1980s, firms from industrialized countries had build up a sizeable stock of foreign direct investments.[12] In this, pharmaceutical firms in general and the Pfizer Inc. in particular were not different from others. Chemical and pharmaceutical firms, however, faced a particular problem. Even among members of the Paris Convention or the Patent Cooperation Treaty (cf *infra*), patent laws differed widely. In some developing countries, therapeutic substances itself were not patentable. Patents were only granted for the technological processes that produced these substances. Therefore, e.g. Indian firms were able to find other methods of producing these substances and so to offer generics at lower prices in the domestic market legally. Moreover, Indian pharmaceutical firms were free to export those generics to other countries that did not consider active ingredients to be patentable subject matters.

The WIPO proved to be an unfortunate venue to push for stronger intellectual property rights (IPRs). Developing countries had joined forces to make their interests as chief importers of technologies heard at the WIPO. In addition, even if future negotiations brought about stronger IPRs to the existing treaties governed by the WIPO, one problem would remain: none of those treaties had an effective enforcement mechanism like the one the General Agreement on Tariffs and Trade (GATT) offered.

Putting an idea on an agenda

Allegedly, Pfizer Inc.'s chief executive officer (CEO), Edmund Pratt, first came up with the idea to push the notion of IPRs as being trade-related once again.[13] To achieve their ends, Pfizer's executives needed support within the business community. They used their networks to spread the idea at business forums and (non-governmental) trade associations. In addition, they lobbied the Advisory Committee on Trade Negotiations and thereby introduced the idea into the political sphere.

Even with the support of the business community and US–American politicians, making IPRs part of the GATT required that they were put on the agenda of the next round of trade negotiations. The Ministerial Conference of Contracting Parties of the GATT set the agenda, and the next meeting was scheduled for September 1986 in Punta del Este (Uruguay). Certainly, the US exerted a considerable influence, but the support of the European Community and Japan had to be ensured to have a realistic chance of linking IPRs to trade aspects. So, Pfizer's and IBM's representatives created the Intellectual Property Committee (IPC) that consisted of 13 major US corporations in March 1986.[14] More than half of the members were highly interested in removing the patent bar to chemical and pharmaceutical *substances* or new plants in developing countries. The protection of the production processes were regarded to be insufficient since inventing around patented processes was possible so that the therapeutic substances could legally be produced and, to a certain extent, even be exported. In June and August, members of the IPC travelled to Europe and Japan to induce their competitors and business partners to make a case for the IPR–trade link with their governments.

Intellectual property rights were put on the Agenda of the Uruguay Round of the GATT negotiations and the TRIPs Agreement became part of the Final Act (Annex 1C) that was signed in April 1994 in Marrakesh.

The significance of the TRIPs

The TRIPs Agreement constitutes a minimum standard for the protection of intellectual property rights that every World Trade Organization (WTO) member has to comply with.[15] Hence, it not only applies for patents, but also for copyrights, trademarks, geographical indications, industrial designs and trade secrets. Virtually all member countries had to adapt their national laws to some extend.

Keeping the history of the TRIPs Agreement in mind, the following provisions bear witness to the efficiency of the IPC's lobbying efforts: According to Article 27,

> [...] patents shall be available for any inventions, whether products or processes, in *all fields of technology*, provided they are new, involve an inventive step and are capable of industrial application. [...] patents shall be available and patent rights enjoyable without discrimination as to the place of invention, the field of technology and *whether products are imported or locally produced.*[16]

As the wording of Article 27 makes clear, an exclusion of certain subject matters from patentability is, with two exceptions, not longer permissible.[17] Countries, as e.g. India that did not protect therapeutical substances, must now grant patents for pharmaceutical products given the application does satisfy the other requirements (cf *infra*).[18] In fact, patents must be available for all (existing and future) fields of technology so that the patent system is at least theoretically highly adaptable.

In addition, patent protection must equally apply whether products based on an invention are imported or locally produced.[19] This effectively declares the provision according to which a patent must be worked in the issuing country unlawful.

A true novelty constitutes Article 28 paragraph 1 (b):

> A patent shall confer on its owner the following exclusive rights:
> [...] where the subject matter of a patent is a process, to prevent third parties not having the owner's consent from the act of using the process, and from the acts of: using, offering for sale, selling, or importing for these purposes at least the product obtained directly by that process.
>
> (WTO, 1994)

As a consequence, new products for which only one production process is yet known are now protected twofold. This is especially important for the pharmaceutical and the chemical industry: even if the patent on the substance itself (product patent) is later revoked for some reason it is still protected by the process patent as long as no other way exists to produce it.

Some scholars have attempted to evaluate the effects of the TRIPs Agreement. McCalman (2005) estimates e.g. the net cross-country profit flows induced by the Agreement for a selected number of countries in the short and long run. He finds, that although developing countries may gain in the long run, industrialized countries are certainly benefiting most from the TRIPs Agreement.[20]

3.2.3 The Patent Cooperation Treaty

Nature and aim

While both the Paris Convention and the TRIPs Agreement are concerned with harmonizing patent law and other laws protecting intellectual property, the Patent Cooperation Treaty (PCT) has different aims. According to Article 1 of the PCT, a Union is established 'for cooperation in the filing, searching, and examination of applications for the protection of inventions' (WIPO 1972: 11). The PCT provides a simplified application procedure for applicants who wish to receive a national and/or at least one international patent for the same invention.

The starting point

After World War II during which patentable research activities were halted, national and international patent applications increased again. Especially for those countries that heavily exported technologies, as e.g. the US, filing patent applications for the same invention in several countries was an arduous task, not only because of divergent material requirements. Every application in a foreign country had to be filed in the respective national language. If e.g. an US inventor were to file an application for the same invention in the US, Germany, Russia and Japan he would need three translations of the description of the subject matter apart from altering the respective applications to meet local patent requirements.

In addition, many countries required foreign applicants to be represented by a local patent attorney. From an applicant's point of view, multiple international applications for the same subject matter were burdensome and extremely costly. On the other hand, the patent offices had to perform the necessary searches for prior art and examinations for applications that had already been examined by other patent offices. From a patent office's point of view, the usually huge backlog could be cut back at least a little if they were allowed to rely on the search results of other patent offices.

Towards the PCT

It is therefore not surprising that the US initiated a dialogue to simplify international filing and examination procedures. A formal proposal was presented to the Bureaux Internationaux Reunis pour la Protection de la Propiete Intellectuelle (BIRPI) in 1966.[21] The BIRPI commissioned a study to identify and assess possibilities to reduce duplicate filings and examination procedures. This was the basis for the first preliminary draft in 1967. During the following years, a number of consultations, at which not only state representatives, but also intergovernmental organizations and non-governmental organizations (NGOs) participated, took place. Expert opinions were heard and the first draft was amended several times. The final draft was signed at the Washington Diplomatic Conference in 1970. Formally, the PCT was enforced in January 1978 and originally included eighteen members.[22]

The principles of a PCT application

An international PCT application consists of an international and a national phase (WIPO, 1972: 746). Inventors of a signatory state usually file the PCT application at the local patent office. However, they may do so at any of the member states' patent offices. With the application, the international phase is entered. Although applicants file only one application, they apply for a patent in each of the designated countries. Thus, several national procedures are opened upon entering the international phase. If the application satisfies the formal requirements, all national procedures are halted for at least 20 months during which an authorized patent office undertakes the international search for relevant prior art and delivers the international search report to the applicant and to the patent office that received the application. The international application and the international search constitute the first stage of the international phase and are mandatory.

The second stage of the international phase is optional and consists of an international preliminary examination. Applicants may demand a preliminary examination after they have received the international search report. Upon entering the second stage of the international phase, national application procedures are suspended for at least another five months.

Either after the first or the second stage, the application enters into the national phase. Only then is the applicant required to provide translations in case national patent offices ask for them. The international search report and, if applicable, the international preliminary examination report are sent to all the national offices involved.

Administration

As at 2009, the PCT numbers 141 contracting states; Peru and Chile joined in 2009. The PCT was amended three times, the last being in force since 2002. This treaty is also administered by the WIPO in Geneva.

3.A Important development steps of patents

In Table 3.1, important development steps of patent systems, historical events as well as certain inventions, are given. The bold dates in the first column refer to developments of patent systems whereas the other dates stand for the year in which the patents for the inventions in the last column have been issued.

Table 3.1 History of the patent system, important inventions and historical events

Time	Development steps in patent law	Historical events
1280s		Eyeglasses in North Italy
1311	*Letter of Patent*	
	First letter of patent issued in England	
1338		'The Hundred Years' War' began
1450s		Gutenberg's movable type print
1431		Jeanne d'Arc burned at Rouen
1455		The War of the Roses began
1474	*Venetian Senate's Act*	
	The first administered patent system. Inventions had only to be registered, no formal examination took place	
1492		Columbus discovered America
16th century	*German Kingdoms*	
	Some of the German princes used patents widely; their patent system was well developed economically	
1517		Luther proclaimed his theses
1609		Microscope
1609		Reign of James I began
1618		The 'Thirty Year's War' began
1620		The *Mayflower* reached Plymouth Rock
1623	*Statute of Monopolies*:	
	The Statute of Monopolies recognizes patents as an exception to the rule against monopolies. The utility requirement appears and 14 years of protection are granted	
1642		Reign of Louis XIV began
	Industrial Revolution	
	The 'written description' requirement was strengthened shifting attention from novel arts and technologies to the underlying knowledge	
1789		French Revolution (1789)
1791		Steamboat
1834	*Zollverein*	
	A customs union between Prussia and most other German states except Austria was established	
1836	Revision of the US Patent Act	Safety matches
	A formal examination procedure was introduced	

(Continued)

Table 3.1 (Cont'd)

Time	Development steps in patent law	Historical events
Mid-19th century	The 'non-obviousness' requirement was introduced	
1849		Safety pin
1850	*Switzerland* Switzerland abandoned the patent system and only reinforced it in 1907	
1869	*The Netherlands* The Netherlands abandon the patent system until 1912	Vacuum cleaner
1871		German Empire under King Wilhelm I
1881		Metal detector
1883	*Paris Convention* Established to help in obtaining global patent protection. 'National treatment' was introduced	
1922		Radar
1953		Maser
1970	*European Patent Convention* Establishment of the European Patent Office (EPO). The EPO issues patents on behalf of the European Union Members	
1972		Computed tomography
1978	*Patent Cooperation Treaty* Came into full force. International application procedure created	
1982	*Court of Appeals for the Federal Circuit* (CAFC) The CAFC was created	
1993		GPS (global positioning system)
1995	*Agreement of Trade Related Aspects of Intellectual Property (TRIPs)* As part of the World Trade Organization (WTO) Agreement in the Uruguay Round. Harmonizing standards on a minimum level in all members of the General Agreement on Tariffs and Trade (GATT)	

4   Foundations of patent systems

The last chapter has revealed that the objectives as well as the instruments of patent systems have changed over time. The *letter of patents* was introduced as a mercantilistic instrument, whereas today patents are frequently seen as an instrument to overcome market failure. Early patent systems required a demonstration that the invention indeed worked. Nowadays, a proof that the invention works is not necessary. Instead, a detailed description of the invention has become a patent requirement. The most important adjustments in the recent history of patents undoubtedly belong to the Agreement of Trade Related Aspects of Intellectual Property (TRIPs) Agreement, as well as the possibility of obtaining patents in new technology fields such as computer software, business methods, genetically modified plants and animals as well as gene sequences in a number of countries. Undoubtedly, new developments in science, technology and society will continue to challenge the patent systems and force the latter to adapt. Indeed, a number of scholars point out the urgency for patent reforms.[1] Yet, how are shortcomings and inefficiencies identified, and how are reasonable alterations to the system selected?

To evaluate the performance of a patent system, the objectives that are to be achieved have to be clearly defined. Various (philosophical) schools and a number of positive and normative theories have attributed different purposes to the patent system. Here, two schools, the natural rights theory and the utilitarian theory, are introduced. Since modern patent systems seem to draw more heavily on the latter, two patent theories belonging to the utilitarian school are described in greater detail.

4.1 Natural rights theory

4.1.1 John Locke and the natural rights theory

John Locke is considered to be the most prominent representative of the natural rights theory.[2] In the second of the *Two Treatises of Government* he develops his theory of political power, i.e. the beginning of societies, their aims, organization and justification.

The starting point of the analysis is the state of nature given by God. For Locke, this state is neither an abstract idea nor does it refer to a time in human evolution that predates human societies. According to Locke's libertarian view, every person is born in this state and the laws of nature is his or her birthright. The laws of nature include the rights (1) to preserve their life, liberty and estates and (2) to prevent others from violating these rights and to punish others for a violation (Locke, 1824: 179, § 87).

In the state of nature, every person has

> [...] a property in his own person: nobody has any right to but himself. The labour of his body, and the work of his hands we may say, are properly his. Whatsoever then he removes out of the state that nature that provided and left it in, he hath mixed his labour with, and joined to it something that is his own, and thereby makes it his property.
>
> (Locke, 1824: 145, § 27)

Thus, property is an immediate consequence of the law of nature. Therefore, natural rights not only justify the existence of property, but also define the rights that should be attached to it: no one has the right to take another person's property (Locke, 1824: 213, § 138). Locke's view on property is absolute. Hence, it is fair to assume that he meant the owner not only to have the exclusive right to possess the property, but also to enjoy the services of it and to transfer the property to others – the modern definition of property rights.[3] Natural rights and property are firmly interlinked and are central to Locke's political theory.

The next step is to explain why societies formed. Although persons have absolute freedom in the state of nature, they must also be prepared to defend their freedom frequently. Locke argues that societies are created with the main purpose to preserve the members' natural rights in general and their property in particular. To this end, society must be endowed with certain rights and powers: legislative and executive powers. However, both are limited to the extend that

> [...] the law of nature stands as an eternal rule to all men, legislators as well as others.
>
> (Locke, 1824: 210, § 135)

4.1.2 Intellectual property and natural rights

The distinction between tangible and intellectual property is meaningless as far as natural rights theory is considered. As long as labour is mixed with unowned resources, property is created and must be protected.[4] Thus, a patent system protecting intellectual property is not only justified according to natural rights theory. It also lays down the principles for its provisions.

For a natural rights' theorist, intellectual property should have the same level of protection as tangible property. This obviously includes the exclusive rights of possessing it, enjoying its services by e.g. licensing it, and transferring it to others. Indeed, these are acknowledged standards for all types of property today. There are also other normative aspects of the equal treatment of all types of property that are unfamiliar since they have not been implemented. In accordance with tangible property, intellectual property rights should not be limited in duration. Most importantly, patents would not be protected against independent discovery (cf Oddi 1996), since this would interfere with other people's property.

Unquestionably, the natural rights theory did play a role in the history of modern patent systems. In modern patent law, however, no traces are left.

4.2 Utilitarian theory

4.2.1 Jeremy Bentham and utilitarianism

According to Eatwell *et al.* (1998: 770), *utilitarianism* has three features:

> (1) individual well–being ought to be the end of moral actions; (2) each individual is to *count for one and no more than one*; (3) the object of social action should be to maximize general utility.

Jeremy Bentham laid the foundations to utilitarianism as we know it today. Although utilitarianism and natural rights theory share some ideas, as e.g. that all human beings are equal and that they pursue good and avoid evil, Bentham rigorously rejected natural rights theory. For him, rights that predate or precede positive laws do not exist – *every* right is created by law and, thus, by a government. Perhaps even more importantly, natural rights theory lacks any guidance as to which measure from the vast number of possible actions a government should take in order to increase social welfare. Bentham's concept provides both, the ends and the means. According to the utilitarian theory, the ultimate object is to maximize general utility, and general utility also helps to decide which actions to choose.

4.2.2 Utilitarianism and patent systems

According to Bentham's utilitarian theory, policymakers should maximize general welfare. This principle also establishes a yardstick that aids in answering the following questions: (a) should the government intervene to strengthen intellectual property, (b) which set of rules should be installed, and (c) how should it be designed?

Too many or too few inventions?

At least in principle, the first question has a simple answer. A policymaker should impose a set of rules if the actual and the welfare-maximizing level of inventions do not coincide. Although it is impossible to calculate the optimal level of inventions, we can identify incentives that cause over- or under-investment into research and development (R&D).

First of all, most inventions are regarded to be socially valuable since they satisfy a human desire more effectively (product innovations) or perform a certain task more efficiently (process innovation). In addition, high R&D and innovation rates are necessary to reach or sustain appropriate economic growth paths according to one branch of modern growth theory.[5] Therefore, we might conclude that governments want to encourage R&D.

Indeed, early utilitarians highlighted either the information good characteristic (Jeremy Bentham and John Stuart Mill) or the public good characteristic (Arthur Cecil Pigou) of inventions. The former refers to the notion that imitation costs are always lower than development costs. Consequently, imitators would successfully drive inventors out of the market if inventions were not protected in some form. Rational inventors anticipating the inventors' actions may decide to divert their resources away from inventions and thereby reduce society's welfare.

The public good argument rests on the fact that inventions essentially consist of information which is non-rival and non-excludable without intellectual property rights. Since inventors are unable to appropriate the full social benefit, they will provide an inefficient level of inventions and innovations. In contrast to most other public goods, inventions affect social welfare in two different ways. Firstly, inventions increase social welfare directly by providing new products and processes. The second channel emphasizes knowledge as an important input factor for further research which itself leads to new products and processes. Thus, welfare is increased indirectly. In the latter function, knowledge is socially desirable in itself and points to a particular problem arising from the cumulative nature of inventions (cf *infra*).

Both the information good and the public good argument arrive at the conclusion that there will be too few innovations as compared to the social optimum unless the government intervenes.

By the time the mechanisms of imperfect markets had been understood better, possible negative consequences of the patent system were pointed out. Plant (1953) e.g. claims that all inventions are spontaneous. Thus, they are made with or without intellectual property rights. Other protective mechanisms are available and have been used for a long time: e.g. trade secrecy, first-mover advantage or lead time. According to Plant granting exclusive rights would lead to over-investment, especially when the research environment is competitive. Although Plant's argument is supported by empirical evidence, a patent system may still be justified since trade secrecy prevents inventions from performing their second material function: disclosing the embodied knowledge so that subsequent inventions can be made.

From a utilitarian point of view, government intervention is justified whenever the level of inventions is sub-optimal. Unfortunately, there are incentives for both over- as well as for under-provision of inventions, and they typically are present at the same time. However, it seems undebated that without a regulatory system more inventions would be protected by trade secrecy which deprives society from valuable knowledge.

Patents, prizes or awards

Even if market failure can be attested, a patent system might not be superior to other alternatives. Thus, the second question is concerned with the relative performance of patents, prizes, awards and procurements.[6] Although the patent system has frequently been criticized, only few scholars tried to compare the different systems.[7]

Suzanne Scotchmer shows that prizes provide the same incentive to innovate as patents, but at lower costs under certain circumstances.[8] Prizes and awards do not entail deadweight loss which inevitably arises in a patent system. Given that prizes and awards are even older than patents and have been used to reward inventors to the present day (Scotchmer, 2004: 41–46), why does the patent system dominate other alternatives? In order to provide socially efficient incentives to innovation using prizes or awards, the value of the desired invention must be known. It may be more easily established in some cases. For the vast majority of cases however the value of an invention remains highly uncertain even after the patent has been issued. This is particularly true in the pharmaceutical industry. Typically, several years elapse until a patented therapeutical substance has been developed into a medicine suitable for clinical tests.[9] These tests are necessary to gain market approval, and the value of the active ingredient is considerably higher if market approval is granted than if it is denied.

The advantage of patents over prizes and awards consists in a patent system's ability to perform reasonably well with comparably little information.[10] This makes the patent system more flexible than either of the alternatives.

The optimal design

The last question is concerned with the optimal design of a patent system. In pursuing this task, one cannot exclusively focus on either social benefits or social costs of inventions since policy instruments increasing the former may also increase the latter. Thus, the question of how to achieve the ultimate object can be re-addressed as follows (see Besen and Raskind, 1991):

1.   Do individuals and enterprises have sufficient incentives to invent?
2.   Is the balance between the incentives to invent and the dissemination of knowledge optimal?
3.   Are inventions generated at minimum *social* costs?

Each of the numerous (normative) patent theories have to answer these questions. However, only two are introduced here: the incentive theory and the disclosure theory.[11] They have been chosen because they each correspond to one of the functions of a patent system: to facilitate technical progress and to disseminate knowledge.

4.2.3 Two patent theories

All utilitarian patent theories have to demonstrate market failure in order to justify the intervention into the market mechanism. Identifying the reasons for market failure is also the starting point for laying down the guiding principles of an appropriate patent system. By nature, they will be incomplete because each theory emphasizes a single factor. In reality, however, all factors of market failure are present at the same time.

Incentive theory

This patent theory focusses on the firms' incentives to innovate. For firms to engage in R&D is just another, highly uncertain investment decision. As every other investment decision, the aim is to at least keep pace with competitors and at best to out-perform the rivals in future. Incentive theory emphasizes that creating a piece of information or knowledge is more expensive than to copy it. Consequently, the profitability of research projects crucially depends on the firms' ability to protect their inventions and know-how.

Using the standard neoclassical framework, it can be shown that the incentives to innovate are optimal only if firms are able to appropriate the entire social benefits from the invention (Scotchmer, 1991). In particular, it is assumed that there is one firm that has the potential to innovate in a perfectly competitive environment where imitation is costless. Neither legal protection nor alternative protective mechanisms exist. In a frictionless world, firms are unable to recoup their research expenditures. Rational actors will anticipate this situation and refrain from R&D. However, if the firm were to receive the entire social benefit, e.g. due to an effective and efficient patent system, it would exert the optimal effort into the R&D project.

Alternative protective mechanisms such as trade secrecy and lead time have been used for a long time to protect inventions.[12] Thus, some research projects will be profitable even without legal protection. Yet, since expected payoffs are lower for both alternative mechanisms, the incentives to invent will not be socially efficient. Strong, legal patent protection therefore seems justified. If there was only one invention in a particular line of technology, an infinite patent term would induce sufficient incentives. However, there is usually a sequence of inventions in the same technology line where later inventions perfect previous ones or find new applications. It is therefore impossible to give every inventor the full social benefit of his or her invention (Scotchmer, 1996). Thus, with cumulative inventions in mind, patent law has reduced the incentives for every inventor to achieve the maximal possible incentives for all inventors in the long run.

Incentive theory has always been criticized for both theoretical and empirical reasons. One may doubt whether the existence of patent protection does increase the number of inventions and, therefore, welfare. According to Cohen *et al.* (2000), firms usually rely on a mixture of legal and alternative protective measures. Thus, the same inventions may have been created without patent protection and therefore at lower social costs. Empirical evidence as well as surveys yield mixed results (cf e.g. Penrose, 1951; Kortum and Lerner, 1998).

Even if patents foster industrial progress as intended, they may also create social costs by creating too much incentive or the wrong kind of incentives. If the market structure is oligopolistic and several firms try to find a solution for a known problem, research costs are duplicated, but the social benefit of the invention remains the same. The incentives created by the patent system may generate competition in research that eventually dissipates the entire social benefit of an invention (cf e.g. Grady and Alexander, 1992; Oddi, 1996). In addition, firms use their patents not solely for the purpose of recouping their upfront investments, but also to pursue (aggressive or defensive) strategies to weaken their competitors (cf Shapiro, 2001). In particular, an attractive patent portfolio may become a necessary prerequisite to negotiate licence agreements in different technology fields. Although this strategy may actually reduce development and production costs for incumbents when existing patent portfolios lead to favourable cross-licensing agreements, it might constitute a prohibitive entry barrier for other firms. The importance of strategic patenting greatly differs across industries. However, it is well documented for the subgroups of the consumer electronics industry and the software industry (Hall and Ziedonis, 2001; Brodley, 1990).

Whether or not the patent system does create *the right amount* of incentives to generate inventions largely remains an empirical question. Presently, the evidence is at best mixed.[13]

Disclosure theory

The second patent theory introduced here looks upon patents as a contract between two parties, society and the inventor.[14] Each party has its rights and obligations. The *traded object* is the knowledge embodied in the invention. The *price* society pays for it is granting the exclusive patent rights. Different from the incentive theory that centres on the welfare effects of new products or processes, the disclosure theory focusses on making information publicly available.

Information has a very peculiar production function.[15] It almost entirely consists of fixed costs. The variable costs for reproducing the same information are negligible. Under these circumstances, the efficient allocation of information is to provide it free of charge to everyone who is interested.[16] However, the creators of information have to cover the fixed costs so that they will usually charge a positive price. An inefficient allocation of information and, therefore, market failure will arise. In case the creators anticipate that potential consumers are not willing to pay for the information, they will not produce the information in the first place unless their private utility for the information exceeds the fixed costs.

Inventions are basically information that are extremely expensive to produce partly because the research process is highly uncertain. Different from creators of many other kinds of information, inventors may still recoup their R&D costs if they can protect their inventions appropriately, i.e. usually by trade secrecy. Thus, as along as a patent system succeeds in revealing the information that would otherwise have been kept secret, it reduces the level of market failure (Beckerman-Rodau, 2002). Since patents are published 18 months after the issuance, patented inventions are invariably revealed.[17]

Publishing inventions may increase welfare further. Especially when R&D processes are envisaged, knowledge is undoubtedly an important input factor. Once a patent has been granted, other researchers may build upon the knowledge and generate new inventions. This makes it possible that e.g. applications for a basis invention can be discovered and brought to the consumer sooner as compared to a situation where the invention was kept secret.[18] Modern growth theory is build upon this concept and links information to economic growth and welfare.[19]

Admittedly, a patent system would not be the first choice of correcting market failure under these circumstances. Prizes that reward inventors and put the invention into a public domain would fare much better as deadweight loss is avoided. As discussed above, however, a prize system is difficult to establish in an uncertain environment, i.e. when the value of the information cannot be assessed. Again, a patent system may perform reasonably well with inventions.

Disclosure theory is rather flexible as far as specific patent regulations are concerned. Different from natural rights theory which would imply an infinite patent term when applied strictly, disclosure theory would specify the lowest possible patent life that induces inventors to use patents rather than trade secrecy to protect their intellectual property. This also describes the general implications of this patent theory for patent systems: to use the necessary and least invasive policy instruments to achieve the disclosure of information embodied in inventions.

5 An introduction to patent law and policy instruments

All components of a patent system, including the question of which instruments are to be used to protect the intellectual property, as well as the market structure itself, potentially affect firms' decisions concerning research projects. It is a quite complex system so it seems expedient to describe it in greater detail in order to understand its workings and mechanisms. Although the Agreement of Trade Related Aspects of Intellectual Property (TRIPs Agreement; World Trade Organization, 1994) has harmonized patent law and therefore also the patent system to a certain degree, there remain considerable differences in patent systems. These distinctions are inconsequential for the analysis in the following chapters so that we decided to refer to only one system, the United States (US) patent system.[1] The first section traces an invention's way through the patent system, i.e. from filing the application to the court rulings concerning remedies for the infringement of a patent.

Some aspects of the patent system, as e.g. the way in which damages are determined or the judges' tendency to uphold challenged patents, can have a huge impact on a firm's inclination to use patents. However, the book focusses on certain provisions of patent law that determine the strength of the patent rights conferred. Consequently, the second section gives a short introduction to patent law. It covers familiar patent requirements that inventions must be new and useful as well as more unfamiliar ones of disclosure and enablement. For each of the included provisions, the principles are outlined according to which patent examiners or courts determine whether the requirements are met in a particular case. Subsequently, potential economic effects are sketched.

Patent law has to concern itself with numerous details to ensure that all cases are treated equally, and it must remain flexible enough to accommodate future developments without stifling the patent system. In addition, patent law has to take care that present inventors are not rewarded at the expense of future ones. Economic models on the other hand cannot and should not deal with all the legal details. They generalize effects and demonstrate how single provisions work. Unsurprisingly, the details of patent law do not easily translate into economic models. Therefore, the third section shows which legal provisions are to be analysed in the remainder of the book, and how they can be treated in a way suitable for economic modelling.

5.1 The patent system

The patent system comprises all steps and provisions that govern patents from filing an application to the issuance of the patent as well as all conflicts over patent rights. Frequently, the patent system is divided into prosecution, i.e. the whole application process, and enforcement. The former includes all administrative steps leading to the issuance or a rejection of a patent. The latter negotiates conflicting interests between a patentee and other parties which possibly arise from the administrative act of granting patent rights.

5.1.1 Patent prosecution

Patent prosecution starts with the application. Except for applications under the Patent Cooperation Treaty (PCT) or the European Patent Convention (EPC), they are filed at the domestic patent office. Applications under the PCT or the EPC can be filed at any patent office of a contracting state.

The application describes the invention and contains the principal information on which examiners base their decisions. As the patent itself, the application is a highly standardized document. In fact, an application and the corresponding patent may differ in the description and the claims of the invention but not in the structure. Therefore, it seems appropriate to discuss the parts of a patent in some detail.

The parts of a patent

A patent has three main parts: the bibliographic data section, the body and the claims.

THE BIBLIOGRAPHIC DATA

The bibliographic data section (cf Figure 5.1) provides general and technology-related information.[2] In the headline, the issuing country and the first inventor are on the left-hand side. On the right-hand side of the headline, the patent number and the issuing date of the patent are given. The general information in the main part consist of a short descriptive title, the inventors and the assignee as well as the application number and the filing date.

Since the full description of the invention is given in the body of the patent, the technology-related information in the bibliographic data section is very brief. It reveals the technology fields to which the invention belongs by listing the appropriate numbers of the domestic and international classification code. Further, the technological fields that the examiners searched for relevant prior art are detailed.[3] Inventors are required to specify all relevant sources that were used in making the invention in the application. These references are part of the bibliographic section and frequently consist of other patents and published scientific papers. Finally, a concise abstract that must convey the essence of the invention as well as its use is given.

United States Patent [19]

Baer et al.

[11] Patent Number: **4,875,096**

[45] Date of Patent: Oct. 17, 1989

[54] ENCODING OF AUDIO AND DIGITAL
SIGNALS IN A VIDEO SIGNAL

[75] Inventors: Ralph H. Baer, Manchester, N.H.;
Kenneth J. Curran, Redondo Beach;
Jay Smith, III, Los Angeles, both of
Calif.

[73] Assignee: Smith Engineering, Culver City,
Calif.

[21] Appl. No.: 898,268

[22] Filed: Aug. 20, 1989

[51] Int. Cl.⁴ H04N 7/04
[52] U.S. Cl. 358/143; 358/147
[58] Field of Search 358/142–147,
358/343; 360/19.1, 27; 375/24

[56] **References Cited**

U.S. PATENT DOCUMENTS

3,492,432	1/1970	Schinpf	375/24
3,549,795	12/1970	Mullin	178/5.6
3,666,888	5/1972	Sekimoto	178/69.5 TV
3,859,458	1/1975	Takezawa et al.	
3,900,887	8/1975	Soga et al.	358/142
3,902,007	8/1975	Justice	178/5.8 R
3,916,092	10/1975	Justice	358/12
3,988,528	10/1976	Yanagimachi et al.	
4,134,127	1/1979	Campioni	358/16
4,233,627	11/1980	Sugihara	358/143

4,318,125	5/1982	Shutterly	358/145
4,321,623	3/1982	Rzeszewski	358/144
4,367,488	1/1983	Leventer et al.	358/147
4,394,690	7/1983	Kobayashi	358/180
4,479,150	10/1984	Ilmer et al.	358/310
4,569,026	2/1986	Best	
4,602,295	7/1986	Moriyama et al.	360/19.1
4,652,919	3/1987	Devino	
4,665,431	5/1987	Cooper	358/143
4,786,967	11/1988	Smith, III et al.	358/143

FOREIGN PATENT DOCUMENTS

0003247 1/1980 Japan 358/142

Primary Examiner—James J. Groody
Assistant Examiner—David E. Harvey
Attorney, Agent, or Firm—Price, Gess & Ubell

[57] **ABSTRACT**

Audio signals and digital commands are encoded into a standard raster format television signal recorded on a cassette for play by a home video cassette unit. The audio signals are encoded in the displayable video as modulated carrier pulses separated by return to median intervals with the audio waveforms being tapered near discontinuities. The digital commands are recorded as binary level pulses, one such pulse occupying substantially an entire video line to permit accurate decoding.

4 Claims, 11 Drawing Sheets

Figure 5.1 Bibliographic data of a patent.

THE BODY

The body contains the main information concerning the invention. Usually, drawings of the main parts of the invention, or flow charts in case of software-related inventions, are presented first. It follows the specification of the invention (cf Figure 5.2) which gives exhaustive information on three points: written description, enablement and the best mode (cf *infra*). Together, the elements constitute the disclosure and enablement requirement which must be met at the filing date of the patent and cannot be amended to include new subject matter during the examination process.

Because all inventions draw upon previously created knowledge, inventors have to describe precisely how their invention is related to the prior art in the written description section. They also have also to make clear what sets their invention apart from the prior art and the cited references, i.e. they have to demonstrate an inventive step.

For a patent to be granted, the invention must be useful which also means that a specific use for the invention has to be given in the application. Both, the enablement and the best mode requirement are concerned with making and using the invention. Specifically, inventions must be outlined in such a way that a person skilled in the technology line is able to make and use the inventions without undue experimentation.

4,875,096

1

**ENCODING OF AUDIO AND DIGITAL SIGNALS
IN A VIDEO SIGNALBACKGROUND OF THE
DISCLOSURE**

The subject invention relates to signal encoding and more particularly to encoding of audio signals and digital commands on a video signal such as may be transmitted to standard television receivers.

In the prior art, techniques have been suggested for encoding audio signals in conjunction with a raster scan format television signal. In general, these techniques prove unsatisfactory for use in consumer oriented products because of the implementation expense involved or because degradation of the video signal in application precludes satisfactory recovery of the transmitted sound or data.

Both of the foregoing factors are exacerbated when encoding a video signal which is to be reproduced by a typical video cassette recorder (VCR) in the playback mode. The available bandwidth of consumer quality VCR's is on the order of 2.5 megahertz. We have found that this bandwidth eliminates a number of apparently feasible encoding methods, particularly those relying on various forms of modulating the audio signals onto chroma frequency subcarriers, see Justice U.S. Pat. No. 3,916,092.

2

to limited bandwith storage media and apparatus, such as presently existing consumer quality VCR's.

It is another object of the invention to provide a format and encoding method for multiple audio signals, as well as digital commands required to effect controlled branching to one of the audio signals at any given time.

In accordance with the invention, a pair of pulses are inserted at the left and right vertical edges of the that portion of each horizontal scan line extending from the end of color burst to the beginning of the next horizontal sync pulse of a standard raster-format television picture. Each signal pulse in these pulse pairs is amplitude modulated with the instantaneous value of an audio signal during the encoding process. Upon playback, the decoding process recovers the audio signals by a sample hold method of decoding. To prevent intermodulation between adjacent pulse pairs, suitable return-to-median levels are interpersed between the pulses. Furthermore, to minimize the effect of the vertical blanking gap, the encoding of audio is tapered or otherwise modified just preceding and forwarding the vertical blanking pulse intervals. These features contribute to successful recovery of usable audio, with the implementation of the sample and hold decoding function being under control of a microprocessor. Encoding of digital data required by the processor into the video signal is accomplished by placing the data in the first

Figure 5.2 The body of a patent.

Naturally, all inventors want their patents to be as broad as possible. One way of achieving it is by listing e.g. a range of materials that can be used instead of naming a single one. The best mode requires inventors to disclose the configuration that has proven to be most successful in the research process.

THE CLAIMS

The last part of a patent consists of one or more claims (cf Figure 5.3, emphasis added). They state in a formalized manner what the patentee claims to have invented. The claims must not contain any information that is not described in the body of the patent. Frequently, they are considered to be the most important part of the patent since they define the scope of the patent rights that are conferred. Naturally, they are rewritten several times in negotiations between the examiner and the inventor or the inventor's attorney during the examination process.

Other steps of the prosecution process

After the application has been filed, examiners have to assess whether the application satisfies all patent requirements (cf *infra*). Therefore, they have to search for prior art above and beyond what the inventors states in the application. Frequently, internal and international patent databases as well as scientific literature are consulted. On the basis of the search result, the examiners determine whether the invention constitutes sufficient technological progress to justify a patent.

What is claimed is:

1. A method of encoding multiple audio and digital signals into a video signal having a plurality of displayable video areas, each area comprising substantially the entire period between a pair of horizontal sync pulses, comprising the steps of:

sampling the audio signals to produce a set of samples;

amplitude modulating said samples onto sampling pulses;

placing the amplitude modulated sampling pulses into a portion of each of a plurality of said displayable video areas; and

encoding digital commands in the form of bits in the video signal, one bit occupying substantially the entire portion of a selected one of said displayable video areas not allotted to the amplitude modulated sampling pulses.

2. The method of claim 1 wherein the video signal comprises:

a horizontal synchronization pulse;

a color burst following the horizontal synchronization pulse;

signals into a video signal having a plurality of displayable video areas, each displayable video area being located between a pair of horizontal sync pulses and recovering said audio and digital signals, comprising:

sampling the audio signals to produce a set of audio samples;

amplitude modulating said audio samples onto sampling pulses, each sampling pulse occupying a pulse interval;

placing the amplitude modulated sampling pulses into said displayable video areas;

encoding digital commands into selected ones of said displayable video areas;

recovering the audio signal by sampling the encoded video signal during the pulse interval to produce a sample value and holding the sample value;

digitizing the encoded video signal to form a digital signal;

identifying a said digital command in the digital signal;

extracting the digital command from the digital signal; and

storing the extracted digital command.

• • • • •

Figure 5.3 The claims of a patent.

In case the examiner rejects the patent application, the claims can be rewritten twice. Usually, this stage is entered when claims were initially poorly defined and too broad. Negotiations between examiner and inventors help to define the proper patent scope or to clarify that the invention does not merit a patent. At the end of this process, examiners either accept the application in which case the patent is granted or they reject it. In the latter case, the applicants may abandon their efforts to receive a patent, file a continuation patent or appeal the decision.

The form of continuation patents is unique to US patent law. Here, the application re-enters the examination process and can be changed or split into several patents to meet the patent requirements. From the patentee's point of view, this procedure has two advantages: the continuation patent retains the 'parent' patent's priority date and continuation patents are usually not published.[4]

Those applications for which patent protection is not sought abroad need not to be published in the US. All other patent applications are to be published 18 months after the filing date.

5.1.2 *Patent enforcement*

Patent enforcement is concerned with matters after a patent has been issued. It settles conflicting interests between patentees and (potential) infringers. In general, two situations may arise. (1) A patentee puts forth an infringement action against a party which, so the patent owner believes, violates his patent rights. (2) A party, as e.g. a potential infringer or another patent owner, brings a declaratory judgement action against the patentee because the former believes that some or all claims are invalid.

In both cases, the validity of the patent can and usually is challenged. However, the (potential) infringer always has the burden of proof. Since a patent has undergone a thorough administrative examination, it is presumed that patents are valid until there is sufficient evidence for doubt.

If the infringement action is successful, the accused party is held to be liable for infringement. Three kinds of remedies may be imposed (cf *infra*): (1) an injunction, where the infringer has to give up producing the product or using the infringing technology, (2) a damage has to be paid, and (3) the legal expenses of the winning party have to be paid. Often, a combination of those measures are imposed.

Since the (potential) infringer usually defends himself by claiming that that patent is invalid in the first place, part of the claims can be declared invalid even if the patentee wins his case.

5.2 Legal policy instruments and their economic effects

The main purpose of this section is to introduce the *legal patent instruments* and to describe their economic effects.[5] Only some of them, i.e. patent eligibility and patent requirements, form the principal subject of the following chapters. Therefore, they are only briefly discussed in this section. The legal patent instruments that are not studied in the following chapters are examined in greater detail here.

Before introducing the main components of patent law, a description of the patent rights are given. According to §154 of USC 35, a patent constitutes

> a grant to the patentee, his heirs or assigns, of the right to exclude others from making, using, offering for sale, or selling the invention throughout the United States or importing the invention into the United States, and, if the invention is a process, of the right to exclude others from using, offering for sale or selling throughout the United States, or importing into the United States, products made by that process, referring to the specification for the particulars thereof.

5.2.1 Patent prosecution

Patent fees

APPLICATION FEES

When inventors file a patent application they have to pay application fees. Throughout the whole examination process, other fees have to be paid which depend on certain characteristics. Typical fees are e.g. search fees, examination fees and fees payable if the patent application has more than a certain number of claims (cf Table 5.2 in the Appendix).[6]

From an economic perspective, a rational inventor will only apply for a patent if the expected value exceeds the expected cost of a patent. Principal components of the expected patent costs are the total application costs as well as litigation costs that may arise in future over validity or infringement issues. To what extent litigation costs will become relevant depends largely on the characteristics of the invention and the patentee (cf e.g. Harhoff and Reitzig, 2004). Application costs comprise application fees as well as the costs for a patent attorney and are sunk.

Application fees are not primarily imposed to increase the patent office's budget (Jaffe and Lerner, 2004: chapter 5), but to stop inventions that do not contribute to the progress of the technology field from entering the patent system. Trivial inventions would not satisfy the patent requirements and would therefore not be granted a patent. Nevertheless, they would bind resources. Although application fees are by far the smallest part of the total expected patent costs, they have the effect of an entry barrier. This effect is amplified by the fact that, as soon a patent application is pursued, attorney costs will also accrue.

The presumption that only trivial inventions are kept out of the patent system is subject to dispute. On the one hand, it has been argued that application fees are still too high for small or young enterprises as well as individual inventors although they are eligible for reduced fees in the US (see Table 5.2 in the Appendix). On the other hand, concerns about the raising the number of poor-quality patents are voiced (Merges, 1999).

MAINTENANCE FEES

Patent fees do not only apply during the examination procedure. Although the patent term is 20 years from the filing date, maintenance fees have be paid to keep the patent in force (Table 5.2). They are progressive, and only about one of three patents cover the entire patent term.

Maintenance fees also work as a sorting mechanism protecting valuable inventions longer than less valuable ones. Rather than imposing a large fee when the patent is issued, smaller instalments are well adapted to the fact that information affecting the value of the patent is gradually revealed over time. Thus, e.g. a pharmaceutical firm may keep the patent in force while clinical tests for a new medicine are carried out. After a rejection of market approval, however, the firm may want to abandon the patent.

Patentable subject matter

After the application reaches the examiners, they have to determine whether the invention is eligible for patent protection, i.e. whether the discovery belongs to a patentable subject matter. Patentable subject matters are broad technology classes for which patents can in principle be obtained. §101 of USC 35 rules that:

> Whoever invents or discovers any new and useful process, machine, manufacture, or composition of matter, or any new and useful improvement thereof, may obtain a patent therefore, subject to the conditions and requirements of this title.

Different from European patent law, US law does not explicitly exclude any fields or classes of technology.[7] However, the wording of the provision leaves no doubt that patents were only intended for technical inventions in a broad sense, i.e. not only for technological processes and machinery, but also materials and biological and chemical substances. This excludes not only artistic expressions that are protected by other forms of intellectual property rights. It has also been the standard of patent law from its beginnings that laws of nature, physical phenomena, abstract ideas, and naturally occurring plants and minerals are generally not patentable. These exceptions are known as the *natural law doctrine*.[8]

History has shown that the §101 USC 35 was initially narrowly construed so that e.g. computer software, business methods and living organisms were initially unpatentable. Over time, however, each of these subject matters became patentable in the US.[9]

Since the expansion of patentable subject matters in an international framework is studied in Chapter 12, general considerations are here limited to the national perspective, i.e. under autarchy. For illustration, take the example of biotechnology and assume that the patent system indeed spurs innovations. Making biotechnology a patentable subject matter has two effects. Firstly, it is important to note that the absence of patent protection does not usually imply that there are no inventions in that field. University research is largely state-funded so that basic research is conducted in every technology class. In addition, private firms that made a discovery in a new technology field may simply resort to alternative protective mechanisms such as e.g. trade secrecy or lead time.[10] In a situation where technological knowledge is growing fast and trade secrecy is used, crucial information remains scattered since trade secrecy prevents its dissemination (cf *supra*).[11] As a consequence, improvements on e.g. a method to alter a particular gene sequence appear on average later, and consumers have to wait longer for practical applications such as new drugs. Biotechnological progress can be expected to increase if the government decides to grant patents in this field. Indeed, Merges (1995: 107) understands intellectual property rights as a device for industrial policy that is capable of subsidizing creative firms in this particular field without burdening the budget.

Secondly, private enterprises are less likely to direct their research efforts to new technology fields for which they cannot obtain patents. Again, a higher technological progress can be expected when a subject matter becomes patentable, not because of more readily available knowledge, but because research expenditures and investments increase in the particular technological class. Regibeau and Rockett (2005) argue that granting patents on *pure gene sequences* would redirect research toward basic research and away from the search of useful applications.

Utility requirement

The utility requirement is derived from §101 USC 35 (cf *supra*), where it is explicitly stated that inventions must be useful to be patentable. In this provision, the utilitarian roots of the patent system become obvious: only inventions that increase social welfare merit the intellectual property rights conferred by patents (cf *supra*).

Formerly, this patent requirement has been used to exclude immoral and dangerous inventions from patentability. Today, the US Patent and Trademark Office (USPTO) largely focusses on technical utility and leaves other government agencies to deal with moral issues and the protection of consumer interests.

The modern view on the issue is that an invention has to pass three tests in order to comply with the utility requirement: (1) practical utility, (2) beneficial utility, (3) operability.

The *operability* test examines whether the invention is capable of accomplishing the utility claimed in the application. Since it is no longer necessary to demonstrate the operability of the invention, the test mainly serves to exclude fantastic claims, as e.g. to have invented the perpetuum mobile, or claims that are based on accidental mistakes made by the inventor.

The *beneficial utility test* assesses whether the invention is in general desirable for society. By this standard, discoveries directed at immoral or socially harmful purposes are unpatentable. Indeed, patent applications on gambling devices have been rejected on moral grounds prior to 1977. However, the USPTO has become more lenient as far as immorality is concerned.

Finally, the invention must have a practical purpose, i.e. *practical utility*. The standard has never been very high. Nevertheless, it frequently becomes relevant for pharmaceutical, chemical or biotechnological inventions.[12] To obtain a patent, it is not sufficient to change e.g. substances or materials that have proved to be socially useful and hope that the new ones will finally turn out to have some purpose – the substance in itself is not useful for society. The inventor must credibly demonstrate how it can be used to the general advantage.[13]

The utility requirement is seldom the stumbling block for an applicant. Economically, the requirement guarantees a minimum level of benefit society receives in exchange for the exclusive rights it confers to the inventor.

It should be pointed out that the USPTO does not consider social usefulness and commercial value to be synonymous during the examination phase. It recognizes that a new substance e.g. to treat malaria is socially desirable even if it does not survive the clinical test phase and, thus, does not have an immediate commercial value.[14] This substance might serve as a starting point for the development of new substances that eventually obtain market approval and successfully cure malaria. Hence, the original substance serves a socially useful purpose although it has no commercial success and, thus, deserves patent protection.

In addition, the utility requirement discourages researchers from filing patents too early and encourages them to find new products and processes *as well as* keeping a practical application in mind.

Novelty and statutory bars

NOVELTY

The novelty requirement is not only derived from §101 USC 35 which states that inventions must be new. §102 of USC 35 stipulates that

A person shall be entitled to a patent unless –

(a) the invention was known or used by others in this country, or patented or described in a printed publication in this or a foreign country before the invention thereof by the applicant for patent [...]

The short passage points at two connected problems: (1) how to measure novelty, and (2) to which point in time the measure should be applied.

With respect to the second question, two concepts are used. Either the invention has to satisfy the novelty requirement at the *invention date* or at the *filing date* of the application. Except for the US, all countries implemented the second concept. Clearly, both concepts differ as a patent application might not be filed immediately for various reasons. Inventors may want to perfect their invention or broaden the potential patent scope by establishing new uses for the invention. Alternatively, the invention might be kept secret for strategic reasons.

A closely related issue is that of who shall be considered to be the inventor of a subject matter. The two above mentioned concepts are used which are also known as the first-to-invent and the first-to-file method in this context. Again, the person who invented the subject matter and the one who applied for the patent first need not be identical. In holding onto the first-to-invent method, the US aim at rewarding the true inventor. Disputes on who did invent a certain subject matter do occasionally arise, and court trials over and again show that the first-to-invent method makes measuring novelty much more complex.

Yet how is novelty actually measured? §102(a) provides that an invention is regarded to be new unless it has been known or used or described in a printed publication before the invention date (cf *supra*). Ultimately, all inventions draw upon knowledge created by others so that parts of them are well-known and used. Then, the question is really about how much of an invention must be described in a reference of the prior art to destroy novelty. The US apply the concept of anticipation. The principle is simple and straightforward. For an invention to be anticipated by prior art, a single published reference must describe each and every element of the claimed invention. In this case, the invention fails the novelty test and is unpatentable. If some elements of the invention are described in one reference and the rest in another publication, the application for the subject matter passes the novelty test. By combining two or more references, the inventor has created something new. Whether such combinations constitute a sufficient technological advance to merit a patent then becomes a matter of obviousness.

From an economic point of view, it is important that patents are only issued for inventions that generate social benefit. Disseminating technical knowledge is one way of increasing welfare. Although not necessarily rewarding the true inventor, the first-to-file method does encourage inventors to patent early. With the first-to-invent method, additional provisions, i.e. the statutory bars (cf *infra*), have to be put into force to achieve a similar and frequently not identical effect (Scotchmer and Green, 1990).

The novelty requirement as such also ensures that society only grants exclusive rights for inventions that benefit society. By conferring patent rights for an invention that already exists does not create an extra benefit. To the contrary, it would result in social costs. In case the subject matter had been patented before, monopoly rights have to be borne longer than necessary. Consumer prices for associated products are higher and the deadweight loss will be greater when a patent is granted for an invention that does not pass the novelty requirement and was not patented before.

STATUTORY BARS

Statutory bars to patents are laid down in §102(b–d) USC 35. They are not primarily concerned with any technological considerations but with external events that have taken place before the filing of the patent application and destroy novelty. In particular, such events are that the subject matter has already been patented (abroad), it has been described or publicly used at least a year before the filing for a US patent or it has been abandoned.

At first glance, the anticipation standard which determines novelty seems too narrow to guarantee a sufficiently high social benefit associated with the protected invention. Before the 1952 US Patent Act, the novelty requirement alone was responsible for preventing trivial innovations from being rewarded patents. Although the doctrine of *inventiveness* had been used for a long time, only the 1952 amendment of the Patent Act introduced a sharp distinction between novelty and non-obviousness.

Non-obviousness

Most commentators consider the non-obviousness requirement to be the heart of modern patent systems. Novelty and utility, although important, are easily met by most inventions. To satisfy the non-obviousness requirement is much harder.

The non-obviousness requirement aims at measuring an invention's contribution to the technological progress in the field and is ruled by §103 USC 35:

> A patent may not be obtained [...] if the differences between the subject matter sought to be patented and the prior art are such that the subject matter as a whole would have been obvious at the time the invention was made to a person having ordinary skill in the art to which the subject matter pertains.

The provision states clearly how a sufficient inventive step is measured: as the difference between the invented subject matter and the prior art. Thus, an invention is unpatentable if a person skilled in the art would find the solution to the underlying problem obvious. Trivial technical changes as well as obvious combinations of prior art that would satisfy the novelty requirement are barred from patent protection by this provision. In practice, the non-obviousness requirement is not easy to apply since the *person skilled in the art* is a hypothetical construct.

Although courts have increasingly ruled in patent validity cases that an invention must have been non-obvious because it had commercial success, the non-obviousness criterion is a measure of technological progress in a specific field.[15] The latter may raise social welfare in several ways. Firstly, in case a sophisticated invention is successful in the market, consumers enjoy new or improved products. Alternatively, they may be able to buy known products at lower prices because production is possible at lower costs. In both cases, the consumers' surplus is higher even though exclusive rights inevitably create a deadweight loss. Secondly, if the invention is not a marketable product, new technological know-how is created so that follow-on research becomes possible sooner. These efforts may eventually lead to marketable products or processes that have commercial success.[16]

Since there is evidence that technical quality and social welfare are positively correlated (Reitzig, 2005), should the non-obviousness standard be as high as possible to maximize social welfare? Weak non-obviousness requirements might have severe *side-effects* as the following example shows. A firm holds process patents for a therapeutical substance and has commercial success, and a second firm improves the production process slightly.[17] If the non-obviousness standard is weak, even trivial improvements receive a patent. As a consequence, the second firm is able to realize profits that do not correspond to the social value it added. However, the value of the patent and the profits of the first firm decline. Under those circumstances, firms behaving rationally may pursue suboptimally small, trivial inventions. Clark (1927) points out that firms may find it profitable to wait for a competitor to make an invention in case intellectual property is insufficiently protected. Weak non-obviousness standards may lead to this situation.

On the other hand, setting the non-obviousness standard too high might also yield suboptimal results. If we assume that the second firm did achieve a major improvement on the production process of the substance so that the drug has fewer side-effects, denying a patent to such improvements will certainly result in lower welfare. A more detailed analysis of the *optimal non-obviousness standard* is dedicated to Chapters 10 and 13.

Disclosure and enablement

The practice of diligently describing an invention arose during the Industrial Revolution when the perception of what society gains in exchange for the exclusive rights changed (cf *supra*). Previously, it was the product or the trade that was introduced and a demonstration of operability or a prototype was frequently required. With the Industrial Revolution, society became more interested in knowledge so that it became necessary that inventions are described in such a way that they can be reproduced. In detail, §112 USC 35 states that

> The specification shall contain a written description of the invention, and of the manner and process of making and using it, in such full, clear, concise, and exact terms as to enable any person skilled in the art to which it pertains, or with which it is most nearly connected, to make and use the same, and

shall set forth the best mode contemplated by the inventor of carrying out his invention.

The main parts of the disclosure and enablement requirement are (1) the definiteness of claims, (2) the written description, (3) enablement, and (4) the best mode. With the exception of the definiteness of claims, all other requirements apply to the specification in the body of the patent application (cf *supra*).

What exactly inventors claim to have invented can be found in the specification section and the claims section of the patent. The claims are the essence of a patent and constitute the legal definition of the patent, i.e. the patent scope. They are first consulted when conflicts, as e.g. infringement or a validity challenge, arise. Therefore, the *claim definiteness* requires that claims are written in such a way that the boundaries of the legal rights that are conferred by the patent can easily be understood by someone skilled in the art.

In the specification section, the invention is more extensively described. To satisfy the *written description* requirement inventors have to make clear what sets the invention apart from existing work. At the same time, there must not be a disparity of what the inventor claims in the specification and claims section of the patent.

According to the *enablement* requirement, applicants have not only to describe the invention itself, they also have to give extensive details on how to make the invention and how to use it. It must be written in such a way that someone skilled in the technology field can reproduce and use the invention without undue experimentation. Inventors are thus not allowed to withhold important pieces of information that enable them alone to work the invention after the patent lapses or expires.

Finally, according to the *best mode* requirement, the inventor must disclose the best mode to make and use the invention when there are certain choices, as e.g. to the pressure to be applied, materials to be used or the way certain parts are joined.

The requirements of disclosure and enablement regulate how much technological know-how is revealed to the public.[18] If the standards are low, inventors will keep part of the information secret and thereby enjoy the best of both protective mechanisms.[19] As a consequence, researchers that want to improve the invention or develop complementary devices have to spend (socially wasteful) resources in order to find out how the original invention works in the first place. Hence, lax disclosure and enablement standards inevitably increase the social costs of the invention (see e.g. Trajtenberg, 1990). Followers have not only to spend resources to rediscover the withheld information, but it takes longer until the improvements or complementary devices become available to consumers and the public at large.[20] Therefore, technological progress and economic growth can be expected to be slower when disclosure and enablement are not applied strictly.

At least in principle, high standards will also minimize disputes over patent rights.[21] The written description and the definiteness of claims requirement ensure that (1) the legal rights cover no more than what the applicant invented and (2) that the legal rights are clearly drawn. Consequently, high standards of disclosure and enablement lead to a higher certainty and encourage inventors to pursue fruitful research *and* to disclose the knowledge by seeking patent protection. At the same time, at least part of costly litigation procedures can be avoided. However, this also depends on a number of other factors.

5.2.2 Patent enforcement

After a patent has been issued, two possibilities arise for legal actions: (1) A potential infringer may seek to invalidate the patent, or (2) the patentee may sue an infringer. Usually, infringers defend themselves by claiming that the patent is invalid in the first place. Since potential infringers have the burden of proof, they have to collect evidence to cast sufficient doubt as to the validity of the patent. Hence, part of the judges' task will be to examine whether the patent indeed meets the patent requirements discussed above.

During an infringement action, courts have to establish whether the infringer's product or process does indeed violate the patentee's rights. Upon a positive finding, they have also to decide on appropriate remedies.

Infringement

§271 USC 35 specifies as to what infringement constitutes:[22]

> [...] whoever without authority makes, uses, offers to sell, or sells any patented invention, within the United States, or imports into the United States any patented invention during the term of the patent therefore, infringes the patent.

It is worth mentioning that it is irrelevant whether the accused infringers knew that the patent exists and whether they intended violate the patentee's rights.[23] Infringement is a matter of fact. If intention is considered at all, it affects the remedies chosen by the court.

Patent claims define the legal boundaries of a patent so that they have also to be consulted when determining whether or not an accused infringer's product or process violates the patentee's rights. Claims are always literally construed, where all the relevant patent documents (description, drawings, and the entire history of the patent) as well as additional materials such as e.g. dictionaries or expert testimonies may be used in guiding the court. However, literal infringement is rare. If infringers did know the patent they would surely change details to increase their chances in court. On the other hand, the probability that independent development leads to the same invention in each and every element is small. Yet, the patent scope as derived from the literal interpretation of the claims can be broadened or narrowed by the *Doctrine of Equivalents* and the *Reverse Doctrine of Equivalents*, respectively.

The Doctrine of Equivalents rests on the presumption that, if the same *functions* are used in the same *way* to obtain the same *result*, the process or product must be the same. This is known as the triple identity test. To declare a patent to be infringed on the basis of the Doctrine of Equivalents, two further prerequisites have to be met. Firstly, equivalence must be established for all elements of a claim and not just some of them. Secondly, a person skilled in the art must have known that the elements in question can be used interchangeably when infringement began. Thus, the Doctrine of Equivalents protects the patent owner against minor, insubstantial variations.

The Reverse Doctrine of Equivalents achieves the opposite effect: it protects the accused infringer.[24] The triple identity test can also be used as a guideline here. Different from the Doctrine of Equivalents, however, the Reverse Doctrine of Equivalents is invoked if the same function is employed in a *substantially different way* to obtain the same result. Under these circumstances, a patent may be found not to be infringed even though the accused device falls into the literal scope of the claims.

Accused infringers usually defend themselves by challenging the patent's validity. Hence, courts ultimately decide whether or not an invention merits a patent grant. This two-step system (the administrative and the judicial part) to ensure that the invention indeed satisfies the patent requirements has advantages and disadvantages. It might actually keep overall costs low. Despite the patent offices examination, there will always be some patents whose subject matter does not meet the patent requirements and have therefore been wrongly issued. However, most of them are not (commercially) valuable so that they are not disputed even if infringed. Yet, social costs in the form of higher prices or increased deadweight loss are negligible because the patent is a commercial failure. Only a minority of cases where inventions are valuable are decided in the courts. Therefore, the two-step procedure helps to keep the overall costs of the patent system low.

Yet, the system also generates a certain amount of uncertainty, since patent holders must face a certain probability that their patents are declared invalid by a court. Accordingly, the most sophisticated patent statute may not accomplish fostering innovations when the courts do not uphold the standards prescribed by law. In case patents are frequently revoked, inventors may turn to trade secrecy to protect their creative work. On a macro-economic level, research expenditures may be directed to other fields of technology or remain on a suboptimally low level across all fields of technology.

As far as infringement is concerned, it serves a as fine-tuning mechanism for the non-obviousness standard, apart from protecting patent holders' rights. The principal tools employed are the Doctrine of Equivalents and the Reverse Doctrine of Equivalents.

If the Doctrine of Equivalents is applied liberally, most of the patent cases will be found to be infringed. Since the doctrine effectively broadens the scope of a patent, follow-on research may be halted as even larger improvements on an existing subject matter will probably violate the original patent. On the other hand, if the Reverse Doctrine of Equivalents is widely deployed, most of the patent cases will be found non-infringing. As a result, the expected value of the patented invention will be lower, thereby generating only insufficient incentives to search for an invention in the first place or to resort to trade secrecy if possible.

Since both the Doctrine of Equivalents and its counterpart adjust the non-obviousness standard, the considerations in Chapters 10 and 13 also apply.

Remedies

The question of remedies only becomes relevant if a patent has been found valid *and* infringed. According to the Supreme Court's opinion, the patentee should be fully compensated for the injury suffered due to the infringement. Courts have several ways of accomplishing this, and they have considerable discretion on what they consider appropriate and how the compensation is to be determined. The principal tools are: (1) injunction relief, (2) reasonable royalty damage, (3) lost profits damage, and (4) wilful infringement.

After a patent has been found valid and infringed, society which, after all, grants the exclusive rights in exchange for the associated technological know-how, has an obligation to ensure that no further violation of the patentee's rights continues, i.e. the patent owner has a right to an *injunction relief*. To grant a permanent injunction relief is the usual procedure. However, there are some cases in which courts denied it on reasons of public interest. Since the patentee is still entitled to compensation, the patentee and the infringer have to agree on a licence. If both parties cannot reach agreement, the court will determine a suitable royalty.[25]

Generally, patent law aims at stopping any wrongdoing as soon as possible. Accordingly, the patentee may seek a preliminary injunction relief that stays in force until the trial ends.[26] However, courts are very cautious in granting a preliminary injunction relief since this could cause irrevocable damage to the accused infringer's business. After all, the findings of the court may eventually establish that the patent is either invalid or not infringed. Although the defendant has a right to be compensated for the interruption of his business, the particular line might be destroyed. The patentee has therefore to show convincingly that his patent is likely to be found valid and infringed by the court in order to get a preliminary injunction.

Reasonable royalty and lost profit damages are measures to compensate the patent owner for the injury he suffered on account of the infringement.[27] Naturally, patentees seek full compensation for any lost profits. The patentee has the burden of proof and the standards are rather high to prevent the infringer from being punished unduly. In case the court finds the patent owner's evidence on the lost profits unconvincing, it calculates the damage on the basis of a hypothetical licence contract both parties would have struck at the time when infringement began.[28]

Finally, if the court's findings demonstrate that the infringer was aware of the patent, *wilful infringement* is presumed. In this case, the infringer is liable to treble damage.

Remedies are imposed to ensure that infringers do not profit from their violation of patentees' rights. It also encourages licence agreements. However, apart from the patentee's willingness to licence, this requires that the infringer is aware of

Table 5.1 Legal and economic patent policy instruments

Legal instruments	Primary test through	Economic instruments	
Patentable subject matter	Patent office	Patentable subject matter	Chapter 12
Utility Novelty Non-obviousness	Patent office	Non-obviousness	Chapter 10, 13
Patent term		Patent term Maintenance fees	Chapter 7
Patent scope (infringement)	Courts	Patent scope Patent breadth	Chapter 8 Chapter 9

the patent before he decides to infringe. The mere awareness of the patent is sufficient to establish wilful infringement in which case the infringer is liable to treble damage. Hence, wilful infringement in its present form leads to a general disincentive to search for patents at any stage of research and development. Not only does it stand in the way of licence agreements, it is also at odds with a patent system that is otherwise designed to disseminate technological knowledge.

5.3 From patent law to economic modelling

Legal patent policy instruments do not easily translate into policy measures.[29] The problem arises because the disciplines serve totally different purposes. Patent law has to define rules and norms which ensure equal treatment of all patent applications and a certain degree of consistency without losing its flexibility. The law must be such that each and every patent case can be dealt with justly. Moreover, each and every case is considered on an individual basis. Economics, on the other hand, has to abstract from particular cases to find general effects and mechanisms. Thus, patent law provides necessarily more details than economic models can and should consider.

The present work focusses only on certain legal policy instruments. They are the ones most directly related to patents as opposed to the entire patent system, i.e. patentable subject requirements, patent requirements, patent term and patent scope. In Table 5.1, they are grouped according to whether the primary test is undertaken by the patent office, i.e. before the patent is issued, or by the courts, i.e. after the patent has been issued.

The question of whether patentable subject matter should be extended is straightforward to model. More interesting insights can be gained in an international framework though. Thus, this question is relegated to Part III.

Utility, novelty and non-obviousness are different patent requirements that ensure that a patent is only granted for inventions that make a sufficient contribution to the technological progress of a particular field. In economics, they can hardly be distinguished. The only requirement that can be operationalized is the non-obviousness standard which measures some sort of quality improvement in a technological field. It is studied in the national as well as the international framework, where the results of the former also serve as a reference point for the latter.

The seemingly straightforward question of the patent life is a more complex problem in economics. We distinguish between the statutory patent life and the effective patent term. This differentiation becomes important if one considers that only around one-third of all patents are maintained for the entire patent life (cf *infra*). Although a number of factors influence the effective patent life, the maintenance fee schedule is the most direct one.

As far as patent scope and infringement is concerned, it is only evaluated if disputes arise and, therefore, after a patent has been issued. In economics, a distinction between patent scope and patent breadth is reasonable. Patent scope measures how different an alternative production process or a product must be to not infringe a certain patent. It protects against competing, *contemporary* technologies and products and, thus, against imitation.

In contrast, patent breadth is assumed to protect against *succeeding inventions* and therefore against trivial quality improvements in the same technological field. The problems of hold-up or blocking patents are closely related but not considered here (see e.g. Ellingsen and Johannesson, 2004).

5.A A comparison of patent fees

Table 5.2 presents the minimum fees an inventor would have to pay to receive and maintain a patent in the US and the European Union (EU). In the US, small entities (e.g. individuals) get a 50 percent reduction on all fees. Depending on how many dependent and independent claims a patent contains, additional fees would become relevant. Here, it is assumed that the hypothetical patent has one independent claim and at least one dependent claim, but no more than ten dependent ones.

In Europe, all fees except for the designation fee are paid only once, independent of the number of EU member countries for which the patent is applied for. The maximum designation fee is €560, i.e. for seven countries.

Table 5.2 Patent fees in the United States (US) and the European Union (EU)

	US in $		EU in €
	Normal	*Small entity*	
Basic fee	300	150	95
Multiple dependent claims	360	180	
Designation fee, max. € 560			80
Search fee	500	250	1000
Examination fee	200	100	1335
Grant fee	1400	700	750

(Continued)

Table 5.2 (Con'd)

	US in $		EU in €
	Normal	Small entity	
Maintenance fees			For Germany
3 year			70
3.5 year	900	450	
4 year			70
5 year			90
6 year			130
7 year			180
7.5 year	2300	1150	
8 year			240
9 year			290
10 year			350
11 year			470
11.5 year	3800	1900	
12 year			620
13 year			760
14 year			910
15 year			1060
16 year			1230
17 year			1410
18 year			1590
19 year			1760
20 year			1940

Source: http://www.uspto.gov/web/offices/ac/qs/fee2006may15.htm for the USPTO, http://www.european-patent-office.org/epo/fees1.htm for EPO, and Annex to §2(1) PatKostG (Law on the Fees of the German Patent and Trademark Office) for Germany.

Part II

Patent policy from a national perspective

6 Introduction

As Chapter 4 has shown, discussions on whether patent systems are indeed beneficial to society or how to design a patent system are as old as patent systems themselves. The first formal-mathematical formulation of a patent policy instrument – the patent length – was developed in the mid-1960s. Since then, the effects of many other patent policy instruments have been studied. Naturally, the first models relied on a purely national framework. The second part of this book introduces the most influential approaches for a closed economy.

Chapter 7 is concerned with the optimal patent term. Clearly, we have to distinguish between the statutory and the effective patent length. The seminal work of Nordhaus (1967) that is introduced in a slightly more general version is concerned with the legal patent term. The derived results are similar to the original version. Although the work of Nordhaus is very important, its relevance was limited even in the mid-1960s. Patents have to be renewed in all industrialized countries so that the usually progressive renewal schemes determine the effective patent term. In fact, only a minority of patents are maintained for the full statutory patent length. Therefore, it seems appropriate to introduce a second group of models that describe the optimal renewal schemes.

Chapters 8 and 9 are both dedicated to policy instruments that define patent rights in relation to the rights of third parties. In particular, Chapter 8 focusses on the question of how many different unpatented or unpatentable products and technologies should not infringe an existing patent. Excluding more alternatives to the product or process patent from its patent scope increases the consumers' surplus today since the patentee's ability to raise prices are limited. However, this may come at the expense of a steady stream of future inventions because the accumulated profits may be insufficient to cover the research costs. The chapter starts with a simple setting in which the patent scope cannot influence a firm's decision on the research effort and imitation is prohibitively expensive by assumption. The remainder of the chapter analyses the effect of these assumptions by removing them.

Patent breadth determines the patent rights of subsequent inventions in the same technology field, i.e. it exclusively applies to cumulative inventions. Chapter 9 characterizes the optimal patent breadth. In the first part of the chapter, the model of Chang (1995) is introduced which relies on a simple scenario of two subsequent inventions. This framework suffices to demonstrate the consequences of wide or narrow patent breadths on the economy. In a sequence of only two inventions, second-generation patents cannot be violated. This fact alters the second inventors behaviour in choosing the research effort. Therefore, the model of O'Donoghue *et al.* (1998) who rely on an infinite sequence of patent races is presented as well.

Finally, Chapter 10 studies the effects of changes in the non-obviousness standard on a closed economy. When studying other patent policy measures, it is usually assumed that the inventions do satisfy all patent requirements, i.e. novelty, utility and non-obviousness (cf *supra*). To pass the non-obviousness test is usually the hardest, and a considerable number of patent applications fail this test. Assuming that patents are effective in increasing the appropriability of the returns in at least some technology fields, changing the non-obviousness standard will have profound effects on the firms' behaviour and on an economy's welfare. Chapter 10 derives some important results that will form the basis of the analysis in Chapter 13 for an open economy.

7   The optimal patent term

It is surprising how little the statutory patent term varied over time. During the early stages of patent systems, the inventor was granted monopoly rights for 14 years. Since apprenticeship lasted for seven years in the Middle Ages and the early Renaissance, this allowed inventors to train two apprentices successively in their trade, thereby passing on skills and knowledge. Before the Agreements of Trade Related Aspects of Intellectual Property (TRIPs Agreement) was signed, the patent term was only slightly longer, i.e. 17 years from the issuing date of the patent, in the United States (US). Even then, most European countries provided for a patent protection of 20 years measured from the application date. The TRIPs Agreement has adopted a similar provision, stipulating that every signatory member has to provide for a patent protection of *at least* 20 years, thereby allowing for even longer patent terms.[1] The patent term has to be granted indiscriminately for all technology fields.

It is also interesting to note that countries do not grant patents for more than 20 years although this would be perfectly in line with the TRIPs Agreement. So, can we conclude that 20 years is the optimal length of patent protection? This chapter probes into this question by introducing two models. The first model is that of Nordhaus (1969) who was the first to formalize a patent policy instrument. He characterizes the optimal (uniform) patent term. We use a slightly more general version of Nordhaus' original model. Essentially, the results remain unchanged, showing that the optimal, uniform patent term depends on certain firm or industry characteristics. This property would make it desirable to offer a differentiated patent policy. In its simplest form it would provide that *larger* inventions as measured by the improvement over the prior art are granted longer patents.

As mentioned above, neither the patent authority nor the patentee itself frequently has accurate information on the size of the invention or its value when applying. This information is slowly and usually asymmetrically revealed over time. Cornelli and Schankerman (1999) show that a progressive renewal fee structure is welfare enhancing as compared to a uniform patent term in these situations. However, owing to information asymmetries, a first-best solution cannot be achieved.

Before introducing both models, the practice of patent renewal and some empirical facts on patent maintenance are presented.

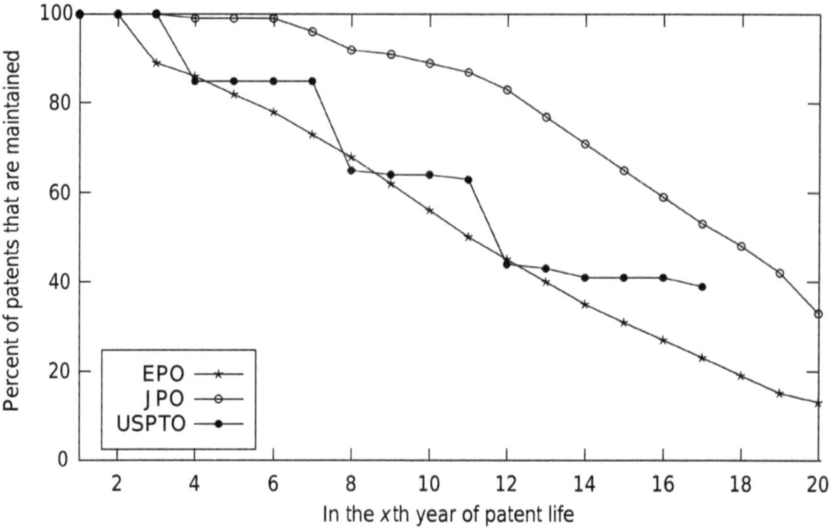

Data source: Trilateral Patent Offices (2006).

Figure 7.1 Patent maintenance at the European Patent Office (EPO), the Japanese Patent
　　　　　Office (JPO) and the US Patent and Trademark Office (USPTO) in 2005.

7.1 Patent maintenance

It is frequently stated that the patent term is 20 years. In fact however, this is merely
the maximal duration of a patent and only a minority extends to the full length. As
mentioned above, patents are subject to renewal in many countries, among them
the US, Japan, and European countries. Only if renewal fees are paid timely is the
patent maintained for another year in Germany and Japan.[2] In the US, renewal
fees are due after 3.5, 7.5, and 11.5 years (cf Table 5.2 *supra*). In case the renewal
fees are not paid within a certain time period, the patent lapses automatically.

　　Whether or not patentees do renew a patent for another year depends on two
factors: the level of the maintenance fees and the expected value (or the expected
profits) of the patent stemming from the extension. The latter is influenced by a
number of circumstances, e.g. whether market approval has been obtained for a
drug whose effective ingredient has been patented or whether a close substitute or
even an improvement has terminated the effective patent life.[3] In any case, only
the most valuable patents will be maintained for the maximum patent term for any
given patent fee schedule.

　　Figure 7.1 shows the share of patents that have been maintained until the
respective year.[4] The three graphs share one feature: they all decline. As it can
be seen, half of the patents are maintained for approximately eleven years in the
European Union (EU) and the US, while in Japan, they are sustained for nearly
18 years in 2005. Grabowski (2002) finds similar figures for drugs. Between 1990
and 1995, the average patent life (including the extension that can be obtained

for drugs) was 11.7 years. Only 13 and 34 percent of patents cover the maximum patent life in the EU and Japan. Assuming that there is a positive correlation between the patent value and the number of years for which patents are maintained, it can be concluded that most patents have a relatively small value while only a fraction of them has a high value.[5]

Do the higher maintenance rates in Japan imply that the most valuable patents are applied for and granted in Japan? Although a thorough application of high patent standards may result in only the most valuable inventions surviving the examination process, nothing in the data supports this hypothesis. It is much more likely that lower renewal fees account for the difference.[6]

7.2 Nordhaus' model of optimal uniform patent life

Over- as well as under-investment into the creation of inventions are plausible scenarios. However, patent laws and international treaties were explicitly designed to facilitate inventions:

> The protection and enforcement of intellectual property rights should contribute to the promotion of technological innovation and to the transfer and dissemination of technology, to the mutual advantage of producers and users of technological knowledge and in a manner conducive to social and economic welfare, and to a balance of rights and obligations.
>
> (World Trade Organization, 1994: Article 7)

Thus, exclusive rights were not made to correct both, over- and under-investment into innovations, but only to alleviate an under-provision of innovations. Exclusive rights always bear monopolistic elements that inevitably create static inefficiencies which result in higher prices and lower consumers' surplus during the patent life. Rather than trying to eliminate these inefficiencies, they are used to accomplish a desired effect — more inventions. Society benefits during as well as after the patent term. New products as e.g. more efficient drugs unquestionably raise social welfare even though the drugs are only available at prices above the competitive ones. After the patent expires, society gains from the correction of the market distortion initiated by the exclusive rights.

Nordhaus was among the first economists to draw attention to the patent length as a policy instrument by which a policymaker can induce firms to create inventions at a social optimally level.[7] His work is introduced here in a slightly generalized version.

7.2.1 Public vs private knowledge as the source for ideas

One may consider ideas as the seeds of innovations.[8] An idea may or may not mature into an invention and it may or may not be turned into an innovation by spending time and resources. Frequently, two approaches are used to describe the nature of ideas. An idea may originate from a pool of *public knowledge*.

This describes a situation in which the next steps on the line of progress in a certain technology field are laid out. Typically, firms in the industry that have research facilities strive to be the first to take the logical next step, i.e. firms engage in a patent race.[9] Although ideas stemming from public knowledge may result in all kinds of innovation, they may more often be associated with non-drastic innovations, i.e. innovations that cannot ensure the monopoly position under monopoly pricing in a perfect competitive market.[10]

On the other hand, the *private knowledge* approach postulates that technical progress has come to a point where all further developments of the technology line seem to be exhausted. New paths have to be explored where previous research experience and success gives perhaps little or no advantage over less experienced competitors. Here, ideas come from private sources of information or inspiration. This situation is incompatible with patent races and may be more frequently associated with drastic innovations, i.e. innovations that put inventors in a monopoly position even though they charge the monopoly price.

The two approaches represent different archetypes. As usual, however, reality blends both types. Successful firms may even pursue both alternatives at the same time. They may exploit public knowledge to create non-drastic innovations to secure success in the short run. At the same time, they may try to push the known boundaries of the technology field to create drastic innovations. The latter will certainly ensure a dominant market position in the long run.

Both approaches have been used extensively in the literature. In the present work, the models presented in Chapters 7 and 9 postulate that private knowledge is the source of ideas whereas Chapters 10 to 13 are based on the public knowledge approach.

7.2.2 The timing of the decisions

The starting point of the analysis is a homogeneous product market. There is a large number of firms so that the market is perfectly competitive in absence of active patents. Accordingly, firms receive zero profits before and after the patent life.

Here, it is assumed that private knowledge is the source of the innovation. Thus, only one firm can undertake the research project that turns the idea into an invention by allocating a certain amount of effort and resources to it. Owing to the assumption of a homogeneous product market, the innovation must be a process innovation. Otherwise, the market would become horizontally or vertically differentiated.

Without loss of generality, it is assumed that the research and development (R&D) process is frictionless and deterministic. In particular, this implies that creating the invention and developing it into an innovation does not take time. Arguably, the R&D process is a very rudimentary one. However, since only one firm had the idea for the innovation, R&D competition does not exist, and a longer R&D process would simply increase research costs. Since the R&D process is deterministic, there is no uncertainty over the quality of the invention or innovation.

Once the invention has been created, the firm applies for a patent.[11] The patent requirements are presumed to be low, i.e. every invention qualifies for a patent and it is issued immediately. The invention is protected for T years and patent rights are broad and absolute so that competitors do not have the possibility to invent around the innovation during the patent's life.[12] It is also assumed that other innovations in the same technology line are not created so that the inventor enjoys the full term of patent protection. After the patent expired, every firm is able to produce and market the invention at no additional costs, the market becomes perfectly competitive again.

Formally, three stages are distinguished: In the first stage, the government chooses the patent term T, $T \in \mathbb{R}_0$. In the second stage, the creative firm creates the invention and is granted the patent. In the last stage, firms set prices $p \in \mathbb{R}_0$ and collect profits. The latter depend on whether the patent has expired yet.

7.2.3 The market stage

Assume that the firm has introduced its process innovation and temporarily occupies the monopoly position created by the patent. The monopoly sets the product price so as to maximize profits and faces a market demand of $Q(p)$. The latter satisfies the usual properties, i.e. market demand is a downward sloping, concave function of the market price: $\partial Q / \partial p := Q_p(p) < 0$ and $\partial^2 Q / \partial p^2 = Q_{pp} \leq 0$.[13]

The production technology shall exhibit constant returns to scale so that total production costs are linear in output. Without fixed costs, the sole effect of the process innovation is to reduce the unit costs of production. Let c_0 and c_1 denote unit costs associated with the production technology before and after the innovation. Then, the monopoly's lower marginal costs c_1 can always be expressed as $c_1 = c_0 - u$, where u measures the size of the innovation.

While the patent is in force, the patentee occupies the monopoly position and is able set a price above its marginal costs c_1. However, depending on the size of the innovation u, the patent holder might not be able to charge the monopoly price without losing the entire market. Assuming that the monopoly cannot discriminate prices and if the process innovation is non-drastic, the monopoly is constrained by the unit costs of the original production technology so that the optimal price p^* is $p^* = c_0$. On the other hand, if the innovation is drastic, the patent holder's optimal decision is to charge the monopoly price p^m that maximizes the profit function $\pi = (p - c_0 + u)Q(p)$ by satisfying the first-order condition

$$Q(p) + (p - c_0 + u)Q_p(p) = 0. \qquad (7.1)$$

In general, the function describing the monopoly's optimal pricing decision can be written as $p^*(u) := \mathrm{argmax}_p \, (p - c_0 + u)Q(p)$.

Lemma 7.1.   Under the above introduced assumptions, a larger process innovation will have the following effects:

$$\frac{\partial p^*}{\partial u} \le 0,$$

$$\frac{\partial \pi^m}{\partial u} = Q(p^*) > 0.$$

In particular, a larger process innovation will have no effect on the optimal price if the innovation is non-drastic. In this case $\partial p^* / \partial u = 0$ holds true. Only if the innovation is a drastic one, the patentee charges the monopoly price which is inversely related to the unit costs of production. Thus, a larger invention will reduce the monopoly price.

Without uncertainty on the demand or the supply side, setting the profit maximizing price leads to a one-to-one relationship between the innovation size and monopoly profit. Consequently, the improvement u can be expressed as a function of the monopoly profit π^m, i.e. $u(\pi^m)$. This function informs us about the size of the process innovation necessary to create a certain profit level.

After the patent expires and all firms are free to use the superior production technology, competition forces firms to set prices equal to marginal costs so that they earn zero profits again.

7.2.4 The inventor's research effort

In order to convert the idea for an improvement into a process innovation, the firm has to exert at least some research effort h, $h \in \mathbb{R}_0$.[14] Since the research process is perfectly deterministic, the R&D process can be represented by a 'production' function $u(h)$. To any research effort of h it assigns a specific reduction in unit costs u. Naturally, we expect the innovation size to increase with the research effort, but at a decreasing rate, i.e. $\partial u / \partial h := u_h(h) > 0$ and $\partial^2 u / \partial h^2 = u_{hh}(h) < 0$. Let $C(h)$ denote the research cost function that has the usual (weakly) convex shape, i.e. with $C_h(h) > 0$ and $C_{hh} \ge 0$.

The rational inventor aims at maximizing the discounted stream of profits. During the patent life T, the firm earns flow profits of $\pi^m(h) = (p^* - c_0 + u(h))Q(p^*)$. After the patent expired, the innovation becomes public knowledge and all firms are free to use the superior production technology. Hence, the product market becomes perfectly competitive again and positive profits are eliminated.[15] In this situation, the present value of future profits V can be written as

$$
\begin{aligned}
V(h, T) &= \int_0^T e^{-rt} \, \pi^m(h) \, dt - C(h) \\
&= \frac{\gamma(T)}{r} \pi^m(h) - C(h),
\end{aligned}
$$

(7.2)

where r is the exogenously given interest rate and γ is defined as $\gamma(T) := 1 - e^{-rT}$. γ takes values in the interval $[0, 1]$.

In accordance with the timing of the game, the patentee treats the patent life T as given when maximizing the present value $V(\cdot)$ with respect to the research effort. The first-order condition to the firm's maximization problem follows immediately with

$$\frac{\gamma(T)}{r} \pi_h^m(h^*) = C_h(h^*), \tag{7.3}$$

where $\pi_h^m = Q(p^*) u_h(h)$ due to the Envelope Theorem (cf Lemma 7.1). As usual, the profit maximizing effort balances marginal benefits on the left-hand side and marginal costs of an additional unit of effort on the right-hand side of the equation.

The assumptions posed on production and research technologies as well as market demand are insufficient to guarantee the existence of a solution to condition (7.3). If marginal costs exceed marginal benefits for all possible effort levels h, the research project is obviously unprofitable for the firm, and a rational firm will abandon it. Specifically, the firm will not dedicate any resources to the invention so that $h^* = 0$ if $rC_h(h) > \gamma(T)\pi_h^m(h)$ for all $h \in \mathbb{R}_0$.

Proposition 7.1. Existence and uniqueness of a solution to condition (7.3) with $h^* > 0$ is ensured at least for some T if

$$\frac{\pi_h^m(0)}{r} > C_h(0), \tag{7.4}$$

where $\pi_h^m(0) = Q(c_0) u_h(0)$.

Figure 7.2 illustrates the Proposition. Intuitively, the condition in (7.4) states that if the patent lasts forever, the firm will develop the invention into a process innovation. Since $\lim_{T \to \infty} \gamma(T) = 1$, the term on the left-hand side of inequality (7.4) is the value of an incremental profit flow created by the first unit of effort when the patent term is infinite. If this value exceeds the associated costs of $C_h(0)$, the firm will choose a positive effort level to realize the invention. By the assumptions posed on the research and production technologies as well as on the market demand, it is clear that every positive optimum h^* is unique.

Even though an innovation may be profitable for an infinite patent life, a firm may not want to develop the invention into an innovation for shorter patent terms. In general, $\pi_h^m(h)/r$ stands for the profits from an additional unit of effort when the patent life is infinite. Consequently, it is also the maximal benefit that can be achieved from an additional unit of research effort. For any finite patent term, an additional unit of effort will yield lower gains of $\gamma(T)\pi_h^m(h)/r$. Given that the innovation is profitable for an infinite patent term and that $C_h(0) > 0$, there exists a patent term $\tilde{T} \in [0, \infty)$ for which the firm is indifferent between developing the process innovation and doing nothing, i.e. $\gamma(\tilde{T})\pi_h^m(0)/r = C_h(0)$. Then, the

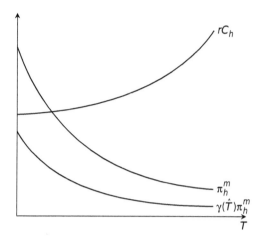

Figure 7.2 The optimal research effort.

process innovation will be created and used for a patent life of $T > \tilde{T}$. On the other hand, the total accumulated profits from the first unit of research effort will not suffice to recoup the initial innovation costs if $T < \tilde{T}$; a patent becomes too short to cover expenses. This situation is illustrated in Figure 7.2 for a patent life of $\hat{T} < \tilde{T}$ years. Note that if $C_h(0) = 0$, i.e. if the first unit of effort is inexpensive, the threshold value $\tilde{T}$ becomes zero so that a unique, strictly positive profit maximizing research effort exists for all $T \in \mathbb{R}_+$.

Given a unique profit maximizing effort level h^* exists, it is a function of the patent life and the properties of the market demand and the research technology. With respect to the patent life we find:

Proposition 7.2.   Given $T \geq \tilde{T}$, the optimal research effort is an increasing function of the patent term T.

The primary effect of a longer patent is that the monopoly profit can be earned for a longer period of time. In turn, total profits from a previously optimal research effort increase without raising the costs. Since the benefits from an additional effort unit are now higher, the inventor can afford to exert a greater effort. Thus, the innovative firm can afford to increase its efforts.

7.2.5 The optimal patent length

In the model introduced here, patent life T is the only policy instrument to encourage innovative activity. As demonstrated in Proposition 7.2, longer patents have indeed the desired effect of stimulating the inventors to exert higher research efforts. In doing so, the innovation size, i.e. the reduction in unit costs, increases and may eventually raise the consumers' surplus as prices decrease due to higher production efficiency (cf Lemma 7.1). At the same time, an extension of the patent term also prolongs the time during which static inefficiencies in the form of deadweight loss reduce the consumers' surplus. From a social point of view, the patent length should extend to the point where social benefits and social costs of an additional year of protection equalize.

It is assumed that the policymaker seeks to maximize welfare. In the current framework, this is achieved by maximizing the welfare stemming from the only available invention. Since inventors are granted exclusive rights, instantaneous welfare during the patent life and after the patent has expired differ. Let Δw and d be defined as follows:

$$\Delta w(h) := \int_{c_0 - u(h)}^{c_0} Q(\tilde{p}) \, d\tilde{p},$$

$$d(h) := \int_{c_0 - u(h)}^{p^*(h)} Q(\tilde{p}) \, d\tilde{p} - \pi^m(h),$$

The function $\Delta w(\cdot)$ measures the entire instantaneous social welfare that can be attributed to the process innovation. It consists of the monopoly profit π^m and the deadweight loss $d(\cdot)$ which only becomes available to society after the patent has been expired. The deadweight loss $d(\cdot)$ represents society's instantaneous costs of the patent system.

Given $\Delta w(\cdot)$ and $d(\cdot)$, the present value of future welfare streams can be written as

$$W(T) = \int_0^\infty e^{-rt} \Delta w(\cdot) \, dt - \int_0^T e^{-rt} d(\cdot) \, dt - C(\cdot),$$

$$= \frac{1}{r} \left[\Delta w(\cdot) - \gamma d(\cdot) \right] - C(h), \tag{7.5}$$

where again $\gamma = 1 - e^{-rT}$, and the deadweight loss has to be deducted from the social benefits during the patent life.

The policymaker's problem is then to maximize the objective function (7.5) with respect to the patent term T and anticipating the firm's optimal choice on the research effort. However, since γ is a monotonically increasing function of the patent life T, the original problem is identical to maximizing function (7.5) with respect to γ. For convenience sake, we use the latter formulation:

$$\max_{h, \gamma} \quad W(h, \gamma) = \frac{1}{r} \left[\Delta w(h) - \gamma d(h) \right] - C(h),$$

$$\text{s.t.} \quad \gamma u_h(h) Q(p^*(h)) - r C_h(h) = 0.$$

Applying the standard techniques to the above problem yields the following generalization of the results derived in Nordhaus (1967):

Proposition 7.3.   The optimal patent term is given by

$$\gamma^* = \max\{0, \bar{\gamma}\}$$

with

$$\bar{\gamma} = \frac{u_h Q(c_1) - \lambda r C_{hh}}{u_h Q(c_1) - \lambda u_{hh} Q(p) + p_u \big(Q(p) - \lambda u_h Q_p\big) u_h} \tag{7.6}$$

$$\lambda = \frac{d(h)}{u_h Q(p)}$$

From equation (7.6) it is clear that not every invention deserves patent protection from a social point of view. In particular, society does not benefit if any research effort is directed into projects or technology lines for which the research costs are expanding rapidly with the research effort, i.e. $C_{hh}(h)$ is large, while the obtained cost reductions are moderate, i.e. $u_h(h)$ remains small. To ensure that a positive optimal patent life T exists, two additional assumptions are necessary. Let the research cost function be linear in h and the innovation be non-drastic so that $C_{hh}(h) = 0$ and $p_u(u(h)) = 0$. Then, equation (7.6) becomes

$$\bar{\gamma} = \frac{1}{1 + \dfrac{d(h)}{u(h)Q(c_1)} \upsilon}, \tag{7.7}$$

where $\upsilon := -u_{hh} u(h)/(u_h)^2 > 0$ measures the curvature of the research technology. It immediately follows:

Proposition 7.4.   Let the research cost function be linear, the innovation be non-drastic and the market demand be (weakly) concave in the market price. Then, the optimal patent term is positive and finite, i.e. a

$$\gamma^* = \bar{\gamma} \in (0, 1)$$

exists.

Equation (7.7) also allows us to derive some inference about the properties of the optimal patent life. $\bar{\gamma}$ is entirely determined by the properties of the market demand and the research technology captured by υ. With respect to the market demand, unambiguous results cannot be obtained unless making specific assumptions on the functional form. However, equation (7.7) shows that industries in which the diminishing returns of research effort are less pronounced, i.e. where υ is low, will have a longer optimal patent life.

7.3 Optimal renewal schemes

The previous section has shown that differences in firm and industry characteristics makes differentiated patent terms desirable. In addition, incentives should be created that induce firms to pursue more socially valuable inventions, i.e. larger ones. This can be achieved by offering stronger patents to larger inventions. Yet, trying to implement a patent system that attempts to differentiate the strength of protection to such a degree is not only impractical due to the enormous costs it would entail. It is also impossible since the necessary information to determine the individually tailored protection is either unavailable or is revealed at an uncertain point in time after the patent application has been made. At the same time, the Agreement of Trade Related Aspects of Intellectual Property (TRIPs Agreement) does not leave much room to accommodate the needs of individual inventions, whole technology classes or industries.

For a long time, the pragmatic solution has been to make longer patents more expensive. Once a patent has been issued, the patent holder has to pay fees in order to maintain his exclusive rights on a regular basis. In case he fails to do so, the patent is simply terminated. Usually, the fees increase over time. In Germany e.g. 70 € are due for the third year and 1,940 € for the 20th year (see Table 5.2 *supra*).

Two factors may have motivated the introduction of renewal schemes: the necessity for funding and the desire that more valuable inventions should receive a higher reward in the form of longer protection. Since a patent holder will certainly not maintain a patent that has outlived its usefulness, e.g. because a new discovery has rendered the previous invention obsolete, a progressive fee structure just achieves the ends. Indeed, roughly 50 percent of patented inventions in the US and the EU are maintained for no more than 10 years (cf *supra*).

Pakes (1986) contrives a model of patent renewal to estimate that value of patents.[16] Since the estimates and the real data on patent renewal are very close, the hypothesis that the actual duration of a patent and its value are positively correlated seems to be supported by empirical evidence.

7.3.1 Asymmetric information on the patent value

The model of Cornelli and Schankerman (1999) is to be introduced here.[17] The basic structure of timing and decision making is identical to the model of Nordhaus (1967). The differences in the assumptions and interpretation of parameters and variables are discussed here.

The previous section merely required that the research cost function is weakly convex in the research effort level. Here, the function $C(h)$ now takes a specific form, it is quadratic (cf Assumption 7.1 *infra*). The assumption that the research process is completely deterministic is maintained so that it can be perfectly described by a research technology function $u(h)$. The model of Cornelli and Schankerman (1999) is not restricted to process innovations, but also applies to product innovations. Consequently, the research technology does not necessarily reduce unit costs but it does affect market demand $Q(p, u)$.

Even with the slightly altered assumptions on the nature of the invention, the analysis of the market stage in section 7.2.3 remains essentially valid. In particular, the optimal pricing decision is a function of the innovation size $u(h)$ alone. Moreover, the monopoly profit π^m remains an increasing function of the innovation size if market demand is an increasing function of u which shall be considered to be true henceforth. The latter property is important because it firstly allows us to express the improvement size u as a function of the monopoly profit π^m. Secondly, it becomes apparent that the important information on the market demand is essentially captured in the profit function provided the pricing is optimal. Consequently, it is sufficient to pose regularity assumptions directly on the profit function. Specifically, the following assumptions shall be maintained:

Assumption 7.1.   The cost and the profit functions are twice continuously differentiable with the following properties:

1. $C(h) = h^2/2$,
2. $\pi_h^m(h, \alpha) > 0, \pi_{hh}^m(h, \alpha) < 0, \pi_\alpha^m(h, \alpha) > 0, \pi_{h\alpha}(h, \alpha) > 0$, where α denotes the appropriation effectiveness.

According to the second assumption, a higher research effort will always increase the monopoly profit, but at a decreasing rate. Inventions for which the returns can more easily be appropriated have a positive effect on profits and make an additional unit of effort more profitable.

For a differentiated renewal scheme to be optimal, some degree of asymmetric information must be present. Otherwise, the central patent authority is always able to determine the optimal patent life for each individual invention. In the present model, appropriation effectiveness is supposed to be private information, i.e. the firm knows the value of α, but the central authority has only information on the general distribution.[18] Specifically, the cumulative distribution function is denoted by $F[\alpha]$, the density function is $f[\alpha]$ and α can take values from the interval $[0, \bar{\alpha}]$.

Before we characterize the optimal patent fee structure, two benchmark cases are introduced.

7.3.2 *The benchmark models*

To compare the performance of a differentiated patent fee structure, Cornelli and Schankerman (1999) use two benchmark situations: the first comprises the *full-information model* where the patent authority can observe the appropriation parameter α, but not the research effort. In the second case, it is postulated that the central authority cannot observe α and therefore decides to implement a *uniform patent life*.

Although there are cases in which the first-best solution can be implemented by appropriate mechanisms, this is certainly not the rule in the presence of asymmetric information. In general, the patent authority would have to observe the appropriation ability α and the research effort h^* in order to realize the social optimum. By knowing both variables, the patent authority could at least in principle calculate the value of the patent and determine the optimal patent length for each combination of $\{h^*, \alpha\}$. Since at least the research effort h^* is unobservable by the patent authority, the *full-information model* and the *model of a uniform patent life* will yield only second-best results.

The full-information model

Assume that the firm chooses the profit maximizing price in the market stage so that the reduced-form profit function $\pi^m(h, \alpha)$ satisfies Assumption 7.1. Then, the firm's problem of choosing the optimal research effort and the first-order condition to this problem remain virtually unchanged to (7.2) and (7.3). The only difference is that the (marginal) profit depends on the appropriation parameter α. The specific form of the research cost function in Assumption 7.1 ensures existence as well as uniqueness of a solution to the first-order condition (7.3).

In the present model, the social benefits are slightly differently divided into their main components. Here, the instantaneous welfare w *during the patent life* is used for the analysis of the patent authority's problem:

$$w(\pi^m) = \int_{p^*}^{\infty} Q(\tilde{p}, u(\pi^m)) d\tilde{p} + \pi^m,$$

$$d(\pi^m) = \int_{c}^{p^*} Q(\tilde{p}, u(\pi^m)) d\tilde{p} - \pi^m.$$

For convenience's sake, the definition of the deadweight loss has been restated. Given both definitions, the present value of the welfare flows can be written as

$$W(\pi^m, T) = \int_0^{\infty} w(\pi^m) dt + \int_T^{\infty} d(\pi^m) dt - C(h),$$

$$= \frac{1}{r}[w(\pi^m) + (1 - \gamma)d(\pi^m)] - C(h), \tag{7.8}$$

where again $\gamma = 1 - e^{-rT}$ and $C(h) = h^2/2$ by Assumption 7.1.

The patent authority's problem is then to maximize the stream of welfare (7.8) stemming from the particular invention with respect to the patent life and subject to the profit maximizing choice of the research effort. The following result ensues for the full-information model:

Proposition 7.5 (Cornelli and Schankerman, 1999, Proposition 1). The full-information, second-best policy $T^{**}(\alpha)$ satisfies the following equation at each value of α

$$\frac{1}{r}[w_\pi + (1 - \gamma)d_\pi]h_T = h^* h_T^* + (1 - \gamma)d(\pi). \tag{7.9}$$

In the first-order condition (7.9), the social benefits from an additional year of patent protection in the full-information scenario are on the left-hand side whereas the social costs are on the right-hand side. As it can be seen from the left-hand side of the first-order condition, there are no direct social benefits from a longer patent life. The benefits work through a higher research effort h. A higher research effort does increase both, the instantaneous welfare flow $w(\pi^m)$ that can be collected during as well as after the patent life and the deadweight loss $d(\pi^m)$ increasing the welfare after the exclusive rights expired.

Unlike social benefits, an additional year of patent protection has direct as well as indirect effects on social costs. According to the right-hand side of equation (7.9), the direct effect captures the fact that society has to wait an additional year before it can appropriate the deadweight loss that has increased due to the higher research effort. The indirect effect $h^* h_T^*$ measures the costs that are associated with the additional resources dedicated to research.

The uniform-patent life model

Again, the problem of the firm to maximize the discounted stream of profits with respect to the research effort remains unchanged so that the first-order condition is given by (7.3).

In the uniform-patent life model, the patent authority cannot observe the appropriation parameter α or the firm's research effort. Thus, the policymaker is not able to condition the patent life on either of the two variables. Facing uncertainty over the appropriation effectiveness α, the patent authorities problem changes to seeking the optimal, uniform patent length that maximizes the *expected* stream of discounted welfare:

$$EW = \int_0^{\bar{\alpha}} W(\pi^m, T) \, dF[\alpha],$$

where E stands for the expectation operator and $W(\pi^m, T)$ is given in (7.8). Cornelli and Schankerman (1999) obtain the following result:

Proposition 7.6 (Cornelli and Schankerman, 1999, Proposition 2).   The optimal uniform patent length T^U satisfies the following equation:

$$\int_0^{\bar{\alpha}} \left[\frac{1}{r} (w_\pi + (1 - \gamma) d_\pi) \pi_T^m \right] dF[\alpha] = \int_0^{\bar{\alpha}} \left[h^* h_T^* + (1 - \gamma) d(\cdot) \right] dF[\alpha].$$

$$(7.10)$$

The optimal uniform patent life equates the expected marginal social welfare and the expected marginal social costs of an additional year of patent protection when the appropriation ability is private information. The expected social benefits consist of the usual components: the increased flow welfare and deadweight loss that can, however, only be appropriated after the patent has expired. Likewise, the expected changes in social costs comprise the private ones, i.e. the higher research costs, and the deadweight loss that arise because monopoly privileges are granted for one additional year of protection. Different from the full-information case, the optimal, uniform patent term also depends on the properties of the distribution function.

Although neither benchmark model achieves the social optimum, it will provide incentives to undertake research. Yet, a uniform patent term will give too much encouragement to firms with low α and will still be insufficient to induce firm with a higher α to pursue larger inventions. A differentiated patent policy can solve the dilemma as demonstrated below.

7.3.3 Optimal differentiation policy

The basic structure

To determine the optimal renewal fee structure that may, after all, consist of a uniform fee for a fixed patent term, the concept of mechanism design is employed. The difference between the mechanism design and other concepts in game theory is that the strategy space of one player, the principal, comprises rules or designs which govern all subsequent dealings.

According to Fudenberg and Tirole (1993: 244) a game of mechanism design typically has three stages:[19] (1) The policymaker (the principal) designs a mechanism. (2) The principal presents the design to the agents who accept or reject it. In case an agent rejects the set of rules, he will receive some fixed compensation that might be zero. (3) The agents that accept the mechanism, play the game specified by the set of rules, and collect the payoffs.

In the context of the model at hand, the game can be specified as follows: There is one principal, the patent authority or the government, and one agent, the firm. Since the appropriation ability α is information private to the firm, the principal's optimal design cannot be conditional on α. Thus, the offer made by the policymaker cannot directly consist of a patent length as a function of the unobservable appropriation ability. Instead, the patent authority will design a menu of patent lengths T and patent fees K in the first step. In the second stage, the policymaker presents the different contracts $\{T, K\}$ to the firm and the latter chooses one. Assuming that the firm has decided for $\{T', K'\}$, the game designed by the menu of *contracts* proceeds in the last step. Here, the firm is granted a patent for T' years in exchange for a fee K'. After the patent expires, costless imitation and market entrance ensures perfect competition.

The revelation principle

The revelation principle simplifies matters in that not all possible combinations of $\{T, K\}$ have to be considered but only *direct mechanisms*, i.e. combinations of patent length and patent fees that directly depend on the unobservable α. Restricting attention to direct mechanisms makes it possible to simplify the game structure. Now, the principal asks the firm to announce its type, i.e. its appropriation efficiency. The firm might or might not reveal its true efficiency α. Subsequently, the patent authority chooses a combination $\{T(\alpha), K(\alpha)\}$ and the *normal* game proceeds. In fact, the relevation principle ensures that if the mechanism $\{T(\alpha), K(\alpha)\}$ maximizes welfare when the firm announces a type then it will constitute an equilibrium for the mechanism design game.

The maximization problem

Let α and $\hat{\alpha}$ denote the true and the announced value of the appropriation ability. The firm knows that the principal will design some rule that links the patent term and the patent fee to its statement on the appropriation effectiveness. Then, the firm's discounted stream of profits can be rewritten as

$$V(\alpha, \hat{\alpha}) = \int_0^{T(\hat{\alpha})} e^{-rt} \pi^m(h^*, \alpha)\, dt - \frac{h^{*2}}{2} - K(\hat{\alpha}). \tag{7.11}$$

Since the parameter α cannot be observed by the authority, the monopoly might find it profitable to conceal the true appropriation ability in order to pay lower patent fees.

The problem of the patent authority is still to maximize the expected stream of welfare subject to certain constraints, i.e.

$$\max_{T,K} \int_0^{\bar{\alpha}} \left[\frac{1}{r}\left\{ w(\pi^m) + e^{-rt} d(\pi^m) \right\} - \frac{h^{*2}}{2} \right] dF[\alpha] \tag{7.12}$$

subject to

$$V(\alpha, \alpha) \geq 0, \ \forall \alpha, \qquad\qquad \text{(IR)}, \qquad (7.13)$$

$$\alpha = \operatorname*{argmax}_{\hat{\alpha}} V(\alpha, \hat{\alpha}), \ \forall \alpha, \hat{\alpha}, \qquad \text{(IC)}. \qquad (7.14)$$

The two constraints (7.13) and (7.14) are necessary on account of the asymmetric information on the appropriation effectiveness. Together, they ensure that the firm does innovate and that it truthfully reveals the parameter α.

Assume that the firm were to announce its true type α. Then, there are some combinations of $\{T, K\}$ for which the firm does not have an incentive to innovate. Consequently, the set of patent terms and patent fees has to be restricted to those combinations for which the firm exerts a positive research effort to realize its idea. This restriction is formulated in (7.13) as the individual-rationality constraint: the patent authority should only consider $\{T, K\}$ that leave the inventor at least indifferent between innovating and doing nothing.

The principal has an interest to induce the firm to reveal the true appropriation ability α. The constraint that restricts the set $\{T, K\}$ so that the inventor signals the true α is the incentive-compatibility constraint in (7.14).

The optimal patent fee structure and its properties

For principal's maximization problem in (7.12), Cornelli and Schankerman (1999) obtain the following result:

Proposition 7.7 (Cornelli and Schankerman 1999, Proposition 3). An optimal differentiated patent policy, $\{T^*(\alpha), K^*(\alpha)\}$, has to satisfy the following necessary conditions for each α.

$$R(T, \alpha) =: \frac{1}{r} \left[w_\pi + e^{-rT} d_\pi \right] \pi_T^m - h^* h_T^* - e^{-rT} d(\pi) = 0 \tag{7.15}$$

$$K^*(\alpha) = \pi^m(T, \alpha) \frac{\gamma(T)}{r} - \frac{1}{2} h^{*2} - \int_0^\alpha \pi_x^m(x, h) \frac{\gamma(T)}{r} \, dx. \tag{7.16}$$

Note that (7.15) is identical to the first–order condition of the full-information benchmark model in (7.9). It determines the optimal patent term for each appropriation ability α.

In the absence of information asymmetries and the patent authorities', ability and willingness to discriminate perfectly between different levels of appropriation effectiveness, the principal would set a patent fee that makes the monopoly indifferent between pursuing the innovation and doing nothing. Hence, it would charge a fee just equal to the private incentive to innovate. With asymmetric information, the patent authority cannot appropriate the entire private incentive to innovate. Otherwise a firm with a high appropriation ability would always announce a lower α and receive a positive profit. The patent fee schedule in (7.16) prevents this by leaving the monopoly an information rent (the last term). Thus, the optimal patent fee structure equals the optimal private value of the innovation less the information rent. In principal, the optimal fees can be negative for small α implying that a subsidy would be optimal for those firms.

Cornelli and Schankerman (1999) study two special cases: one in which the monopoly profit is a linear function of the research effort and the other, where welfare and deadweight loss are proportional to profits.

Assumption 7.2. The monopoly profit, the flow welfare and the instantaneous deadweight loss shall take the following functional forms:

1. $\pi^m(h, \alpha) = \alpha h,$
2. $w(\pi^m) = (1 - \sigma)\pi^m$ and $d(\pi^m) = \delta \pi^m.$

Both assumptions seem rather restrictive at the first glance. In fact, the monopoly profits take this functional form for non-drastic process innovations, where the demand schedule and the production cost function as well as the research technology are linear, i.e. for a special configuration of the Nordhaus (1967) model. Likewise, the second assumption merely serves to rule out pathological cases in which e.g. flow welfare $w(\pi^m)$ is smaller than the monopoly profits or the deadweight $d(\pi^m)$ loss is larger than the monopoly profits. Both cases would violate its definitions given above.

When the monopoly profit is linear, Cornelli and Schankerman obtain:

Corollary 7.1 (Cornelli and Schankerman, 1999, Corollary 1).   Under Assumptions 7.2 (1), $h^* = \gamma(T(\alpha))\alpha/r$ and the optimal differentiated patent policy $\{T^*(\alpha), K^*(\alpha)\}$ satisfies the following necessary and sufficient conditions for each α:

(i)
$$R(T,\alpha) = \frac{\alpha^2}{r}\left[w_\pi + e^{-rT(\alpha)}d_\pi - \gamma\left(T(\alpha)\right)\right] - d(\pi^m) = 0$$

(ii)
$$K^*(\alpha) = \frac{\alpha^2}{2r^2}\gamma\left(T(\alpha)\right)^2 - \int_0^{\bar\alpha} \frac{x}{r^2}\gamma\left(T(\alpha)\right)^2 \, dx$$

(iii)
$$-\frac{d(\pi^m)}{r} + d_\pi < \frac{\alpha^2}{r}\left[w_{\pi\pi} + e^{-rT}d_{\pi\pi}\right] \le 1 + 2d_\pi$$

Equations (i) and (ii) are the necessary conditions stated in Proposition 7.7. The inequalities in (iii) are the sufficient conditions. The inequality on the right-hand side is the second-order condition for the welfare maximization. The inequality on the left-hand side stems from the incentive constraint (7.14) which, in fact, requires that the optimal patent length is an increasing function of α. The precise functional form is determined by (i).

The second-order conditions depend on the properties of welfare and deadweight loss. Let $b(\pi^m)$ stand for the instantaneous welfare after the patent expired. Then, $b(\pi^m) = w(\pi^m) + d(\pi^m)$. If total welfare $b(\pi^m)$ is concave in the monopoly profit, the second term of (iii) is negative so that the second-order condition of the patent authority's problem is always satisfied. However, in this situation, the incentive-compatibility constraint may fail to be satisfied. Then, the patent fee schedule in (ii) cannot induce firms to reveal their true type α and a uniform patent term would turn out to be optimal. In case total welfare is a convex function of the monopoly profit, it is more probable that the incentive-compatibility is satisfied. Cornelli and Schankerman (1999) point out that a convex total welfare function may arise from two sources: Firstly, larger innovations generate R&D spillovers to a larger degree than marginal ones. Secondly, the demand elasticity for products based on larger innovations may be smaller than the elasticity for products from marginal innovations.

Given that both second-order conditions are met, Corollary 7.1 states that the optimal patent length will be differentiated for different types of firms. The selection takes place through the patent fee schedule that implies larger fees for greater appropriation abilities α.

For the second case, the following result ensues:

Corollary 7.2. Under Assumption 7.2, it is optimal to set a uniform patent life equal to

$$T^U = \frac{1}{r}\big[\ln(1+2\delta) - \ln(\delta - \sigma)\big].$$

If welfare and deadweight loss are also linear functions of the research effort, it becomes optimal to choose a uniform patent life for all types of firms. This result arises because the patent length is independent of the appropriation ability, $T_\alpha^* = 0$. Then, a higher appropriation ability of a firm does not alter the distribution between private and social costs and benefits.

In case the welfare and deadweight loss are proportional to the monopoly profits and the latter are a convex function of the research effort, a uniform patent length is not necessarily optimal. Yet, similar to the first case in Corollary 7.1, a concave profit function makes it more probable that the second-order condition of the welfare maximization is met as opposed to the incentive–compatibility constraint.

The optimal renewal fee schedule

So far, the results characterize the optimal direct mechanism that can, however, be linked to the different indirect ones, one of which is a renewal fee scheme. Referring to the mechanism design game, the patent authority announces a patent fee schedule $k(t)$. The innovative firm accepts it and decides on the scale of the research project. As research is deterministic, the firm makes the discovery immediately and receives a patent.

Different from the Nordhaus (1969) model, the patent is not granted for a specified number of years. Rather, the firm has yearly to pay the specified renewal fees $k(t)$ in order to maintain the patent for the next year or some predefined time span.

The optimal patent length as a function of the parameter α is given by (7.15). Assuming the minimum patent life $T^*(0)$ is non-negative, then the initial fees $k(0)$ are derived with $k(0) = K^*(0)$ where $K^*(0)$ is derived from (7.16). All other renewal fees are given by

$$K^*(\alpha) = \int_0^{T^*(\alpha)} e^{-rt} k(t)\, dt.$$

In this way, firms that have higher appropriation abilities and that, after all, generate larger inventions and innovations, get higher rewards. As long as the patent holder is able to afford the increasing patent renewal fees, he signals that the invention's private value still exceeds the patent fees.

Renewal fee schedules have another advantage. Often, the commercial value of an invention is uncertain when the application is filed. The patent holder certainly expects to profit from it either by commercialization or by being able to negotiate favourable licence agreements. As time evolves, additional information become available such as market demand or the willingness of partners to enter into licence negotiations. In case expectations turn out to be too optimistic, the patent holder can terminate the patent by not paying the fee. In contrast, if the invention proves to have previously unexpected applications, the patent holder can simply extend the patent length up to the maximum time. Thus, renewal fee schedules are flexible enough for a variety of situations without raising administration costs unduly.

Observe that the optimal renewal fee structure depends on the profit and the research cost functions. Since the elasticity of demand and the development costs may vary across sectors, it would be optimal to employ sector-specific renewal fee schemes. The administration of patent systems would certainly be unduly burdened if such a degree of differentiation would be attempted. Thus, the current practice of a renewal scheme for all inventions improves on simple uniform patent life and patent fees but it remains a compromise.

7.A Proofs to the lemmata and propositions

Lemma 7.1.   *Case 1*: Non-drastic innovation

Assume that the innovation remains non-drastic as the innovation size becomes slightly larger. Then, the optimal price remains $p^* = c_0$ and $dp^*/du = 0$. The monopoly profit is given by $\pi^m = uQ(c_0)$ so that $d\pi^m/du = Q(p^*) > 0$

Case 2: Drastic innovation

Let the innovation size be such that the innovation is drastic. Then, the first-order condition $G := Q(p) + (p - c_0 + u)Q_p(p) = 0$ can be used to find the derivative

$$\frac{dp^*}{du} := -\frac{Q_p}{2Q_p + (p - c_0 + u)Q_{pp}}.$$

Both the nominator and denominator are negative under the standard assumptions imposed on the demand function so that the monopoly price decreases with the quality of the innovation.

By the Envelope Theorem, $d\pi^m/du = Q(p^*)$.   □

Proposition 7.1.   See Figure 7.2 and the discussion in the text.   □

Proposition 7.2.   Let the first-order condition be written as: $G := \gamma Q(p^*)u_h(h) - rC_h = 0$. Then, $G_h h_\gamma^* + G_\gamma = 0$ so that

$$h_\gamma^* = -\frac{G_\gamma}{G_h} = -\frac{Q(p^*)u_h(h)}{Q_p p_u u_h^2 + Q u_{hh} - rC_{hh}}.$$

With the assumptions posed on the market demand, the research technology and the research cost function, the denominator is negative and the nominator unambiguously positive. Since γ is a monotonically increasing function of the patent life T, it immediately follows that h_t^* is positive whenever h_γ^* is.   □

Proposition 7.3. The Lagrange function to the planer's maximization problem reads

$$\mathcal{L} = \frac{1}{r}\left[\Delta w(h) - \gamma d(h)\right] - C(h) + \lambda\left[\frac{\gamma}{r}u_h(h)Q(p(u(h))) - C_h(h)\right].$$

The first-order conditions are

$$\frac{\partial \mathcal{L}}{\partial \gamma} = -\frac{d(h)}{r} + \lambda\frac{u_h Q(p)}{r} = 0,$$

$$\frac{\partial \mathcal{L}}{\partial h} = \frac{1}{r}\left[\Delta w_h - \gamma d_h\right] - C_h + \lambda\left[\frac{\gamma}{r}\left\{u_{hh}Q + u_h Q_p p_u u_h^2\right\} - C_{hh}\right] = 0.$$

The first derivative yields the equation for the parameter $\lambda = d(h)/\left(u_h Q(p^*)\right)$. Using the definitions of the change in the total social benefit $\Delta w(h)$ and the deadweight loss $d(h)$ and solving the second derivative with respect to γ yields equation (7.6). $\square$

Proposition 7.4. Given that all components in (7.7) are positive, the result is straightforward. $\square$

8   Patent scope

Patent claims determine the boundaries of the exclusive rights with respect to other patents as well as to alternative products or technologies. The present chapter explores how many contemporary, unpatented, alternative products or technologies should fall within the scope of protection and, therefore, be declared as infringing the patent. A narrow protection allows a larger number of alternative products or technologies to be used legally. This tends to increase instantaneous consumers' surplus since the alternative products and technologies make competition more intense so that the inventors' ability to charge premium prices are limited – consumers can switch to non-infringing substitutes. With a narrow patent, there will always be the danger that cumulated flow profits will be insufficient to cover research expenses owing to the more intense competition. In this situation, firms may either choose not to patent the invention or even not to engage in research at all.[1]

Rather than focussing on a single patent instrument, we are characterizing the optimal mix between the patent scope and the patent term. The combination of these two policy instruments is the obvious one to study since both are substitutes from a firm's point of view: wider and longer patents increase the present value of an invention. For the policymaker, the simplest setting would be a situation where patent protection is perfect, i.e. infringement does not occur, and the decision on the optimal research effort only depends on the present value of profits to be earned. In particular, the latter is independent of the patent policy instruments. Then, the principal question is how to design a patent system that consists of two policy measures: patent scope and patent term. This question is addressed in Section 8.1. Subsequently, we allow the patent policy mix to influence the firm's decision on the research effort. Thus, in Section 8.2, patent scope directly affects the flow profits. For both situations, we demonstrate under which conditions a narrow but infinite patent will be optimal.

The existence of patent systems is frequently justified by the threat that an imitation of a patented product or technology may pose to technological progress and economic growth.[2] Yet, imitation does require time and resources as numerous authors have pointed out. This has immediate consequences for the design of patent systems. Especially when studying patent scope, the fact that imitation is not without cost does affect the optimal policy mix as Gallini (1992) demonstrates. The last section presents a slightly more general version of their seminal work.

8.1 Exogenous patent value

If patent cases are judged on an individual basis, the questions of the optimal policy mix between patent term and patent scope and how to create sufficient incentives to innovate can in principal be studied separately. If inventors can be sure to receive a reward that (nearly) equals the social value of their inventions, research will be profitable and inventors will choose the profit-maximizing effort level, given the policy mix. Assuming the *social* value of the invention is known, the problem reduces to the following question which is the focus of the current section: how should the patent system be designed so that the inventor earns a pre-defined reward.

Restricting our attention to fixed-value problems has obvious consequences. Firms care only about the total profits they are able to receive from an invention. In particular, they are indifferent between all combinations of patent scope and patent length that generate the same reward. Consequently, decisions such as how much effort should be invested solely depend on the expected profits as well. In this section, we mainly rely on the works of Gilbert and Shapiro (1990) and Klemperer (1990) to characterize the optimal policy mix.

8.1.1 The general framework

Patent scope, profits and welfare

Assume that the patent authorities have agreed to bestow upon the inventor a certain reward V.[3] Let T and y, $T, y \in \mathbb{R}_0$, denote patent life and patent scope respectively. Patent scope is defined by the claims of the patent. Here, it is understood to include all potential variations of the patent holder's technology that would infringe the patentee's rights. Most importantly, all alternatives to the patented technology are considered to be (imperfect) substitutes, i.e. none is of superior quality.[4]

Clearly, the model is not restricted to a particular type of invention. For expositional reasons, assume that a firm created a non-drastic process innovation. With perfect patent protection, a wider patent scope implies that competitors can use fewer, less efficient, production technologies. It is therefore reasonable to assume that wider patents yield higher profits during the patent life.[5] Instead of explicitly modelling the market stage, we impose certain regularity assumptions directly on the reduced form profits. In particular, the following assumption is maintained.

Assumption 8.1. Let $\pi^m(y)$, $\pi^m(y) \in \mathbb{R}_+$, and π^c, $\pi^c \in \mathbb{R}_0$, denote the patent holder's flow profit during and after the patent life respectively. Then,

1. $\pi_y^m(y) > 0$, $\pi_{yy}^m(y) < 0$, $\sup_{y \to \infty} \pi^m(y) = \bar{\pi}$ and
2. $\bar{\pi}/r > V \geq \pi^c/r$,

where subscripts again denote partial derivatives.

The first assumption deals with the effect of the patent scope on the monopoly flow profits. It formulates the notion that wider patents restrict the number of available non-infringing production technologies so that competitors have to use less efficient alternatives or have to spend more resources to invent around the patented technology. This increases the inventor's market power so that profits rise during the patent life. However, even infinitely wide patents yield finite profits $\bar{\pi}$. Hence, a firm's earning possibilities are always limited by market demand even though all potential competition is eliminated by declaring all potential alternatives to the patented technology as infringing. Thus, it is reasonable to assume that monopoly profits are concave in y.

The second assumption ensures that a patent system is feasible and desirable. $\bar{\pi}$ is the flow profit of an infinitely wide patent so that $\bar{\pi}/r$ denotes the value of an infinitely wide patent that lasts forever. Then, the first inequality restricts our attention to situations in which a combination of patent scope and patent life is able to bestow on the inventor the pre-defined reward V – the patent system is feasible. The competition profit π^c denotes the flow profit after the patent expired. Thus, π^c/r is the present value associated with an expired patent or equivalently with no patent protection. Hence, the inequality on the right-hand side of the second assumption requires that receiving the pre-defined value V is at least as large as the value of the invention when protection of the intellectual property does not exits, i.e. a patent system is desirable.[6]

The competition profit π^c might be zero as well as strictly positive so that the product market might be imperfectly competitive after the patent expired. Different scenarios might explain this market structure. Either there are natural barriers to entry so that all firms earn a positive, possibly identical competition profit.[7] Alternatively, only the inventor is able to earn positive profits after the patent expired. This will frequently occur when the patentee is able to retain part of the competitive advantage gained by the invention.

In any case however, the inventor's competitive profit π^c is independent of the patent scope. At a first glance, this assumption seems implausible. A positive correlation between patent scope y and competition profit π^c would require that the *number* of infringing variations on the inventor's technology would affect the profit after the patent expired. It is more likely that the size or quality of the invention has a bearing on the competition profit. However, both size and quality of an invention is not necessarily correlated to the patent scope.

We imposed certain regularity assumptions on the reduced form profits rather than explicitly formulating the market stage. As a consequence, the properties of the instantaneous welfare cannot be derived from the market stage either. Instead, the following assumptions concerning the relationship between monopoly profits and instantaneous welfare are maintained:

Assumption 8.2.   Let $w(\pi^m)$, $w(\pi^m) \in \mathbb{R}_0$, and $\bar{w}$, $\bar{w} \in \mathbb{R}_+$, stand for the instantaneous social welfare during the patent term and after the patent expired respectively. It is assumed that social welfare is a decreasing function of the patent scope, i.e. $w_\pi(\pi^m) < 0$ and $\bar{w} \geq w(\pi^m)$.

The parameter $\bar{w}$ denotes the flow welfare after the patent life has expired and might be regarded to be the abbreviation for $w(\pi^c)$. It comprises the consumers' surplus, any profits earned by the patentee and the competitors and at least part of the deadweight loss that exclusive rights created during the patent life.[8] Since society will appropriate at least part of the deadweight loss, the flow welfare during the patent life $w(\pi^m)$ will always be smaller than instantaneous welfare after the patent lapsed $\bar{w}$. That $\bar{w}$ does not depend on the patent scope itself shows that the consumers' surplus, and thus demand, is assumed to be independent of the patent scope y.

The instantaneous welfare $w(\pi^m)$ during the patent life only consists of the consumers' surplus and the profits of the patentee and all rivals. The patent scope y influences the instantaneous welfare only through the profits of the firms. By Assumption 8.1, the profit of the patentee increases with the patent scope which has a positive effect on flow welfare. As the profits π^m increase, so does the inventor's market power and, therefore, the deadweight loss. This has a negative effect on welfare. However, the increase in profits is usually larger than the raise in the deadweight loss so that the joint effect should be positive. The assumption that the flow welfare $w(\pi^m)$ does negatively react to an increase in the patent scope must therefore stem from a business-stealing effect, i.e. the profits of the patentee's rivals decrease as a consequence of a wider patent.[9]

To the patentee, the present value of an invention is the discounted stream of profits accruing from it, i.e.

$$V(T,y) := \int_0^T e^{-rt}\pi^m(y) \, dt + \int_T^\infty e^{-rt} \pi^c \, dt$$

$$= \frac{\gamma(T)}{r}\pi^m(y) + \frac{1-\gamma(T)}{r}\pi^c,$$

where again, $\gamma(T) = 1 - e^{-rT}$. By the same token, the total social welfare stemming from the invention in question can be determined with

$$W(T,y) := \int_0^T e^{-rt}w(\pi^m(y)) \, dt + \int_T^\infty e^{-rt}\bar{w} \, dt$$

$$= \frac{\gamma(T)}{r}w(\pi^m(y)) + \frac{1-\gamma(T)}{r}\bar{w}.$$

The maximization problem

Again, we assume that the policymaker aims at maximizing the present value of social welfare from a given invention. In choosing the optimal policy mix between patent scope y and patent term T, the patent authority is restricted to such combinations of $\{T, y\}$ that bestow upon the inventor the pre-defined reward of V. Thus, the maximization problem reads:

$$\max_{T,y} W(T,y) = \frac{\gamma(T)}{r}w\big(\pi^m(y)\big) + \frac{1-\gamma(T)}{r}\bar{w}, \tag{8.1}$$

$$\text{s.t. } V = \frac{\gamma(T)}{r}\pi^m(y) + \frac{1-\gamma(T)}{r}\pi^c. \tag{8.2}$$

Observe that innovation costs do not enter the government's problem here since the object is to find the optimal policy mix for a given invention. For the overall success of such a policy in the long run, the reward V must at least exceed the innovation costs.

The relation between patent scope and patent length

Before fully characterizing the optimal design of the patent system, the relationship between patent scope and patent length is explored. The maximization constraint in (8.2) restricts the conceivable combinations of $\{T, y\}$ to those which are actually able to guarantee a reward of V for the inventor. Thus, $y(T)$ denotes the scope of the patent that leaves the patentee with a reward of V if the patent length is T. From (8.2) immediately follows:

Proposition 8.1.　Under Assumption 8.1,

1. the patent scope y is a decreasing function of the patent term T, and
2. there are a minimum patent scope y_{min} and a minimum patent term T_{min} given by

$$y_{min} = \pi^{m^{-1}}(rV), \quad T_{min} = -\frac{1}{r}\ln\left(\frac{\bar{\pi}-rV}{\bar{\pi}-\pi^c}\right) \geq 0$$

so that the inventor would earn less than V if either $y < y_{min}$ or $T < T_{min}$.

The proposition shows that the policy instruments are strategic substitutes for the policymaker: wider and shorter patents are equivalent to narrower and longer patents when the inventor's reward is to be V.

For narrow patents $y < y_{min}$, the patent holder will be unable to collect profits that amount to V even though the patent lasts forever. Similarly, if the patent term is too short, i.e. for $T < T_{min}$, even infinitely wide patents that declare all alternative production technologies infringing will be insufficient to guarantee a reward V. Observe that $T_{min} = 0$ if and only if $rV = \pi^c$. Consequently, a positive patent life is required if the inventor is to receive a reward that exceeds the value of the invention without patent protection. Proposition 8.1 also shows that both the minimum patent term and the minimum patent scope increase in the level of the reward V.

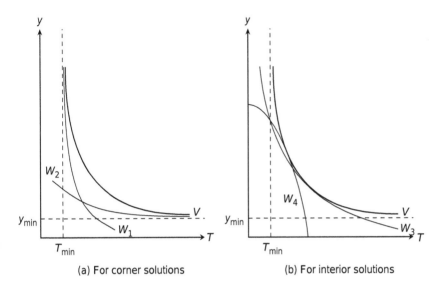

(a) For corner solutions   (b) For interior solutions

Figure 8.1 The optimal combination of patent scope and patent length.

8.1.2 General results

To derive the principal results, a graphical approach is chosen which is presented in Figure 8.1. We first determine the shape of the maximization constraint (8.2). Subsequently, we discuss different scenarios for the objective function (8.1) and demonstrate under which conditions a finite patent length and scope will be optimal.

The maximization constraint in (8.2) determines the combinations of the patent term and the patent scope $\{T, y\}$ that guarantee the inventor a reward of V. According to Proposition 8.1 and Assumption 8.1, the set of graphs representing different levels of V are downwards sloped and convex in a T/y-diagram (cf Figure 8.1). Higher levels of the reward V (not shown in the figure) are located to the North-East of the example given in Figure 8.1. The slope of the graph V can directly be obtained from (8.2):

$$y^V := -\frac{\gamma_T}{\gamma} \frac{\pi^m(y) - \pi^c}{\pi_y^m} < 0. \tag{8.3}$$

By Assumption 8.1, the slope is unambiguously negative.

The present value of the welfare function $W(T, y)$ in (8.1) can also be represented by a set of graphs in the T/y-diagram. The slope of the function can be determined with

$$y^W := \frac{\gamma_T}{\gamma} \frac{\bar{w} - w(\pi^m(y))}{w_\pi \pi_y^m(y)}. \tag{8.4}$$

By Assumptions 8.1 and 8.2, the slope is unambiguously negative as well.

The original maximization problem of the patent authority was stated in (8.1) and (8.2). In graphical terms, the maximization problem is equivalent to choosing the point on the graph V where the slope of the welfare function is tangent to V, i.e. where $y^V = y^W$. From Figure 8.1 it is clear that an interior solution need not to exist.

Maximum patent length or patent scope

Figure 8.1(a) characterizes situations in which either an infinite patent scope (W_1) or an infinite patent length (W_2) will be optimal.

First consider the case of W_1 in Figure 8.1(a). Here, the slope of the welfare function W is steeper than the slope of the constraint V for all $T > T_{min}$. Then, the optimal policy is to grant maximum patent scope and minimal patent length $\{T^*, y^*\} = \{T_{min}, \infty\}$. Conversely, the case of W_2 in Figure 8.1(a) shows a situation in which the slope of V is everywhere steeper than the slope of the welfare function W. Under these circumstances, a combination of the minimal patent scope and the maximal patent length $\{T^*, y^*\} = \{\infty, y_{min}\}$ will be optimal.

Comparing equations (8.3) and (8.4) which define the slopes of the objective and value function yields the following condition:

$$-w_\pi \underset{>}{\overset{\le}{}} \frac{\bar{w} - w(y)}{\pi^m(y) - \pi^c}$$

In fact, it decides whether minimal or maximal patent length will be optimal. Yet, $-w_\pi$ will exceed the term on the right-hand side if and only if $w_{\pi\pi} < 0$, i.e. if the flow of welfare during the patent term is a concave function of monopoly profits.[10]

Proposition 8.2. The optimal patent policy is characterized by

$$\{T^*, y^*\} = \begin{cases} \{T_{min}, \infty\} & \text{if } w_{\pi\pi} > 0, \\ \{\infty, y_{min}\} & \text{if } w_{\pi\pi} < 0 \end{cases} \tag{8.5}$$

for all $T \in [T_{min}, \infty)$.

Proof. See text above. □

If the instantaneous welfare is convex in the monopoly profit ($w_{\pi\pi} > 0$), the optimal policy mix is to declare all variations of the patented technology to be infringing for the shortest possible time T_{min}. Observe that under $\{T_{min}, \infty\}$, the inventor earns maximal profits $\bar{\pi}$ and society receives minimal flow welfare $w(\bar{\pi})$ during the patent life. This policy is justified because the monopoly profit associated with even a small patent scope y_{min} entails a large loss in welfare as compared to the situation after the patent expired. Then, to allow patentees to collect maximal profits for the shortest possible time is best for society.

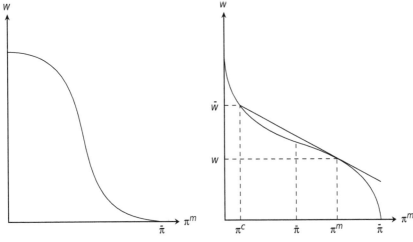

(a) Yielding a convex welfare function W_3 (b) Yielding a concave welfare function W_4

Figure 8.2 Welfare functions.

In contrast, if the instantaneous welfare is concave in the monopoly profits ($w_{\pi\pi} < 0$), small monopoly profits $\pi^m(y_{min})$ result in small welfare losses as compared to $\bar{w}$ that is attained after the patent expired. Thus, it is a reasonable policy to minimize the number of infringing activities. In this situation, monopoly profits are minimal, but flow welfare is maximal.

Finite patent length and patent scope

From Proposition 8.2 can also be concluded that an interior solution to the maximization problem (8.1) and (8.2) exists if $w_{\pi\pi} = 0$, i.e. if the flow welfare function w has both convex and concave parts. Figure 8.2 presents two examples of the social welfare function w that correspond to graphs W_3 and W_4 respectively.

The second-order condition of the maximization problem is only satisfied if the instantaneous welfare is locally concave at the equilibrium point, i.e. if $w_{\pi\pi} \leq 0$. Graphs with a shape as depicted in Figure 8.2(a) and equivalently W_3 in Figure 8.1(b) have to be excluded from consideration. Thus, it can be concluded:

Proposition 8.3 (Gilbert and Shapiro, 1990, Proposition 1). Let $w_\pi(\pi^m) \gtreqless 0$ for $\pi^m \lesseqgtr \tilde{\pi}$. Then, there exists a unique interior solution for the maximization problem in (8.1) where y^* solves

$$-w_\pi\left(\pi^m(y)\right) = \frac{\bar{w} - w\left(\pi^m(y)\right)}{\pi^m(y) - \pi^c} \tag{8.6}$$

and T^* is subsequently derived from the constraint in (8.1).

Proof.   See Gilbert and Shapiro (1990).   □

Observe that the first-order condition in (8.6) is independent of both, the reward V and the patent length T for an interior solution. The optimal patent scope y^* is solely affected by the properties of the profit function $\pi^m(y)$ and social welfare function $w(\pi^m)$. Since y^* is independent of the reward V, the optimal patent scope y^* maximizes the unconditional problem in (8.1). Subsequently, the patent life is set so that the patentee receives the pre-defined reward V.

So far, as little as possible structure has been imposed on the analysis to obtain general results. Yet, studying some details may be instructive. The next section examines the composition of the deadweight loss in greater detail.

8.1.3 The optimal policy design for horizontal product differentiation

Klemperer (1990) studies the same policy mix, but in a slightly different setting. Different from Gilbert and Shapiro (1990), he chooses a differentiated product market so that a patent is granted for a product innovation. He also uses richer structure to distinguish between different sources of the deadweight loss and to analyze whether the policy mix should be adjusted accordingly. Before introducing the model, it is demonstrated that minimizing social costs as Klemperer (1990) does is actually equivalent to the maximization problem (8.1) and (8.2) in the model of Gilbert and Shapiro (1990).

Minimizing social costs or maximizing social welfare

Patent protection bestows upon the patent holder a certain market power so that deadweight loss inevitably arises. After the patent expires, society appropriates the entire deadweight loss under perfect competition. In case some market power persists after the patent lapsed because e.g. the market is too small, the deadweight loss at least decreases.[11] Using the notation of the previous section, $\bar{w} = w(\cdot) + d(\cdot)$, where $d(\cdot)$ stands for the deadweight loss created by the exclusive rights. Then, the objective function in (8.1) can be written as

$$W(T,y) = \frac{1}{r}\bar{w} - \frac{\gamma}{r}d(y). \tag{8.7}$$

Since $\bar{w}$ is constant by assumption, the maximization problem in (8.1) and (8.2) is equivalent to the following problem

$$\min_{T,y} \int_0^T e^{-rt}d(y)\,\mathrm{d}t$$

$$\text{s.t. } V = \int_0^T e^{-rt}\pi^m(y)\,\mathrm{d}t, \tag{8.8}$$

where the competition profit π^c is now zero indicating that perfect competition is achieved after the patent expired. With the additional assumption on the market structure Klemperer (1990) obtains:

Proposition 8.4. The optimal policy design is characterized by:

$$y^* = \underset{\pi^{m-1}(rV) \leq y \leq \infty}{\text{argmin}} \quad r(y) := \frac{d(y)}{\pi^m(y)},$$

$$T^* = \frac{1}{r} \ln\left(\frac{\pi^m(y^*)}{\pi^m(y^*) - rV}\right). \tag{8.9}$$

Similar to the results described in Propositions 8.1–8.3, the optimal patent scope y^* solves the unconditional minimization problem, while the optimal patent term is chosen such that the inventor receives the pre-determined reward V.

In the next section, different sources of the deadweight loss are discussed.

Different sources of the deadweight loss

In Klemperer's (1990) model, patent scope consists of the number of varieties that infringe on the inventor's patent. This is probably best envisaged by Hotelling's model of a linear city ,(Hotelling, 1929). All variants of a product are located on a potentially infinitely long line. The degree of product differentiation is measured by the distance to the patentee's variety: the nearer the alternative variant the more similar are the variants.

In the most popular interpretation of Hotelling's model, consumers differ in their preferences over the product varieties.[12] Here however, consumers agree in the their preference structure, i.e. all consumers prefer the patentee's variant over non-infringing substitutes.[13] Yet, they experience different levels of disutility x per unit of product differentiation when not purchasing their most preferred variety. Let $f[x]$ denote the density function of the distribution over x. The function $F[\tilde{x}] := \int_{\tilde{x}}^{\infty} f[x] \, dx$ measures the probability that a given consumer has a disutility that exceeds $\tilde{x}$.

In case the patent holder is the sole supplier of the differentiated product, e.g. because the patent scope comprises all possible product variants ($y \to \infty$), the patentee faces a demand of $Q(p)$ at price p. Assume that production costs are zero so that the lowest possible price is zero as well. For simplicity, the maximal demand $Q(0)$ is normalized to one.

If the patent scope is such that there are some product varieties that do not infringe on the patentee's patent, competitors will soon supply those variants. It can be postulated that the variants not covered by the patent are marketed under perfect competition. With zero production costs, the price of every non-infringing variety will be zero as well. However, consumers who buy a non-infringing substitute have to bear a disutility that equals xy.[14]

Clearly, consumers will only buy the patent holder's variety if their disutility from buying a non-infringing substitute is greater than the price of the inventor's variety, i.e. if $xy > p$. Since $F[p/y]$ denotes the probability that a given consumer has a disutility parameter $x > p/y$, the expected demand for the inventor is

$$EQ(p) = Q(p)F[p/y], \tag{8.10}$$

where E is the expectation operator.

The patent holder chooses the price $p^*(y)$ so that the profit is maximized. Let $\pi^m(y)$ be defined as $\pi^m(y) := \max_p p \, EQ(p)$. Then, total deadweight loss is obtained with

$$d(y) = \int_0^{p^*(y)} EQ(p) \, dp - \pi^m(y). \tag{8.11}$$

Klemperer (1990) distinguishes three sources for the deadweight loss:

- $d_n(y)$ stems from those (*non-travelling*) consumers who purchase their ideal variety, i.e. the inventor's one, but they buy a smaller quantity as compared to a situation with perfect competition.
- d_{t1} denotes the part of the deadweight loss that is caused by the disutility experienced by the (*travelling*) consumers who decide in favour of the non-infringing variety instead of the patentee's one.
- d_{t2} is also connected to the *travelling* consumers. It arises because consumers purchase less than they would do if the non-infringing substitute were the most preferred variety.

As Klemperer (1990) points out, d_{t1} are the social costs that are generated because consumers buy the *wrong* variety. Henceforth, this part of the deadweight loss is called the *variety effect*. In contrast, d_n and d_{t2} together describe the social costs that stem from the fact that consumption in this particular product class is reduced. The expenditures that would have been otherwise spent for this product are now diverted into an entirely different product class. This effect is henceforth referred to as the *product class effect*. Clearly, a policymaker cannot minimize both the variety effect and the product class effect by deciding for one level of patent scope. When all product variants are infringing (infinite patent scope), all consumers buy the patent holder's product and travelling does not occur. Then the variety effect vanishes, but all consumers suffer from the traditional source of deadweight loss $d_n(\cdot)$. To demonstrate that the variety and the product class effect play different roles in the optimization problem, note that the function $r(y)$ can be written as

$$r(y) = \frac{\int_0^{p^*(y)} EQ(\rho) \, d\rho}{p^*(y)EQ(p^*(y))} - 1. \tag{8.12}$$

Lemma 8.1 (Klemperer, 1990, Lemma 1).   Assume that a monopolist with zero costs facing demand $Q(p)$ has a unique optimal price, p^m. Then,

$$\lim_{y \to \infty} r(y) = \frac{\int_0^{p^m} Q(p) \, dp}{p^m Q(p^m)} - 1.$$

This lemma is concerned with the product class effect. As the patent scope increases, fewer consumers are willing to purchase the non-infringing substitute because the disutility of doing so becomes larger as compared to the monopoly price. Thus, the significance of the variety effect decreases. At the limit, only the product class effect remains. The situation becomes increasingly similar to the one where only one monopolist supplies a homogeneous product. Lemma 8.2 is concerned with the opposite extreme.

Lemma 8.2 (Klemperer, 1990, Lemma 2).   Assume that a monopolist with zero costs facing demand $F[\tilde{p}]$ has a unique optimal price, $\tilde{p}^m$. Then

$$\lim_{y \to 0} r(y) = \frac{\int_0^{\tilde{p}^m} F[p] \, dp}{\tilde{p}^m F[\tilde{p}^m]} - 1.$$

Here, the disutility of purchasing a sub-ideal variant becomes negligible as the narrow patent scope allows competitors to offer products that are very similar to the patented one. This restricts the patent holder's ability to raise his price above the competitive price. At the limit, social costs entirely consist of the d_{t1}-type and the product class effect vanishes.

The optimal policy mix

With the richer structure, it is clear that meaningful results can only be obtained for special configurations. Klemperer (1990) considers cases where consumers have identical disutility parameters and where they have the same reservation price. According to the first alternative, he finds:

Proposition 8.5 (Klemperer, 1990, Proposition 2).   If all consumers have identical transport costs, then infinitely lived patents with minimum possible width are optimal if

1. the elasticity of $Q(p)$ is non-decreasing in p, or
2. the value of the patent to be awarded, V, is sufficiently small.

If all consumers have the same disutility parameter x, there exists a certain threshold value $\bar{p}$ for the monopoly price such that all consumers buy the patented variety as long as the inventor charges $p < \bar{p}$. On the other hand, the monopoly loses all customers to the supplier of the nearest non-infringing substitute if it chooses a price $p > \bar{p}$. Since all firms have identical production costs, the patent holder can always set a price $p < \bar{p}$. Thus, all consumers purchase the inventor's variety in equilibrium, i.e. for a given patent scope and patent length.

In this situation, the social costs d_{t1} and d_{t2} associated with travelling vanish as consumers do not buy the non-infringing substitute in equilibrium. The sole component of the social costs in equilibrium then consists of the deadweight loss d_n, which is also present in homogeneous product markets. A greater market power increases d_n so that it seems reasonable to choose the lowest possible patent scope. This minimizes social costs as the patent holder will have limited power to raise prices above the competitive one in this situation.

Restricting the market power of the patentee by choosing the minimal patent scope compatible with a reward V naturally decreases the profits and, thus, the social welfare. Consequently, the policy mix of minimal patent scope and maximal patent length can only be optimal if lower prices induce social costs to decrease by a larger amount than social welfare. This condition is expressed in condition (1) of Lemma 8.1.

Concerning the second case, Klemperer (1990) obtains:

Proposition 8.6 (Klemperer, 1990, Proposition 4).   If all consumers have identical reservation prices for the most-preferred product variety and if there is a shortest allowable patent life, then this patent lifetime is optimal with maximum possible width if

1. the elasticity of $F(x)$ is non-decreasing in x, or
2. the value of the patent awarded, V, is sufficiently large.

Here, the central argument is that the patent holder chooses a price equal to the reservation price if the latter is identical for all consumers. In this situation, a deadweight loss for the non-travelling consumers does not ensue, i.e. $d_n(y) = 0$ since the consumers' surplus is completely appropriated by the patentee. The social costs only comprise $d_{t1}(y)$ and $d_{t2}(y)$ arising from the disutility associated with not buying the preferred variety and from consumers purchasing less of the sub-ideal variety than they usually would. Clearly, the instantaneous social costs arising from travelling vanish if patent scope is maximal. As a consequence, patent length has to be as short as possible. Otherwise, the inventor is rewarded more than V.

For the numerous situations in which consumers do have heterogeneous disutility parameters and reservation prices, one can expect that the optimal policy mix of patent scope and patent length consists of values between the extremes, i.e. a finite patent scope and patent term.

8.2   Endogenous patent value

The models of Gilbert and Shapiro (1990) and Klemperer (1990) implicitly rely on the presumption that the firm's research decision is only determined by the present value of profits V that are generated by the exclusive rights. The policy mix between patent scope and patent length does not affect the firm's decision in any other way. This also means that patent policy cannot be used to influence or direct research.

The model of Denicolò (1996) introduced here extends the models of the previous section in that the research decision of firms is explicitly taken into account.[15] Thus, Denicolò does not only characterize the optimal combination of patent scope and length, but more importantly studies the effect of both patent instruments on the research effort.

8.2.1 A patent race with endogenous research effort

As the previous models, Denicolò (1996) focuses on a single inventions rather than an entire sequence of inventions (cf *infra*). Different from the previous models, however, he allows for competition in innovation as well as the product market. As a consequence, all firms participating in the research competition derive their ideas from a public stock of knowledge so that the model bases on the patent race literature (cf *supra*).[16]

Timing

The model has three stages. In the first stage, the policymaker chooses the determinants of the patent system, i.e. patent length and patent scope $\{T, y\}$. The n firms in the industry observe the government's decision and set the research effort level $h_j, j = 1, \ldots, n$.

In the second stage, the research projects are carried out. Denicolò (1996) acknowledges that research is an inherently uncertain process. Firms can increase the probability of making the discovery sooner by increasing the research effort, but the completion date of the invention remains a random variable. Thus, there remains a non-negligible risk of losing the patent race despite expending considerable effort. The second stage ends when the first firm completes the research project. The successful firm applies for a patent and receives it immediately.

In the last stage, firms compete in the product market.

The market stage

Before the patent race starts, the n firms are identical. However, after the patent race has been concluded, one firm is different. Consequently, we can define a state z which describes to which group the firm belongs: either it was successful and won the race (z^I) or it was unsuccessful (z^C). As there can be only one winner of the patent race, only one firm can be in state z^I and $n - 1$ firms are in state z^C when they enter the market stage.

Naturally, a firm's earnings possibilities depend on both the state z and the patent scope y. Let $\pi_j(z, y)$ denote the flow profit during the lifetime of the patent if firm j is in state z. An unsuccessful firm's profit need not to be zero during the patent term. Competitors of the patent holder may sell older, less sophisticated products or use a less efficient technology. One might also regard a positive $\pi_j(z^C, y)$ to stem from the unsuccessful firms' ability to offer or employ non-infringing substitutes. As the model in the next section shows, however, this notion is misleading if imitation is not costless. After the patent expired, all firms are assumed to earn identical profits π^c which are independent of the patent scope. Concerning the flow profits the following is maintained:

Assumption 8.3. The instantaneous profits satisfy

1. $\pi_j(z^I, y) \geq \pi^c \geq \pi_j(z^C, y)$,
2. $\pi_{jy}(z^I, y) > 0$ and $\pi_{jy}(z^C, y) < 0$.
3. $\pi(z^I, 0) = \pi(z^C, 0) = \pi^c$.

By the first assumption, the profits $\pi_j(z^I, y)$ for the patent holders are at least as large as the profits π^c they earn after the patent expired. Profits $\pi_j(z^C, y)$ of the unsuccessful firms are at most as large as the ones they earn after the patent expires.

In addition, it is postulated that wider patents increase the patentee's profits while they decrease the competitor's profits during the patent life. This can be justified by the *business-stealing* effect: the more product variants infringe on the inventors' patents, the lower will be the demand for the their competitors.

Denoting by $V_j(z, y, T, \tau)$ firm j's value of being in state z we obtain:

$$V_j(z^I, y, T, \tau) = \int_{\tau}^{T+\tau} e^{-rt} \pi_j(z^I, y)\, dt + \int_{T+\tau}^{\infty} e^{-rt} \pi^c\, dt,$$

$$V_j(z^C, y, T, \tau) = \int_{\tau}^{T+\tau} e^{-rt} \pi_j(z^C, y)\, dt + \int_{T+\tau}^{\infty} e^{-rt} \pi^c\, dt,$$

(8.13)

where τ, $\tau := \min\{\tau_1, \ldots, \tau_n\}$, is the date at which the first firm completed its research project and, thus, receives a patent. Since $\pi_j(z^I, y) \geq \pi_j(z^C, y)$, the value of being successful in the patent race is at least as large as the value of being unsuccessful, $V(z^I, y, T, \tau) \geq V(z^C, y, T, \tau)$.

The research process

Uncertainty in research takes different forms. When firms undertake research projects, they aim at more or less specific targets within a certain time period. The research targets define the technology field as well as the intended improvement over the prior art. Yet, neither aspect can precisely be laid out beforehand. The invention, e.g. a new material, a new function in a software program or a more efficient way to produce a certain drug, may have the properties sought for, but also additional, surprising ones.[17] Moreover, the invention may take less or more time than expected. Here, only one aspect of uncertainty in research projects is considered: the development time. By choosing a higher research effort h_j at the beginning of the second stage, firms can decrease the *expected* development time, but they cannot ensure that they will win the patent race.

Different from the completion date, the size of the invention and the research costs $C(h_j)$ are known and observable. We assume that every invention is patentable regardless of its size and that patents are perfectly enforceable.

As usual, it is assumed that the arrival dates follow a Poisson process. In particular, we presume that the Poisson parameter is the research effort h_j so that the effort directly affects the expected duration of firm j's research project. Then, the distribution of firm j's development time τ_j is exponentially distributed with density $h_j(1 - e^{-h_j \tau_j})$. In addition, it is postulated that the development times are independently identical distributed for all firms.

The firm's objective function

The value functions in equation (8.13) are the present values of a firm that wins the patent race and the $n - 1$ firms that have been unsuccessful. Clearly, at the beginning of the second stage, when firm j decides on the research effort h_j, it is ignorant as to whether it will win the patent or not. With the individual development time being exponentially distributed, the *expected* present value of future earnings can be determined with

$$
V_j(z^0; \cdot) = \int_0^\infty e^{-(H+r)\tau} \left(h_j V_j(z^I; \cdot) + a^I V(z^C; \cdot) - C(h_j) \right) d\tau,
$$

$$
= \frac{h_j V_j(z^I; \cdot) + a^I V_j(z^C; \cdot) - C(h_j)}{r + h_j + a^I}.
$$

(8.14)

The new state variable z^0 indicates that the patent race has not yet started. From firm j's point of view, the parameter a^I is the aggregated research effort of the other firms so that $a^I := \sum_{l \neq j} h_l$. It also stands for the instantaneous probability that one of the $n - 1$ competitors of firm j will make the discovery before firm j. Likewise, the parameter H has a dual interpretation. On the one hand, it denotes the total industry research effort, i.e. $H := h_j + a^I$. On the other hand, it measures the instantaneous probability that any of the n firms in the market will make the invention between time t and dt.

$C(h_j)$ are the research expenditures that have to be spent every period until the patent race ends. All firms undertake research in the same way so that the research costs function is identical for all firms. The cost function is assumed to be convex in the effort, i.e. $C_h(h_j) > 0$ and $C_{hh}(h_j) > 0$.

8.2.2 The optimal investment decision

Firms seek to maximize the ex-ante expected present value $V_j(z^0; y, T)$ in (8.14) by choosing a research effort h_j. We find the following:

Proposition 8.7. Let $I(h, y) := a^I \left(\pi(z^I; y) - \pi(z^C; y) \right) + r \left(\pi(z^I; y) - \pi^c \right)$ and $K(h) := (r + nh)C_h(h) - \pi^c - C(h)$. Then, a unique symmetric equilibrium exists with the optimal research effort satisfying

$$\frac{\gamma(T)}{r}I(h,y) = K(h). \tag{8.15}$$

According to Denicolò (1996) the function $I(h,y)$ measures a firm's incentive to innovate. It consists of two components: the *profit incentive* $(\pi(z^I; \cdot) - \pi^c)$ measuring the extra profit in case the firm is successful and the *competitive threat* that is the difference between being a successful and an unsuccessful firm respectively $(\pi(z^I; \cdot) - \pi(z^C; \cdot))$. The latter effect is weighted with the probability that a competitor makes the discovery first. Observe that the expression $K(h)$ is independent of both, the patent scope y and the patent length T.

The first-order condition uses the fact that all firms are identical at the point in time when the decisions concerning the research effort has to be made. Consequently, all firms will use the same level of research effort. The equation in (8.15) defines how firms react to changes in the policy instruments $\{T, y\}$.

Proposition 8.8. Under Assumption 8.3, the optimal research effort is an increasing function of both the patent length and the patent scope.

Both longer and wider patents encourage firms to invest more into their research projects, yet they do it in different ways. Given a particular patent length, wider patents have two opposing effects on firms. On the one hand, a larger patent scope increases the *prize* for the winner by raising the flow profit so that firms are inclined to increase their research effort. On the other hand, the increase in the winner's flow profit comes at least partly at the expense of the competitors which suffer a decrease in their profits. At the point in time when the decision on the research effort has to be made, firms do not know whether they will win or lose the patent race. With even a modest number of firms, the probability of being unsuccessful is non-negligible which has a negative effect on firms' incentive to do research so that they are inclined to exert less effort. Proposition 8.8 proves that the positive effect of the patent scope dominates.

For any given patent scope y, longer patents increase the time during which the monopoly profits can be collected. Again, being successful in the patent race becomes more attractive so that firms will increase the research effort in order to increase the chances of winning.

8.2.3 The socially optimal policy design

As explained above, patent races incorporate the notion that the next steps on the path of technological progress are well-known, but the associated problems are yet unsolved. Consequently, all firms that have research capabilities in the respective technology field will strive to patent first in order to gain the most advantageous position for the competition in the product market. From a social point of view, competition in innovation always results in a suboptimal level of research effort. They stem from two sources. (1) Only the successful firm is eventually able to patent the invention. Yet, *n* firms participate in the patent race so that competition in innovation leads to *socially wasteful* duplication in research, i.e. a suboptimally high level of total research effort is necessary to create the innovation. (2) Even if one acknowledges that competition in innovation is necessary despite the duplication of research, the individual level of research effort is still suboptimal. This inefficiency arises because each firm neglects the overall effects of its own decision, i.e. the acceleration of the patent race. Accordingly, the individual research effort tends to be too large.

Denicolò (1996) postulates that the socially optimal level of the individual research effort $\bar{h}$ is known to the policymaker. In this case, equation (8.15) determines the combinations of the patent length and the patent scope $\{T, y\}$ that induce firms to choose the optimal research level $\bar{h}$.

Then, the policymaker's problem is to maximize social welfare subject to equation (8.15) evaluated at the socially desirable research effort $\bar{h}$. Similar to the constraints in the decision problems in (8.1) and (8.8), the relation (8.15) defines minimum values for the optimal patent scope and the optimal patent length that are able to induce firms to choose the socially optimal level of research $\bar{h}$.

It has been demonstrated in Section 8.1.3 that maximizing social welfare is equivalent to minimizing the present value of the deadweight loss. Thus, the policymaker's decision problem can be written as

$$\min_{T,y} \int_0^\infty e^{-(H-r)\tau} \int_\tau^{T+\tau} e^{-rt} d(y) \, dt \, d\tau = \frac{\gamma(T)}{r} d(y),$$

(8.16)

$$\text{s.t. } \frac{\gamma(T)}{r} I(\bar{h}, y) = K(\bar{h}).$$

Here, the present value of social costs is evaluated at the point in time when the patent race ends and the innovation becomes available to the consumers. Note also, that the right-hand side of the constraint is constant at the pre-defined effort level $\bar{h}$.

The following result ensues:

Proposition 8.9 (Denicolò, 1996, Proposition 1). Assume that $d(y)$ is an increasing function of the patent scope y. Then, a combination of the maximum patent length and the minimum patent scope will be optimal if $d_{yy} \leq 0$ and $I_{yy} \geq 0$. Conversely, in case $d_{yy} \geq 0$ and $I_{yy} \leq 0$, a combination of the maximum patent scope and the minimum patent length will maximize welfare.

The Proposition states sufficient conditions for the minimum (maximum) patent scope to be the optimal policy instrument. Therefore, both policy designs may prove optimal although the sufficient conditions are not met in special situations. Denicolò (1996) considers several specific examples, including cases for product and process innovations, for Bertrand or Cournot competition.

Although Denicolò (1996) explicitly includes the firms' innovation decision, the structure of the model remains essentially the same as in Gilbert and Shapiro (1990) and Klemperer (1990). In Gilbert and Shapiro (1990) and Klemperer (1990), the policy instruments are chosen so that welfare is maximized *and* the inventor earns profits that amount to a pre-specified reward V. As Denicolò (1996) presumes that the policymaker knows the socially optimal effort level $\bar{h}$, the optimization constraint in fact limits the policy instruments to combinations of $\{T, y\}$ that induce a fixed, pre-specified discounted incentive to undertake research that exactly covers the expected research costs $K(\bar{h})$.

Consequently, the graphical approach and the intuition used in Section 8.1 essentially remains valid. The seemingly additional sufficient condition on the investment incentives I is due to the fact that π^m was assumed to be a concave function of the patent scope that is bounded from above. This ensured that the restriction labelled V in Figure 8.1 is convex. In the model of Denicolò (1996) the restriction $\gamma I/r = K$ is also convex in a T/y-diagram if $I_{yy} > 0$.

Unsurprisingly then, Denicolò (1996) confirms the findings of Gilbert and Shapiro (1990) rather than provides new insights. By assuming that the socially desirable level of the research effort $\bar{h}$ is exogenously determined, Denicolò (1996) implicitly presumes that the policymaker employs different yardsticks against which different objectives are measured. While the patent policy mix is chosen to maximize the usual welfare function in (8.16), the socially optimal research effort $\bar{h}$ is determined using another, unspecified objective function. If both problems, the one of finding the optimal policy design and the one of determining the socially optimal research effort, were to be integrated, results would be less straightforward.

8.3 Patent scope and costly imitation

Until now, the possibility that competitors can offer non-infringing substitutes of the patented product has largely been neglected. In Gilbert and Shapiro (1990) and Denicolò (1996), imitation does not play any role. Although some interpretation that includes imitation may be devised, it remains independent of patent policy. The same essentially holds true for Klemperer (1990) as imitation does not require resources. However, especially when the patent scope is considered as a policy instrument, the question of imitation may be decisive: narrow patents makes inventing-around less expensive and reduces the static inefficiencies. The following considerations are based on the seminal work of Gallini (1992).[18]

8.3.1 A model with endogenous research effort and costly imitation

Gallini's original model is extended to include a patent race so that the results become comparable to those obtained by Denicolò (1996). The model emphasizes different protection mechanisms: the inventor may apply for a patent or protect his work by trade secrecy.[19] Firms that lost the patent race, i.e. the challengers, have certainly the knowledge necessary to invent around the patent. Yet, developing non-infringing substitutes requires additional expenditures that are positively correlated to the patent scope. For simplicity y is here interpreted as the imitation costs.

Formally, the problem of finding the optimal patent scope and length when imitation is costly is described by a four-stage game. In the first stage, the policy-maker decides on the patent length and the imitation costs $\{T, y\}$. Subsequently, n firms decide on the research effort h_j. Firms carry out their projects and one firm wins the patent race. The successful firm, i.e. the incumbent, has now to decide whether to patent the invention or to keep it secret. Lastly, some or all of the $n - 1$ unsuccessful firms choose to invent around the innovation. In case the invention was patented, each competitor has to incur fixed costs y and the imitation becomes available with certainty. If the discovery is protected by secrecy, imitation is costless.[20] However, success is not certain. p_D denotes the probability that the original innovation is independently discovered within a short period of time. If all firms are unsuccessful after this short time interval, all attempts to imitate are abandoned and the innovator gains the monopoly position forever.

Imitation is assumed to be perfect so that consumers do not prefer the original product over the non-infringing substitutes.[21] In addition, all firms are equally efficient in both research and production, so that their cost functions are identical. As a consequence, profits excluding the imitation costs are the same for all firms that are active in the product market. Let m denote the number of imitators and $\pi(m)$ the flow profits each of the $m + 1$ firms earns. Then, $\pi(0)$ stands for the monopoly profit.

8.3.2 The firms' decisions

The decision to imitate

Depending on whether the inventor kept his invention secret, imitation is either costly or costless. Consider first the case of a patented invention. If all competitors decide *not* to imitate the patented product, the inventor's discounted stream of profits amounts to

$$V_j^{PN}(z^I) = \int_0^T e^{-rt} \pi(0) \, dt = \frac{\gamma(T)}{r} \pi(0),$$

since perfect competition reduces profits to zero after the patent expired. Here, the present value is measured at the point in time when the innovation becomes available so that the duration of the patent race can be neglected. The superscripts P and N stand for *patent* and *no imitation* respectively. As the competitors did not try to invent around the patent, they receive zero profits.

As long as $V_j^{PN}(z^I)$ is smaller than the imitation costs y, imitation is unprofitable for all challengers. Thus, $T_I(y)$ with

$$T_I(y) := \left\{ T \in \mathbb{R}_0 : \gamma(T)\pi(0)/r = y \right\} \tag{8.17}$$

is the patent term for which the *first* challenger is indifferent between imitating and not imitating.

Given the patent scope y, imitation occurs for any patent length $T > T_I(y)$. In this situation, all firms, i.e. the patent holder and all imitating firms, earn identical profits $\pi(m)$. Free market entry determines the number of competitors m for which inventing around is profitable: $V_j(z^C) = \gamma(T)\pi(m)/r - y = 0$. Obviously, the challengers earn zero profits due to free entry. On the other hand, the patent holder's value of being faced with m competitors equals $V_j^{PI}(z^I) = y$. Summarizing, the inventor's value of patenting is

$$V_j^P(z^I) = \begin{cases} \gamma(T)\pi(0)/r & \text{for } T \leq T_I(y) \\ y & \text{for } T > T_I(y) \end{cases} \tag{8.18}$$

Now consider the case where the inventor decides to keep his discovery secret. Then, he earns a perpetual profit of $\pi(0)$ if none of the competitors makes an independent discovery. Alternatively, all firms receive zero profits due to perfect competition and zero imitation costs. As the former event occurs with probability $1 - p_D$, the expected value of keeping the invention secret is

$$V_j^S(z^I) = \frac{1 - p_D}{r}\pi(0). \tag{8.19}$$

The decision to patent

The inventor will only patent the discovery if the payoffs from doing so exceed the ones expected from trade secrecy. Observe that the present value of profits from patenting when imitation does not take place V_j^{PN} is smaller than the imitation costs y for all $T < T_I(y)$. This is a direct consequence of (8.17). Accordingly, if $V_j^S(z^I) > y = V_j^{PI}(z^I)$, the inventor always prefers secrecy over a patent. This decision is independent of the patent length.

In contrast, if $V^S(z^I) < y$, the decision to patent depends on the patent policy. Let T_P denote the patent length for which the inventor is indifferent between patenting and keeping the discovery secret, i.e. $T_P := \{T \in \mathbb{R} : V_j^S = V_j^P\}$. Then, patenting the invention is not profitable if the patent length is too short, $T < T_P$.

The innovator's payoffs for all possible configurations can be summarized as

$$V_j(z^I) = \begin{cases} (1-p_D)\dfrac{\pi(0)}{r} & (A) \text{ for } y < V_j^S, \\[2mm] (1-p_D)\dfrac{\pi(0)}{r} & (E) \text{ for } y \geq V_j^S \text{ and } T < T_P, \\[2mm] \gamma(T)\dfrac{\pi(0)}{r} & (C,D) \text{ for } y \geq V_j^S \text{ and } T_P \leq T < T_I(y), \\[2mm] y & (B) \text{ for } y \geq V_j^S \text{ and } T_I(y) \leq T, \end{cases} \tag{8.20}$$

where the bracket terms refer to Figure 8.3. Observe also that the competitors' payoffs are always zero due to free market entry and perfect competition.

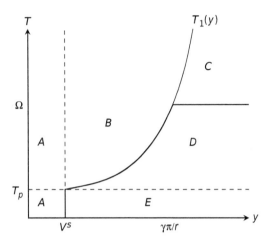

Data source: A, Secrecy Imitation; B, Patent, Imitation; C, Patent, No Imitation;
D, Patent, No Imitation; E, secrecy, No Imitation.

Figure 8.3 Imitation and patenting behaviour depending on the patent policy.

The optimal research effort

As in Denicolò (1996), n firms participate in the patent race. They have to decide on the research effort h_j knowing that a higher effort does only increase the probability of winning, but cannot guarantee success in the patent race. The value of being successful is given in (8.20) while the value of being unsuccessful is $V_j(z^C) = 0$. Then, equation (8.14) changes to

$$V_j(z^0) = \frac{h_j V_j(z^I) - C(h_j)}{r + h_j + a^I}. \tag{8.21}$$

The following two results can be obtained.

Proposition 8.10. For all combinations of the patent length and patent scope (imitation costs) a unique symmetric equilibrium exists.

Proof. See Proof to the Proposition 8.7. ☐

Proposition 8.11. The optimal research effort h^* has the following properties:

– It is independent of the patent policy if secrecy is optimal.
– The imitation costs exert a positive influence on the optimal research effort only when the inventor patents the invention and the competitors imitate the discovery.

–   When the inventor applies for a patent, but the competitors choose not to imitate, the optimal research effort increases with the patent term, but it is independent of the imitation costs.

By comparing Propositions 8.8 and 8.11, the differences from the previous models are revealed. Denicolò (1996) did not consider the possibility that the inventor might prefer secrecy over patent protection. Consequently, his model cannot predict that the optimal research effort remains unaffected by the patent policy if the inventor chooses trade secrecy for protection. Given that the successful firm does patent, however, both models find that stronger patent protection increases the research effort. In the present model, however, the effectiveness of either instrument depends on whether or not imitation occurs. Thus, construing $\pi(z^C, y)$ as the profits of challengers that develop non-infringing substitutes of the patented product or technology is misleading at least for the case of costly imitation.

8.3.3 The optimal patent length and patent scope when imitation is costly

We commence by specifying the policymaker's objective function. Note that we can exclusively focus on the case where the inventor does apply for a patent since the policy instruments cannot affect welfare given the discovery is to be protected by trade secrecy.

Again, let $\bar{w}$ denote flow welfare after the patent expired and $w(\pi)$ stand for the flow welfare during the patent life. Then, the discounted present value of welfare can be written as

$$W = -my + \int_0^T e^{-rt} w(\pi)\, dt + \int_T^\infty e^{-rt} \bar{w}\, dt. \tag{8.22}$$

Since $d(\pi) = \bar{w} - w(\pi)$, and $\gamma(T)\pi(m)/r = y$ by the free-entry condition, the welfare function can be rewritten as

$$W = \frac{\bar{w}}{r} + \frac{\gamma(T)}{r}\Big(d(\pi) + m\pi(m)\Big).$$

Using again the free-entry condition, it follows that maximizing the welfare function in (8.22) is equivalent to the following problem

$$\min_y \quad y\frac{d(\pi) + m(\pi)\pi}{\pi}, \tag{8.23}$$

where $m(\pi)$ is the inverse of the profit function $\pi(m)$.

The following result ensues:

Proposition 8.12 (Gallini 1992, Proposition 3). The optimal patent policy consists of choosing a patent scope (imitation costs) wide enough to make imitation unprofitable. The patent length is adjusted so that a reward for the successful firm ensures sufficient participation in the patent race.

If, as in Denicolò (1996), the research effort only influences the probability of winning the patent race and neither affects the profits $\pi(0)$ and $\pi(m)$ or the maximal flow welfare $\bar{w}$, the policymaker effectively disregards a potential feedback of his choice on the firm's research effort.

Nevertheless, differences occur in the results of the works introduced above. Whereas in the models of Gilbert and Shapiro (1990), Klemperer (1990) and Denicolò (1996) a policy mix between minimal patent scope and a maximal patent length can be optimal under certain circumstances, this policy mix is suboptimal when imitation is costly.

8.A Proofs to the lemmata and propositions

Proof. *Proposition:* **8.1** *Part 1*: Using total differentiation on the constraint in (8.1) yields

$$y_T = -\frac{\gamma_T(\pi^m(y) - \pi^c)}{\gamma \pi_y^m(y)},$$

which is negative since $\gamma_T > 0$ and $\pi_y^m > 0$ according to 8.1.

Part 2: Let $G := \gamma(T)\pi^m(y)/r + (1 - \gamma(T))\pi^c/r$. Then,

$$\lim_{T \to \infty} G = \frac{\pi^m(y)}{r},$$

since $\lim_{T \to \infty} \gamma(T) = 1$. Consequently, there is a minimum patent scope compatible with bestowing a pre-defined reward V on the inventor satisfying $V = \pi^m(y)/r$.

Now consider the case where the patent scope grows to infinity. As $\lim_{y \to \infty} \pi^m(y) = \bar{\pi}$, solving the constraint in (8.1) yields

$$T_{\min} = -\frac{1}{r}\ln\left(\frac{\bar{\pi} - rV}{\bar{\pi} - \pi^c}\right).$$

This expression is positive since $\bar{\pi} \geq rV \geq \pi^c$ by Assumption 8.1. $\qquad\square$

Proof.   *Proposition*: **8.4** Solving the integrals, the minimization problem can be rewritten as

$$\min_{T,y} \frac{\gamma(T)}{r} d(y)$$

$$\text{s.t. } V = \frac{\gamma(T)}{r} \pi^m(y).$$

Using the constraint to replace the discount factor yields the unconstrained optimization problem

$$\min_{y} V \frac{d(y)}{\pi^m(y)}. \tag{8.24}$$

Since V is constant, it can be neglected. Therefore, y^* satisfies the problem (8.24). T^* solves $V = \gamma(T)\pi^m(y^*)/r$. □

Proof.   *Proposition*: **8.7** The first-order condition can be written as $F(h_j, a^I) = \gamma(T)I(h_j)/r - K(h_j)$. By the implicit function theorem, the best response function $\psi_j(a^I) = \{h_j \in \mathbb{R}_0 : F(h_j, a^I)\}$ is continuously differentiable in a^I. The function $\Psi := (n-1)\psi(a^I)/n$ has a unique fixed point by Tarski's Theorem (see Vives, 2000, 39) since $\psi(a^I)$ and $\Psi(a^I)$ are quasi-increasing in a^I and continuously differentiable. □

Proof.   *Proposition*: **8.8** The first-order condition of the optimization problem can be written as

$$F(h, a, y, T) = \frac{\gamma(T)}{r}\left[a^I\left(\pi(y, z^I) - \pi(y, z^C) + r(\pi(y, z^I) - \pi^c)\right)\right]$$

$$- (r + h + a)C_h(h) + \pi^c + C(h) = 0.$$

Using the total differential yields

$$h_T = \frac{\gamma_T}{r(r+nh)} \frac{a^I\left(\pi(y, z^I) - \pi(y, z^C) + r(\pi(y, z^I) - \pi^c)\right)}{C_{hh}},$$

$$h_y = \frac{\gamma(T)}{r(r+nh)} \frac{a^I\left(\pi_y(y, z^I) - \pi_y(y, z^C)\right) + r\pi_y(y, z^I)}{C_{hh}}.$$

Since $\gamma_T > 0$ and $C_{hh} > 0$, both expressions are positive due to Assumption 8.3. □

Proof.   *Proposition*: **8.11** The first-order condition for the firm's problem reads

$$(r + h_j + a^I)\left(V_j(z^I) - C_h\right) - \left(h_j V_j(z^I) - C(h_j)\right) = 0.$$

Part I: Since $V_j(z^I)$ is independent of the patent policy $\{T, y\}$ when trade secrecy is optimal (case A and E in Figure 8.3) the result ensues.

Part II: The function $V_j(z^I)$ only depends on the imitation costs y when patent policy prescribes case B in Figure 8.3. Therefore, the optimal research effort is solely influenced by the imitation costs.

Part III: Similar considerations apply here.   □

9   Patent breadth

Different from patent scope, patent breadth protects against technologies that have a slightly superior or inferior quality than the patented one and belong to the same technology field. Patent breadth affects first and foremost cumulative inventions, i.e. inventions that directly build upon each other and can therefore be regarded to be improvements upon the predecessor.

Patent systems should at least partly solve the general problem of positive externalities associated with inventions. With cumulative inventions, however, the problem presents itself in a particular shape. A basic invention might inspire other inventors to improve the original idea, develop useful applications or complementary devices. If patents are narrow, even small improvements are non-infringing. In this case, the second-generation inventor does not need to negotiate a licence agreement with the first patentee. As a consequence profits that can be earned during the patent term might still be insufficient to cover research expenses and inventions will have a suboptimally low inventive step. On the other hand, if patents are broad, only few improvements are non-infringing. Most second-generation inventors who wish to utilize their invention have to negotiate licence agreements. Then, incentives to develop improvements might be insufficient and the average improvement size would be too high. Patent breadth is a policy instrument that may be used to correct deficient incentives to invent when later discoveries become possible because a previous one has been made.

The first section introduces the model of Chang (1995).[1] Here, the division of profits between two successive inventions is studied where the government employs a mix of patent breadth and anti-trust regulations to achieve the highest possible welfare level. Although the model gives valuable insights into the interrelations between two successive innovations, the results are limited by the assumption that only two inventions occur. Then, the second-generation inventor may infringe on the first-generation patent owner's rights, but his own rights cannot be violated. The second section therefore presents the model of O'Donoghue *et al.* (1998). The authors consider an infinite sequence of inventions so that all inventors except the first one may infringe older patents when their own patent is issued. Later on, their patent rights may be infringed by succeeding inventors.

9.1 A simple model without patent length

In this section we study a simple setting of two subsequent inventions in the same technology line. Different relationships between the two inventions are possible. On the one hand, the first invention might be a basic one without an immediate practical use and the second inventor created an application for the first innovation. Alternatively, the first invention might represent a fairly advanced and widely used technology and the second invention is an improvement over the first, but without any new elements. For both cases, the policymaker has to decide whether the second invention is to be declared infringing on the first one or not. If the second does infringe the first patent's rights, a hold-up situation[2] arises in which the second inventor cannot market his product without the permission of the first patentee; licence agreements have to be negotiated.[3] A situation where the second inventor infringes on the first patent strengthens the first patent owner's bargaining position in licence negotiations. Therefore, patent breadth can become an important tool to stimulate incentives for either the first or the second inventor.

9.1.1 A sequence of two inventions

The game structure

This simple model of cumulative inventions studies two firms, 1 and 2, over two periods. Chang (1995) distinguishes between an idea (invention) and an innovation.[4] The former consists of a pair $\{u_i, C_i\}$ where u_i denotes the improvement upon a previous invention.[5] The parameter C_i stands for the investment costs that turn the invention into an innovation or marketable product. The values of $\{u_i, C_i\}$ may be unknown or unobservable by the firms or the courts in the various stages of the game (cf in more detail *infra*).

At the beginning of the first period, firm 1 has the idea $\{u_1, C_1\}$. By investing the amount C_1, the inventor develops a marketable product with certainty. Only if the first inventor did invest C_1, a second firm can observe and study the product which result in an idea for an improved version of firm 1's product. The invention $\{u_2, C_2\}$ is received at the beginning of period 2 and the second inventor may or may not develop a marketable product.

Here, it is assumed that courts decide on whether or not the second patent infringes on the first invention. After they announce their findings, the firms may negotiate a licence agreement, where certain provisions of the agreement are affected by the court's anti-trust policy. Finally, both firms collect their profits.

Information and timing

Not all parameters of the inventions are known or observable to all parties, i.e. firms and courts, at all points in time. Rather, some parameters are revealed slowly over time and others remain private knowledge.

In particular, it is assumed that each firm learns the values $\{u_i, C_i\}$ when creating the invention. In case a patentee develops his invention into a marketable product by incurring the costs C_i, the quality improvement u_i becomes observable by all participants. Accordingly, when deciding on whether or not to invest innovation costs C_1, the first inventor is uncertain about the future improvement size u_2. The patentee only knows that the improvement will be drawn from the interval $[0, \bar{u}_2]$ according to a probability distribution $F[u_2]$ and the associated density function $f[u_2]$. The characteristics of the distribution function are common knowledge at the beginning of the first period.

Different from the social value u_i of an invention that is observed when the associated product has been developed, the costs C_i remain private information of the firms. However, it is commonly known that the innovation costs are uniformly distributed on the interval $[0, \bar{C}_i]$. Differences in the maximum innovation costs reflect disparities in the expertise with which firms conduct the development of an idea into a marketable product.

The policy instruments

Chang (1995) also uses two policy instruments: patent breath and anti-trust measures. Different from other approaches (cf *infra*), Chang does not introduce parameters to measure different levels of either policy instrument. Rather, he assumes that courts can credibly commit themselves to certain *patent–anti-trust* regimes.

Generally, patent breadth can be envisaged as a certain quality step that an invention has to take in order to not infringe on the rights of a previous patentee. When patents are broad, more quality levels of second-generation inventions and innovations are on average declared to infringe on the first-generation invention. As a consequence, the value of the first invention increases as competition from slightly improved products are prevented. How broader patents exactly affect the first inventor's stream of profits depends on the industry's innovation rate and on the anti-trust regulations in force. Since Chang (1995) does not consider uncertainty over the arrival of inventions, the first factor does not play a role here (cf *infra*).

The second policy instrument to be considered here consists of anti-trust measures. There exists a natural tension between anti-trust policy and patent policy since the latter uses the temporary suspension of competition by granting exclusive rights to foster innovations. Moreover, profit-maximizing behaviour usually implies that firms will restrict competition whenever they are given the opportunity to do so. It is therefore hardly surprising that courts have had a watchful eye on all firms' activities connected to patents. Indeed, technology licensing has e.g. been used to limit competition directly[6] or indirectly. In order to ensure the benefits of patent policy, it has to be accompanied by suitable anti-trust regulations. Otherwise, the negative welfare effects of anti-competitive behaviour may outweigh the benefits of the invention.

Literature distinguishes two types of licence agreements: ex-ante and ex-post licensing. The former refers to situations where negotiations are started *and* concluded after the idea has been conceived, but before any investments have been undertaken. In contrast, ex-post licences are struck after research (and development) costs have been incurred. Naturally, many licence agreements are mixtures of the two pure types, where some expenses have already been made to develop the idea to some degree, but further (joint) investments form a part of the agreement.[7]

It is clear from the previous discussion that Chang (1995) neglects the possibility of ex-ante licensing. Therefore, he implicitly assumes the ex-ante licence agreements either violate anti-trust regulations or are prohibitively costly to conclude. A direct consequence is that a social optimum cannot be reached by indirect policy measures, i.e. by committing to a certain patent–anti-trust regime as opposed to directly intervening into the economy.[8]

Although ex-ante licensing, mostly in the form of research joint ventures, is observed (Siebert and von Graevenitz, 2006), the associated costs can be considerable. Several factors are important. Firstly, assuming that the first inventor is well known, he may be unwilling to enter an agreement as long as he cannot assess the quality of the improvement over his own idea as well as the second inventor's ability to develop the improvement successfully. The former case may require the second inventor to reveal some reliable information on the improvement which will probably only be available if the second inventor has already sunk some resources. In this case however, the potential agreement cannot be classified as pure ex-ante licensing. The latter case, i.e. when the first inventor is uncertain about the second inventor's expertise to successfully carry out the project, is one of asymmetric information that frequently is afflicted with moral hazard and may therefore result in the breakdown of negotiations.

Secondly, imperfect information may also apply to the identity of the participants. Even though the first-generation inventor may be well known in the industry, many potential second-generation inventors may race to find an improvement. Thus, before the patent race has been concluded, the first-generation inventor cannot know who the winner will be and, therefore, who to approach with the ex-ante licence negotiation.

Considering these practical problems in reaching ex-ante licences, it seems reasonable to exclude this type from further consideration. The courts' anti-trust policy is then exclusively concerned with ex-post licensing. Here, an obvious characteristic to study is whether or not price-restricting clauses that allow for joint profit-maximization are permitted. Even if anti-trust regulations are strict so that collusion is not feasible for the inventors, ex-post licence agreements positively affect the first inventor's profits since he can collect royalties.

The effect of policy instruments on firms' profits

Firms are faced by identical consumers who purchase one unit of the consumption good in each period. The mass of consumers is normalized to one. Provided prices do not exceed the reservation price, total demand equals one as well under these circumstances. Here, prices are assumed to be equal to the quality of the product offered.[9]

The profits of a firm are not only determined by the demand structure, but also by the market structure as well as the policy instruments in force. Independent of the patent policy, however, the market is either served by a monopoly or a duopoly in the present model. Moreover, it is assumed that both firms set prices and that production takes place at no cost. Given the game structure described above, firm 1 holds a patented technology and is the monopoly in the first period. Accordingly, it charges the reservation price u_1 during the first period since patent protection is perfect. Firm 1 will remain in the monopoly position and sets the reservation price u_1 in the second period again, if the firm 2 does not to invest C_2 into the improved idea. This situation will typically arise if the costs C_2 are high relative to the improvement u_2.

In case the second firm does choose to develop the invention into a marketable product, the second-period profits depend on the patent policy in force. Profits can take any value between zero and the monopoly profit. The former will e.g. be realized if courts find that the second invention does not infringe on the first inventor's patent rights. In this situation, price competition will drive profits to zero if anti-trust policy makes collusion infeasible. Then, the effect of the patent–anti-trust policy on the firms' second-period profits can be represented by a function that maps the improvements $\{u_1, u_2\}$ into the space of profits $\{\pi_1, \pi_2\}$. Hence, the second-period profits can be written as $\pi_i(u_1, u_2)$. Yet, even under the most favourable patent policy, the maximum of the producers' surplus cannot exceed the second firm's total product quality (and reservation price) so that $\pi_1 + \pi_2 \leq u_1 + u_2$.

The decision to innovate

Given a particular patent–anti-trust policy, firms will only innovate if the associated profits exceed the costs C_i. Since both parameters, u_i and C_i are random variables that are independently distributed, some inventions are too costly to be turned into marketable products even under the most favourable policy regulations. The second inventor who collects profits only in the second period will invest if $\pi_2(u_1, u_2) > C_2$. To make the problem more interesting, Chang (1995) poses the following assumption.

Assumption 9.1.   For any given u_1

$$\bar{C}_2 \geq \pi_2(u_1, u_2)$$

for all u_2 and all possible policy configurations.

The assumption ensures that for any quality of the first invention u_1 there are at least some second-generation inventions that are not developed further when the costs attain its maximum $\bar{C}_2$.

With the decision rule of the second inventor concerning the development of a marketable product, the expected social value of the second invention can be defined as follows:

$$w(u_1) = \int_0^{\bar{u}_2} \int_0^{\pi_2(u_1,u_2)} \frac{u_2 - C_2}{\bar{C}_2} \, dC_2 \, dF[u_2].$$
(9.1)

The expression $u_2 - C_2$ measures the social value of the second invention. However, the realization of the social value depends on whether or not the second inventor finds it profitable to develop his idea at costs C_2. For a given quality improvement u_2, the inner integral takes only those situations into account in which a marketable product is developed, i.e. where $\pi_2(u_1, u_2) \geq C_2$. Then, the outer integral includes all potential quality improvements u_2.

The decision rule according to which the first inventor develops his idea further has also to be obtained. Different from the second-generation inventor, his total profit not only consists of the returns generated by selling his product, but also of potential royalties payable by the second firm if its innovation violates the first-generation inventor's patent rights. Let $\delta\pi_1(u_1, u_2)$ denote the change in firm 1's second-period profits that arise because the second inventor chooses to innovate. Note that $\delta\pi_1(u_1, u_2)$ depends on the patent–anti-trust policy and can take negative values. When the first inventor has to decide on whether or not to incur the innovation costs C_1, $\{u_2, C_2\}$ is uncertain. Thus,

$$P(u_1) = \int_0^{\bar{u}_2} \int_0^{\pi_2(u_1,u_2)} \frac{\delta\pi_1(u_1, u_2)}{\bar{C}_2} \, dC_2 \, dF[u_2]$$
(9.2)

is the expected change in profits induced by firm 2's innovation. Again, only those combinations of $\{u_2, C_2\}$ that result in the development of a marketable product are taken into account.

Owing to the assumption that demand is completely inelastic for prices below the reservation price, deadweight loss does not exist in this model economy. Consequently, any policy design does merely change the distribution of the total welfare between consumers' and producers' surplus given the price does not exceed the reservation price. Under these circumstances, a first-best policy would consist of rewarding both inventors with the social value that their innovations create for society. However, when inventions are cumulative so that the first invention prompts or inspires further developments, the mere existence of a subsequent invention is part of the social value of the first invention. Yet, if two different firms are likely to hold patents on subsequent inventions, the total revenues from the improved product $u_1 + u_2$ are insufficient to reward each firm the total social value it creates. Green and Scotchmer (1995) as well as Chang (1995) conclude:

Lemma 9.1 (Chang, 1995, Lemma 1).   Any patent policy (optimal or otherwise) will offer firm 1 less than the expected social value of its innovation.

This has two immediate consequences: Firstly, a first-best patent policy is not feasible with cumulative inventions and, secondly, any patent policy has to weigh the incentives to invent for the first inventor against the ones for the second inventor. Lemma 9.1 immediately leads to:

Lemma 9.2 (Chang, 1995, Lemma 2).   The welfare-maximizing court would allow firm 1 to charge the monopoly price u_1 in the first period and, if firm 2 does not invent, in the second period as well.

Given that the socially optimal price for firm 1's product is u_1 in the absence of a second innovation, the second-period profit can be written as $\pi_1(u_1, u_2) = u_1 + \delta\pi_1(u_1, u_2)$. Since $\delta\pi_1(u_1, u_2)$ can be positive or negative, the second period profit for the first inventor may be larger or smaller than the monopoly profit u_1. The expected stream of total profits is therefore

$$2u_1 + P(u_1). \tag{9.3}$$

Accordingly, firm 1 is willing to develop marketable products if the expected profits in (9.3) exceed C_1. Again, Chang (1995) poses an assumption so that there are at least some inventions u_1 that are not developed into marketable products when firm 1 faces maximum innovation costs:

Assumption 9.2.   For all possible patent–anti-trust policies, the following shall hold true

$$\bar{C}_1 \geq 2u_1 + P(u_1).$$

The welfare function

Social welfare can be measured as the sum of both innovations' contribution to society over the periods. Conditional on being developed, the first innovation is used in both periods so that its social value is $2u_1 - C_1$ when the second innovation is not made. Given the decision rules of both firms, the expected welfare is derived with:

$$W(u_1) = \int_0^{2u_1+P(u_1)} \frac{2u_1 + w(u_1) - C_1}{\bar{C}_1}\, dC_1,$$

$$= \frac{2u_1 + P(u_1)}{\bar{C}_1}\left[2u_1 + w(u_1) - \frac{2u_1 + P(u_1)}{2}\right]. \tag{9.4}$$

The first term is the probability that firm 1 chooses to develop the idea. The second component of the welfare function is the expected net social benefit from the first innovation, where the fraction within the bracket term stands for the expected development costs for a marketable product of firm 1.

As it can be seen in equation (9.4), patent–anti-trust regulations do not exert a direct effect on social welfare. Policy changes work through the expected change of firm 1's second-period profits $P(u_1)$ and changes in the expected social value of the second invention $w(u_1)$. The following result summarizes both effects:

Lemma 9.3 (Chang, 1995, Lemma 3).   Welfare given any particular u_1, $W(u_1)$ is non-decreasing in $w(u_1)$ and strictly increasing in $P(u_1)$. Furthermore, if either $u_1 > 0$ or $P(u_1) > 0$, then $W(u_1)$ must be strictly increasing in $w(u_1)$.

9.1.2 The optimal patent–anti-trust policy

The different patent–anti-trust regimes

It has been assumed that courts can only commit themselves to certain patent–anti-trust regimes rather than trying to specify the optimal policy for each individual invention. In particular, this means that every point in the quality improvement space $\{u_1, u_2\}$ is assigned to a particular policy regime before the first stage. This *policy program* is announced so that both firms are perfectly informed about the outcome of potential future infringement actions.[10]

Concerning patent policy, courts find either infringement (I) or non-infringement (NI). With respect to the anti-trust regulations, collusion can either be permitted (C) or not permitted (NC). Accordingly, four patent–anti-trust regimes are possible:

- $I \cap C$: infringement and collusion,
- $I \cap NC$: infringement and no collusion,
- $NI \cap C$: no infringement and collusion,
- $NI \cap NC$: no infringement and no collusion.

In case both firms develop a marketable product, firm 1 may call a court to decide whether or not product 2 infringes on its patent rights.[11] After the court announces its findings, firms may enter into licence negotiations.

There are several possibilities for distributing patent rights between licensor and licensee: one-sided or two-sided. In a one-sided transfer, one firm assigns its rights exclusively to the competitor, collects royalties, but does not itself offer the product. In this case, the licensee serves the entire market with the improved product. A two-sided transfer involves the mutual exchange of patents (cross-licensing). Here, usually both firms remain active in the market. It is assumed that the common surplus of the licence agreement is evenly split between the parties for one-side and two-sided agreements.

A court's finding that the second product does or does not infringe on the first-generation invention is of vital importance to both firms since it defines the threat points for later licence negotiations. First consider the case of *infringement*. Here, firms face a hold-up problem. Although holding a valid patent on the improvement u_2, firm 2 cannot sell its improved product without permission of firm 1. Similarly, firm 1 cannot use the improvement without consent of the rival. Owing to the fact that the second-generation invention has been declared a subservient patent, firm 2 has to negotiate a licence in order to earn positive profits. In contrast, without a licence, firm 1 continues to offer its product of inferior quality u_1. Consequently, the threat point for negotiations under regimes $I \cap C$ and $I \cap NC$ is $\{\bar{\pi}_1, \bar{\pi}_2\} = \{u_1, 0\}$.

($I \cap C$): With collusive clauses being permitted, charging the monopoly price $u_1 + u_2$ can be stipulated by the licence contract. In this situation, one-sided as well as two-sided transfers of patent rights are feasible and yield the same distribution of second period profits. As their presence on the product markets is important to firms, a cross-licence agreement with an explicit monopoly pricing provision seems to be the most likely outcome.[12] In this situation, each firm would serve half of the market with the improved product being offered at price $u_1 + u_2$. Net licence fees of $u_1/2$ are paid to firm 1 so that total second-period profits are $u_1 + u_2/2$ for firm 1 and $u_2/2$ for firm 2.[13]

($I \cap NC$): Here, collusion that ensures monopoly pricing is not permitted under the anti-trust regulations. However, the total social value $u_1 + u_2$ can be appropriated by firms if one firm attains the monopoly position. With firm 1 having been the monopoly in the first stage and because of its stronger bargaining position, it is reasonable to assume that firm 1 licences the improvement u_2 and firm 2 merely collects royalties without maintaining production facilities itself. In this case firm 1 charges the monopoly price $u_1 + u_2$ and serves the entire market. The licensor (firm 2) receives revenues of $u_2/2$ so that total second-period profits are $u_1 + u_2/2$ and $u_2/2$ for firm 1 and 2 respectively.[14]

Comparing the firms' second-period profits with those earned in the ($I \cap C$)–regime shows that they are identical. The reason for this lies in the fact that firm 2 is found to be infringing on firm 1's patent in both cases so that the second-generation inventor's only option to earn a positive profit is to enter some form of licence agreement. Firm 1's bargaining position is better in that it cannot do worse than receiving u_1 due to the court's findings.

The situation changes when courts rule that product 2 does *not infringe* on the first patent owner's rights. Then, firm 2 earns a positive profit with or without a licence contract. Since production costs are zero, firm 1 is prepared to offer its inferior product at a price as low as zero. In this situation, firm 2 is able to charge a price of at most u_2 to capture the entire market. In case it raises the price above this level, consumers would prefer to buy the *older* version of the product at a price sufficiently close to zero. As a consequence, by setting the price slightly lower than u_2, firm 2 becomes the monopoly and firm 1 quits the market. Thus, the threat point for licence negotiations is $\{\bar{\pi}_1, \bar{\pi}_2\} = \{0, u_2\}$.

($NI \cap C$): Since collusion is permitted under the anti-trust regulation, the most likely form of a licence agreement is cross-licensing. Under this contract, each firm sells the improved version of the product to half of the customers at the monopoly price $u_1 + u_2$. As firm 2 does not infringe on the rights of firm 1, the bargaining position of the second-generation inventor is much stronger so that firm 1 has to make a net payment of $u_2/2$ for the exchange of patents.[15] Accordingly, the total second-period profits amount to $u_1/2$ and $u_1/2 + u_2$ for firm 1 and 2 respectively.

($NI \cap NC$): Without the option of collusion sanctioned by anti-trust regulations and with product 2 found to be non-infringing on the first patent, firm 2 does not have any incentives to enter into a licence agreement. Firm 1 is prepared to reduce its price to zero, but cannot really compete with product 2 that has, after all, the superior quality. In order to capture the entire market, firm 2 cannot charge a higher price than u_2. Thus, second-period profits are $\{0, u_2\}$ for firm 1 and 2 respectively.

Since firms receive the same profits whether or not collusion is permitted under the anti-trust policy when product 2 infringes on the first-generation invention, the regimes $I \cap NC$ and $I \cap C$ are subsumed under I (infringement) henceforth.

The optimal patent–anti-trust policy

The object of society and, therefore the courts, is to assign to each pair of quality improvements $\{u_1, u_2\}$ the policy regime that maximizes social welfare (9.4). Since the principal components of the welfare function W are the expected social value $w(u_1)$ of the second invention and the expected private return $P(u_1)$, those functions are studied in greater detail. For every quality improvement u_1, the interval $[0, \bar{u}_2]$ has to be divided into smaller subsets for which the policy regimes I, $NI \cap C$ and $NI \cap NC$ are to be applied. This involves the setting of upper and lower boundaries for each policy regime and every u_1. To keep notation simple, the subscripts I, $NI \cap C$ and $NI \cap NC$ indicate the respective subsets of $[0, \bar{u}_2]$.[16] We obtain

$$
w(u_1) = \int_I \frac{3}{8} \frac{u_2^2}{\bar{C}_2} \, dF[u_2] + \int_{NI \cap C} \frac{1}{8\bar{C}_2} (4u_2^2 - u_1^2) \, dF[u_2]
$$
$$
+ \int_{NI \cap NC} \frac{1}{2} \frac{u_2^2}{\bar{C}_2} \, dF[u_2],
$$

$$
P(u_1) = \int_I \frac{u_2^2}{4\bar{C}_2} \, dF[u_2] + \int_{NI \cap C} \frac{1}{4\bar{C}_2} (-u_1^2 - 2u_1 u_2) \, dF[u_2]
$$
$$
+ \int_{NI \cap NC} \frac{-u_1 u_2}{\bar{C}_2} \, dF[u_2].
$$

(9.5)

In particular, Chang (1995) proves:

Proposition 9.1 (Chang, 1995, Proposition 2). For any $u_1 > 0$, the optimal patent–anti-trust policy is infringement for u_2 below a cut-off value, which lies strictly between zero and $\bar{u}_2$, but non-infringement (either with or without collusion) for u_2 above this cut-off value.

In line with court rulings in reality, the optimal patent policy will protect early inventions against small improvements by declaring negligible second-generation inventions to be infringing. According to (9.5), the expected net social welfare $w(u_1)$ of the second invention might even become negative when the quality improvement u_2 approaches zero and courts apply regime $(NI \cap C)$. The best society can achieve from the second innovation under these circumstances is an expected social value of zero in regime I or $NI \cap NC$. Regime I differs from $NI \cap NC$ in that it provides larger incentives for the first inventor by improving his bargaining position in licence negotiations. Indeed, in regime $NI \cap NC$ the first patentee is unduly punished since $P(u_1)$ becomes zero for second-generation innovations of negligible size according to (9.5). This is due to the fact that the second inventor is able to drive the former monopoly out of the market when his product does not infringe on the former monopoly's patent rights.

Depending on the quality improvement u_1, the incentives to create marketable products might even become insufficient for the first inventor. Thus, infringement either with or without collusion is the optimal policy regime when u_2 becomes very small. Then, the second inventor is required to negotiate a licence agreement to earn positive profits. The fact that he cannot use his invention without permission of the first patentee puts him in an unfavourable bargaining position. As a consequence, part of the gross social value generated by the second-generation innovation is transferred to the first innovator to compensate him for the positive externality that the subsequent inventors enjoy.

One might expect a monotonic relationship between u_1 and the threshold for u_2 that divides infringing from non-infringing improvements. In particular, one might argue that a higher initial improvement u_1 corresponds to a lower threshold that second-generation improvements u_2 have to take to be non-infringing because the first-period profits are sufficient to induce the investment of C_1 (Merges and Nelson, 1990). Yet, Chang (1995) demonstrates in the next two results that the threshold dividing quality improvements u_2 that should be declared infringing from those that should be found non-infringing is a non-monotonic function of u_1.

Proposition 9.2 (Chang, 1995, Proposition 3).   As u_1 approaches zero, the cut-off value for non-infringement (either with or without collusion) rises toward $\bar{u}_2$. For $u_1 = 0$, the optimal patent–anti-trust policy is infringement for any u_2.

Proposition 9.3 (Chang, 1995, Proposition 5).   As u_1 grows very large relative to $\bar{u}_2$, the cut-off value for non-infringement (without collusion) rises toward $\bar{u}_2$.

First consider Proposition 9.2. According to equation (9.5) the expected net social value of the second innovation $w(u_1)$ would attain its maximum in regime $NI \cap NC$ when the initial improvement is negligible, i.e. when found to be non-infringing. Yet, as $P(u_1)$ and the first-period profits of firm 1 are zero in this case, the first inventor cannot recover the development costs C_1 to turn the invention into

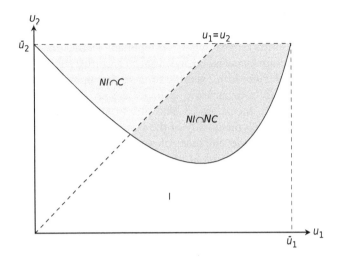

Figure 9.1 An example of the optimal patent–anti-trust policy.

an innovation: the incentives to innovate are clearly insufficient under $NI \cap NC$. As u_1 approaches zero, it becomes more and more important to increase the first inventor's incentives to develop a marketable product by increasing $P(u_1)$. Hence, as u_1 approaches zero, it is optimal to find larger quality improvements u_2 to be infringing (cf Figure 9.1).

When u_1 grows larger and the expected profits from an innovation are sufficient to cover the development costs C_1, non-infringement and price-restricting clauses being not permitted ($NI \cap NC$) is still the best policy to increase the net social value of the second invention $w(u_1)$. Since u_1 is strictly positive, firm 1's expected change in profit from the second invention $P(u_1)$ becomes negative in this case. Switching from $NI \cap NC$ to the infringement regime will increase social welfare because the private value from the second invention $P(u_1)$ increases considerably without decreasing the net social value $w(u_1)$ too much (cf Lemma 9.3).

By Propositions 9.1–9.4, it becomes clear that providing sufficient incentives for the first inventor is society's principal concern for very large and very small first-generation innovations. Only if u_1 attains medium values, non-infringement of the second product and, thus, sufficient incentive for their development are of interest to society.

As to anti-trust regulations, Chang (1995) finds:

Proposition 9.4 (Chang, 1995, Proposition 4). For sufficiently small u_1, collusive licensing agreements will be optimal for all non-infringement cases. For sufficiently large u_1, including any $u_1 > u_2$, however, it will be optimal to prohibit collusive licensing agreements in all non-infringement cases.

From the previous discussion it is clear that anti-trust regulations do not affect firms' profits and, therefore, social welfare when the infringement regime is optimal. Hence, Proposition 9.4 is only concerned with quality improvements $\{u_1, u_2\}$ for which the non-infringement regime is optimal. Under the non-infringement regime, a licence agreement is concluded only if anti-trust regulations permit a collusion to be formed. Since firm 2 is in the stronger bargaining position, it receives part of its competitor's revenues $u_1/2$ under the provisions of the contract and, thus, has excessive incentives to innovate. In addition, firm 2's incentives to innovate increase with the quality of the first innovation and with it the probability of the inefficient development of marketable products. Yet, in contrast to the situation where collusion is not permitted, the first inventor at least retains part of his profits so that the $NI \cap C$ regime offers some incentives for firm 1 to turn an invention into an innovation. Consequently, non-infringement and collusion may be regarded as necessary for small values of u_1 in order to ensure that the first-generation invention is brought to the markets.

9.2 An infinite sequence of inventions with patent term

In the previous section, the smallest possible sequence of innovations has been studied. In this setting, it was possible to examine how a policy regulating patent breadth and competitive behaviour affects the division of profits between the two inventors.

In practice, however, we observe a potentially infinite sequence of inventions. Consequently, each inventor may infringe previous patents at the time when his own patent is issued. Later on, his rights may be violated by subsequent inventors when his patent is about to expire. This problem can only be addressed when more than two succeeding inventions are considered. Therefore, the model of O'Donoghue *et al.* (1998) is introduced here.

9.2.1 A sequence of innovations and patent instruments

The research process

As in the previous section, all innovations belong to the same technology class. Here, however, the first innovation is followed by an infinite sequence of subsequent innovations. Innovation k improves upon the previous one by u_k so that the cumulated quality is given by $U_k = U_{k-1} + u_k$.

Each invention is the outcome of a research process that is at least subject to two sources of uncertainty: (1) the time t_k at which it is achieved and (2) the improvement size u_k. The arrival times t_k of inventions are again assumed to governed by a Poisson process with parameter λ. Private knowledge is supposed to be the source of ideas (cf *supra*) so that the parameter λ applies to all firms as a group. The appearance of inventions can be envisaged as follows. First, the next arrival date t_k is drawn from the body t of all arrival dates. Subsequently, the

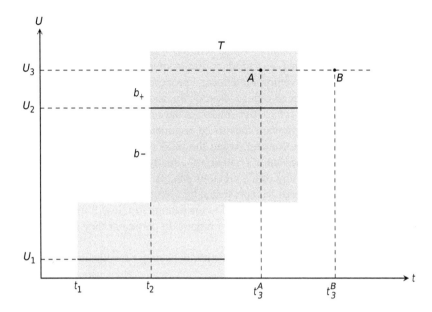

Figure 9.2 Patent breadth and patent term.

identity of the firm that is to receive the idea is randomly chosen. To keep the model tractable, O'Donoghue *et al.* (1998) assume that the number of firms is large so that one particular firm does not make two subsequent inventions.[17] The quality improvement u_k of a particular invention is also a random variable. It is drawn from a cumulative distribution function $F[u_k]$, with a corresponding density function $f[u_k]$.

As in the previous section, an invention is essentially a pair $\{u_k, C\}$ where C denotes the investment costs that are necessary in order to develop a marketable product. The development costs are independent of the inventive step u_k and are assumed to be exogenously given. Even with this additional assumption as compared to Chang (1995), the essential feature that some ideas are too costly so that they are not developed further is also present in the model of O'Donoghue *et al.* (1998).

Patent instruments

The authors study two patent instruments: patent breadth b and the patent term T. Different from Chang (1995), O'Donoghue *et al.* (1998) distinguish between lagging b_- and leading b_+ breadth. Both policy instruments and their effects are illustrated in Figure 9.2.

Assume that invention 2 has just been made at t_2. Since $t_1 + T > t_2$, the first patent has not yet expired. The inventive step u_2 is quite large and equals $U_2 - U_1$. Lagging patent breadth b_- covers inferior technologies, i.e. the area below U_2.

In contrast, leading breadth b_+ protects the second inventor against superior, future technologies, i.e. the shaded area above U_2 in Figure 9.2. The patent term gives the second inventor monopoly rights over his invention for T years so that his patent will expire in $t_2 + T$. Accordingly, with patent term, lagging and leading patent breadth as policy instruments, any product that is situated in the darker shaded area infringes the second inventor's intellectual property rights.

When the next inventor receives his idea at t_3^A, the second patent is still in force. Since the improvement $u_3 < b_+$, it infringes on the second inventor's patent.[18] Consequently, a licence agreement has to be negotiated in order to produce a product with quality U_3. In contrast, when the third inventor receives his idea later, i.e. at t_3^B, the second inventor's patent has already expired so that the third invention does not infringe any of the previous patents.

In general, patent policy can be represented by a vector $\{b_-, b_+, T\}$ specifying lagging and leading patent breadth as well as the patent term. It will frequently be convenient to consider only certain configurations. In particular they are:

- $\{u_k, 0, \infty\}$: complete lagging breadth without leading breadth and an infinite patent life,
- $\{0, b_+, \infty\}$: finite leading breadth with infinite patent life and zero lagging breadth,
- $\{0, \infty, T\}$: and infinite leading breadth with a finite patent term and zero lagging breadth.

Patent law and (lagging and leading) patent breadth

Different from what is suggested by Figure 9.2, leading and lagging breadth need neither to be strictly positive nor to be identical for all inventions. Indeed, a patent system that merely protects inventions for T years, but allows all inferior and superior technologies to be non-infringing has little value since small changes from the wording of the claims result in non-infringing inventions. Such patent systems will provide insufficient incentives to engage in research and development.

One principle of patent law is that rights are only bestowed for the subject matter the applicant really invented. This suggests that leading breadth is zero and lagging breadth automatically coves the entire quality gap $U_2 - U_1$ (not illustrated in Figure 9.2). Yet, this notion is misleading. The second inventor e.g. did not discover *everything* between $U_2 - U_1$.

Lagging (leading) breadth is essentially determined by the wording of the claims together with the Reverse Doctrine of Equivalents (Doctrine of Equivalents). Lagging breadth will usually be positive, but in reality neither covers the entire quality gap $U_2 - U_1$ or fills the gap to the leading breadth of the first invention. However, we usually assume one of the two alternatives to hold true. This is merely a simplifying assumption for the fact that a technology having a quality U', $U' \in (U_1 + b_+, U_2 - b_-)$, so that it neither infringes on the first or the second invention, will not be patentable since it would be found to fall short of either the novelty or the non-obviousness requirement.

9.2.2 A model of homogeneous tastes

The basic model

The economy is populated by identical consumers. Total demand is inelastic and normalized to one. Consumers are prepared to pay a price that equals the monetary equivalent of the cumulated quality of the latest product U_k.

As described in the previous section, a large number of firms is active in the industry. Each of them is able to conduct research and is searching for new approaches within the field of technology considered. The overall industry invention process is governed by a Poisson process with parameter λ as laid out above. Individual firms maximize profits by choosing prices with production costs being zero. Naturally, the concrete price to be chosen depends on a firm's market position, i.e. which product quality it is able to provide, as well as on the patent policy. The latter determines e.g. the net licence payment it receives.

With respect to licensing, O'Donoghue *et al.* (1998) assume that ex-ante licensing is feasible and takes place. Given patent policy $\{b_-, b_+, T\}$, the creator of an idea $\{u_k, C\}$ knows exactly whether courts will find any products developed on the basis of the latest invention to infringe on the previous inventor's rights. In case products of the latest quality infringe ($u_k < b_+$), the inventor could approach patent holder $k - 1$ to negotiate a licence agreement before he invests costs C that are necessary actually to develop the product of the latest quality. If it is possible to ensure the bargaining partner about the quality of the own invention without giving away any details, there will be scope of an ex-ante licence agreement.

In the previous section, it has been mentioned that, although ex-ante licensing can make the first-best solution feasible, it is seldom observed. However, O'Donoghue *et al.* (1998) make the assumption merely to simplify the analysis. Qualitatively, all results remain unchanged if ex-post licensing were to be employed instead.

With an infinite sequence of inventions and a possibly infinite patent life, products based on the latest invention may infringe on a number of previous patents, not just one. Consequently, licence agreements will have to be negotiated with each of the potentially injured parties separately. In the present model, this fact does not pose a problem, partly because of the assumption that firms can hold at most one patent. Here, it is postulated that the incremental profit facilitated by the licence agreement is divided among the parties such that: (1) each one receives a non-negative share and (2) the owner's share is non-increasing in the number of infringed patents.[19] In practice, however, the probability that a licence agreement can be reached with all holders of potentially infringed patents decreases with the number of involved parties. In addition, transaction costs increase with the number of potentially infringed patents.[20]

Independent of patent policy $\{b_-, b_+, T\}$, an innovation of size u_k contributes this inventive step to society for an infinite length of time since future improvements build on the kth invention. Thus, the social value (exclusive of development costs) of an invention of size u_k is u_k/r measured at the time of the invention t_k.

From a social point of view, all inventions that have an social value greater than the development costs C should be developed into marketable products. Let u^o be defined by $u^o := rC$. Then, u^o denotes the minimum inventive step that should be developed into marketable product from a social point of view.

In what follows, the rate of innovations Φ is used to compare different policy instruments. Given the Poisson parameter λ as well as the distribution function $F[u]$ for the inventive steps, the rate of innovation can be expressed as

$$\Phi(\underline{u}) := \lambda \int_{\underline{u}}^{\infty} u \, dF, \tag{9.6}$$

for any $\underline{u}$ so that all inventions satisfying $u \geq \underline{u}$ become innovations. Clearly, when $\underline{u} = u^o$, the innovation rate is socially optimal.

Lagging breadth without leading breadth

O'Donoghue *et al.* (1998) show that lagging breadth without leading breadth provide insufficient incentives for firms to innovate in the sense that the rate of innovation is lower than $\Phi(u^o)$. In order to prove this, they specify values for the lagging breadth b_- and the patent term T that are most favourable for innovations. In particular, this involves granting the patent for an infinite time span and protecting the entire quality gap u_k to the previous invention u_{k-1}. Accordingly, patent policy can be described by $\{u_k, 0, \infty\}$.

In general, the kth inventor can offer a quality of U_k, whereas the previous patent owner's product has at most quality U_{k-1}. With zero production costs and the consumers' reservation price being U_k, the kth inventor sets a price u_k under Bertrand competition and captures the entire market. Thus, gross profit flows are u_k as well and firm k obtains the monopoly position. With no leading breadth, however, an invention of the smallest inventive step would supersede the previous one. Thus, the actual patent term ends when the $k+1$st invention arrives.

Assume that all inventions have made a contribution to the technology field of $u \geq \underline{u}$, and let τ_k denote the time period until the kth invention arrives. Then, τ_k is distributed according to a exponential distribution with parameter θ, $\theta := \lambda(1 - F[\underline{u}])$. Accordingly, the expected profit is given by

$$E\,\pi_k(u_k, \underline{u}) = \int_0^{\infty} \frac{u_k(1 - e^{-r\tau_k})}{r} \theta(\underline{u}) e^{-\theta(\underline{u})\tau_k} \, d\tau_k - C = \frac{u_k}{r + \theta(\underline{u})} - C. \tag{9.7}$$

O'Donoghue *et al.* (1998) define an equilibrium as the inventive step u^* such that $E\,\pi(u^*) = 0$ and all inventions having a $u \geq u^*$ are turned into innovations.

Proposition 9.5 (O'Donoghue et al., 1998, Proposition 1). The equilibrium rate of innovation is suboptimal, that is $\Phi(u^*) < \Phi(u^o)$.

Thus, a patent policy without a leading breadth $\{b_-, 0, T\}$ will generally provide insufficient incentives to generate innovations as long as lower quality products are available. The reason for this result is straightforward. While the statutory patent life is infinite, the actual patent term is determined by the point in time when the next innovation supersedes the present one. Since a Poisson process governs the industry's invention frequency, the expected patent life is $1/\theta$ and finite. Thus, in order to recoup the development costs C, firms will not invest into ideas with $u_k \in (u^o, u^*)$ although they should become innovations from a social point of view in equilibrium.

Finite leading breadth

In this section, patent policy $\{0, b_+, \infty\}$ is studied in greater detail. Here, leading patent breadth is finite and statutory patent life is assumed to be infinite. Nevertheless, the actual patent term ends when a new, non-infringing invention arises. In the previous section all new inventions were non-infringing since leading breadth was assumed to be zero. Here, however, some inventions may violate the previous patent holders' rights so that licences have to be negotiated.

Consider a leading breadth of $b_+ < u^*$. It is easy to see that this choice cannot be optimal. Observe that for any arbitrary level of $b_+ < u^*$, all inventions with a quality improvement $u_k \leq b_+$ infringe on the previous non-infringing patent. Note also that inventions with $u_k < u^*$ would never be pursued under the *no leading breadth* policy $\{u_k, 0, \infty\}$ that defines the equilibrium value u^*. According to the definition of an equilibrium, the expected value of profits $E\,\pi(u^*)$ becomes just zero at u^* so that any lower quality innovation $u_k < u^*$ does on average not cover their development costs C. Consequently, all levels of leading breadth $b_+ < u^*$ are ineffective in raising the rate of innovation above $\Phi(u^*)$.

Now consider the case of $b_+ \geq u^*$. Ideas with $u_k > b_+ > u^*$ are non-infringing. Since all $u_k > u^*$ would be turned into innovations even without leading breadth, inventors having ideas $u_k > b_+$ will invest the development costs and, thus, become the new monopoly. The expected time until the next non-infringing innovation arrives is $1/\theta(b_+)$ which is larger than the expected patent life $1/\theta(u^*)$ without leading breadth.

Next, there are the inventions for which $u_k \in [u^*, b_+]$. Under the *no leading breadth* policy, they would form the basis for the development of marketable products as demonstrated above. Now, however, their associated products will infringe at least one patent so that licence agreements have to be negotiated. Assume that the owner of the latest non-infringing patent considers to licence the idea. The common surplus created by the kth invention is the expected profit it generates in the market. By analogy to equation (9.7) we find

$$E\,\pi_k(u_k, b_+) = \frac{u_k}{r + \theta(b_+)} - C > \frac{u_k}{r + \theta(u^*)} - C = E\,\pi_k(u_k, u^*) \geq 0.$$

It immediately follows that an idea of any quality $u_k \in [u^*, b_+]$ has a strictly higher expected profit under a patent policy with finite leading breadth than under a policy without leading breadth. Accordingly, the inventor holding the latest non-infringing patent is certainly willing to licence any invention satisfying

$u_k \in [u^*, b_+]$ and, subsequently, turn the idea into an innovation. An agreement between the parties is ensured as long as $E \pi_k(u_k, b_+)$ is positive.

Finally, there are the ideas $u_k < u^* < b_+$ that are on average unprofitable under a patent policy without leading breadth because the expected profits fall short of the development costs. Expected patent life is, however, longer under a patent policy with a positive leading breadth. Therefore, expected profits gross of development costs will increase as leading breadth rises. As a consequence, some ideas that are unprofitable under a policy without leading breadth are now profitable enough to cover the development costs.

An equilibrium under a patent policy $\{0, b_+, \infty\}$ with $b_+ \geq u^*$, is a minimum inventive step $u^b(b_+)$ such that $E \pi(u^b, u^b) = 0$ and all inventions having $u_k \geq u^b(b_+)$ become innovations. Note, that $u^b \leq u^*$ so that more ideas are realized when leading breadth is positive as opposed to a policy without leading breadth. A direct consequence is that the rate of innovation is generally higher under a policy with leading breadth than without leading breadth, i.e. $\Phi(u^b(b_+)) \leq \Phi(u^*)$; incentives to innovate increase when leading breadth becomes broader.

In addition it can be demonstrated:

Proposition 9.6 (O'Donoghue et al., 1998, Proposition 2). The equilibrium rate of innovation $\Phi(u^b(b_+))$ is increasing in b_+, and $\lim_{b_+ \to \infty} \Phi(u^b(b_+)) = \Phi(u^o)$.

Thus, the rate of innovation approaches the optimal one when patent breadth becomes infinite. Recall that all inventions with an inventive step larger than u^o and a social value u^o/r that just covers the development costs c should become innovations in the social optimum. With a statutory patent life being infinite, an infinite patent breadth makes all innovations infringe the first one. In this situation, the decision of the first inventor decision of the first inventor to licence a subsequent infringing social planner's one:

$$\lim_{b_+ \to \infty} E \pi_k(u_k, b_+) = \frac{u_k}{r} - C \geq 0 \quad \text{if} \quad u_k \geq u^o.$$

Infinite leading breadth

Here, we consider a patent policy $\{0, \infty, T\}$ with a finite patent term T and infinite leading breadth. Different from the patent policies discussed before, patents issued after $t_k + T$ will not infringe on the kth invention independent of how small or large the improvement actually is. Figure 9.3 presents two examples.

In Figure 9.3(a), the second innovation infringes on the first one since $t_2 < t_1 + T$. Hence, the first and the second inventor have to negotiate a licence agreement. In t_3^A, the third invention is made. As $t_3^A > t_2 + T$, it does neither infringe the first nor second invention so that the third inventor does not need to does not need to negotiate licence agreements with previous inventors.

Figure 9.3(b) shows essentially the same situation with one difference. Here, the third invention arrives earlier. Since $t_1 + T < t_3^B < t_2 + T$, it infringes the second but not the first patent. The immediate consequence is that the second and

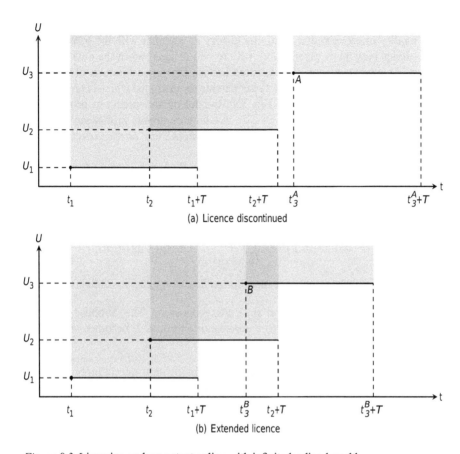

Figure 9.3 Licensing under a patent policy with infinite leading breadth.

third patentee enter licence negotiations. Assume that they are successful. Assume further that the second inventor licences his technology out so that his market profit is augmented by the licence revenues. Since negotiations are usually over the total returns that are facilitated by a licence agreement, the fees received from licensing out the second invention should be included in the negotiations between the first and the second inventor. However, at t_2 at which the negotiations between the first and the second patentee take place, it is uncertain when the next invention will arrive so that the *expected* licence fees $L(\cdot)$ have to be included rather than the actual ones. Thus, the expected profit from an invention reads

$$\mathrm{E}\,\pi_k(u_k, T, g_k) = \frac{u_k}{r}\gamma(T) + L(T, g_k) - C,$$

where $\gamma(T) = 1 - \mathrm{e}^{-rT}$ as before. The first component is the discounted market profit that can be collected during the patent life T. The second stands for the expected licensing fees.

Let G_k denote the set of possible patent histories that have led to t_k, and let g_k stand for a particular path through history that records all previous invention dates and quality improvements. Then, the history g_k together with the patent term T determines how many patents are likely to be infringed when the next invention arises. As a consequence, the expected licence fees are a function of T and g_k. Clearly, when patent life is short, fewer patents are infringed which *ceteris paribus* increases the expected licence fees. Yet, the discounted stream of profits of the next invention falls since the time span in which monopoly profits can be earned is shorter. Overall, the total effect of a shorter patent life T on the expected licence fees for a given history g_k is a priori ambiguous.

An equilibrium under patent policy $\{0, \infty, T\}$ is a pair $\{u^T(T,g), g \in G\}$ such that all inventions with $u_k > u^T(T,g)$ become innovations and $u^T(T,g)$ satisfies $E\,\pi_k\left(u^T, T, g\right) = 0$ for each $g \in G$. The corresponding rate of innovation obtained by

$$\int_G \Phi\left(u^T(T,g)\right) dZ[g,T] = \lambda \int_G \left(\int_{u^T(T,g)}^{\infty} u \ dF[u]\right) dZ[g,T],$$

where $Z[g,T]$ is the cumulative distribution describing the possible histories.

Proposition 9.7 (O'Donoghue et al., 1998, Proposition 3).   Suppose that for each $g \in G$, $L(T,g)$ converges to a nonnegative limit as T becomes large. Then for each $g \in G$, $\lim_{T \to \infty} \Phi\left(u^T(T,g)\right) \geq \Phi(u^o)$.

The result shows that under $\{0, \infty, T\}$ the innovation rate is higher than the optimal one when the patent term becomes large, i.e. some inventions that a social planner would turn down become innovations here.

Comparison between the policies with leading breadth

Both policies $\{0, b_+, \infty\}$ and $\{0, \infty, T\}$ stimulate research and development (R&D) as compared to a policy without leading breadth $\{u_k, 0, \infty\}$. A comparison between Propositions 9.6 and 9.7 shows that the former two are not equivalent since $\lim_{b_+ \to \infty} \Phi(u^b(b_+)) \leq \Phi(u^o) \leq \lim_{T \to \infty} \Phi(u^T(T,h))$. O'Donoghue *et al.* (1998) state in their Proposition 4:

Proposition 9.8 (O'Donoghue et al., 1998, Proposition 4).   Suppose two policies $\{0, b_+, \infty\}$ and $\{0, \infty, T\}$ induce the same rate of innovation. Then:

1. Policy $\{0, \infty, T\}$ has a shorter effective patent life or $T < 1/\theta(b_+)$.
2. Policy $\{0, b_+, \infty\}$ has lower total R&D costs.

With static inefficiencies being absent, policy $\{0, b_+, \infty\}$ is preferable since it would achieve the same rate of innovation at lower costs. This policy has another advantage. It does not create claims against future inventions through a third party. Take the example depicted in Figure 9.3(b). The probability that the second invention is infringed by a future one so that licence revenues are created for the second inventor is taken into account when the first and the second inventor negotiate the licence agreement. The third invention does not actually need to violate the first inventor's rights. The fact that it infringes on the second inventor's patent suffices to transfer part of the third innovations market profit to the first inventor. In contrast, under policy $\{0, b_+, \infty\}$, an infringing idea does not create claims against future innovations that are not already owned by the original patent holder.

9.2.3 Heterogeneous tastes in a model of a natural oligopoly

In the model with identical consumers, firms were always able to appropriate the entire consumer surplus. In this special situation, static inefficiencies that usually arise with exclusive rights do not occur. In order to re-establish their results, O'Donoghue *et al.* (1998) adapt the basic model to allow for heterogeneous consumers and two firms. Their model bases on the one of Shaked and Sutton (1983) who show that the number of firms a market can accommodate depends on the properties of the consumers' income distribution.[21]

The basic model of a natural duopoly

Consumers are presumed to be identical except for their willingness to pay for quality. Each consumer has unit demand and receives utility

$$\zeta U_k - p_k$$

when consuming a product of quality U_k. The parameter ζ measures the willingness to pay and is supported on the interval $[\zeta_l, \zeta_u]$. The ratio ζ_u/ζ_l determines the number of firms that the market can at most accommodate. To keep analysis as simple as possible, O'Donoghue *et al.* (1998) assume that two firms, a low-quality and a high-quality firm, can serve the market. A third firm cannot capture a positive market share. Again, production costs are assumed to be zero and market entry is only possible at small fixed costs ε.[22]

Lemma 9.4. Let $4 \geq \zeta_u/\zeta_l \geq 2$ and k denote the latest innovation. Then, there are exactly two firms in the market each producing one product with

$$U_h = U_k, \qquad\qquad\qquad U_l = U_{k-1}, \quad u = u_k$$

$$p_h = \frac{u}{3}(2\zeta_u - \zeta_l), \qquad\qquad p_l = \frac{u}{3}(\zeta_u - 2\zeta_l),$$

$$\pi_h(u) = \bar{\pi}_h \frac{(2\zeta_u - \zeta_l)^2}{9}u, \qquad \pi_l(u) = \bar{\pi}_l \frac{(\zeta_u - 2\zeta_l)^2}{9}u,$$

$$q_h = \frac{1}{3}(2\zeta_u - \zeta_l), \qquad\qquad q_l = \frac{1}{3}(\zeta_u - 2\zeta_l).$$

According to the lemma, each innovation has to conclude a cycle of two periods. In the first one, the innovation is new so that the associated product has the highest quality U_h. After the next innovation arrives, the former incumbent produces the good with the low-quality. Equilibrium prices and profits are proportional to the quality gap u. Clearly, the high-quality firm sets the higher price and receives the larger profit. Lemma 9.4 also shows that the demand for the high- and the low-quality good are independent of the quality gap and solely depend on the properties of the distribution of the consumers' willingness to pay for quality and, hence, the market size.

Further, let B denote the sum of all consumers' willingness to pay and l the share that corresponds to the demand q_l. Then, the flow welfare is given by $BU_h - lu$. In a duopoly, market distortions arise so that $B - l > \bar{\pi}_h$.

Lagging breadth in a natural oligopoly

Again, it is demonstrated that complete lagging breadth $\{u, 0, \infty\}$ provides insufficient incentives for firms to innovate. In the richer framework, however, the results have to be qualified.

In the natural duopoly framework, expected profits stem from two periods: (1) as the market leader and (2) as the market follower. Here, market leadership is identical with being the quality leader. The end of each period occurs when an invention arrives that is considered to be profitable enough to justify further development costs C. Assume that all inventions with $u \geq \underline{u}$ are turned into innovations. Then, the expected quality gap between the current innovation and the next invention conditional on the latter qualifying for an innovation is determined by

$$\mathrm{E}\, u(\underline{u}) = \frac{1}{1 - \theta(\underline{u})} \int_{\underline{u}}^{\infty} u \, dF[u].$$

A new innovation can collect profits over two periods. The flow profits of the quality leader depends on the inventive step he achieved. In contrast, the profit of the market follower is not determined by the own quality gap he created a period earlier, but by that of the current market leader. As a consequence, flow profit is $\bar{\pi}_h u$ in the first period, but $\bar{\pi}_l\, \mathrm{E}\, u(\underline{u})$ in the second period since the quality gap to be achieved is uncertain yet. Expected profits for any firm k that produces the high quality good is

$$\mathrm{E}\, \pi_k(u_k, \underline{u}) = \int_0^{\infty} \frac{\pi_h u_k}{r} \left(1 - e^{-r\tau_1}\right) \theta(\underline{u}) e^{-\theta \tau_1}\, d\tau_1 + \int_0^{\infty} \theta(\underline{u}) e^{-(\theta + r)\tau_1}$$

$$\times \int_0^{\infty} \frac{\pi_l\, \mathrm{E}\, u(\underline{u})}{r} \left(1 - e^{-r\tau_2}\right) \theta(\underline{u}) e^{-\theta \tau_2}\, d\tau_2\, d\tau_1 - C \qquad (9.8)$$

$$= \frac{\pi_h u_k}{r + \theta(\underline{u})} + \frac{\pi_l\, \mathrm{E}\, u(\underline{u})}{r + \theta(\underline{u})} \frac{\theta(\underline{u})}{r + \theta(\underline{u})} - C.$$

τ_1 and τ_2 denote the duration of the first and second period respectively. Both are exponentially distributed with parameter $\theta\underline{u}$.

The first term is the expected profit as the high-quality firm. Here, the expectation is over duration of the first period τ_1. Likewise, the second term measures the expected profit during the second period as a market follower. There are three sources of uncertainty in the second period: firstly, the quality gap achieved by the next market leader is uncertain so that the flow profit $\pi_l E u(\underline{u})$ during this stage is unknown as well. Secondly, the duration of the second period is uncertain. This effect is measured by the inner integral. Lastly, the second period only starts when the first one is concluded. The uncertainty over the start date is captured by the outer integral of the second term.

Different from the model with homogeneous tastes, the expected profit $E\,\pi(0,0)$ may be strictly positive.[23] When the own contribution to the technological progress is negligible ($u_k = 0$), the expected profits from being the market leader are zero according to equation (9.8). Since the expected quality improvement of the next invention is positive, the expected profits as a quality follower are positive because $\theta(0) = \lambda$. Thus, if the expected profit from being the market follower exceeds the development costs, $E\,\pi(0,0)$ is positive and $u = 0$ constitutes an equilibrium. More generally, the equilibrium under a policy $\{u, 0, \infty\}$ is

$$\tilde{u}^*(\lambda) = \begin{cases} \tilde{u} & \text{if } E\,\pi(\tilde{u}, \tilde{u}) = 0 \\ 0 & \text{if } E\,\pi(0,0) \ge 0. \end{cases}$$

Consequently, all inventions with $u \ge \tilde{u}^*$ become innovations.

The properties of the equilibrium can be summarized with:

Lemma 9.5 (O'Donoghue et al., 1998, Lemma 1). $\tilde{u}^*(0) = \hat{u}$, and $\tilde{u}^*$ is either non-decreasing or U-shaped, where $\hat{u}$ satisfies $\pi_h\hat{u} = C$.

An example of the equilibrium minimum inventive step is shown in Figure 9.4. The example illustrates a situation where $\tilde{u}^*$ is always positive so that the expected profits from being a market follower never exceed the development costs C. To show that the equilibrium under policy $\{u, 0, \infty\}$ does create suboptimal incentives to innovate, the social optimum and, thus, the social welfare function has to be considered.

Assume that all inventions with $u \ge \underline{u}$ become innovations. Then, the social welfare function can be derived with

$$W^*(\underline{u}) = \frac{\theta(\underline{u})}{r}\left[\frac{B}{r}E\,u(\underline{u}) - \frac{l}{r+\theta(\underline{u})}E\,u(\underline{u}) - C\right]. \tag{9.9}$$

The bracket term measures the expected social benefit when the minimum inventive step that becomes an innovation increases by a unit. The first term represents the value if the increase of quality would benefit all consumers immediately. However, part of the consumers with low willingness to pay for

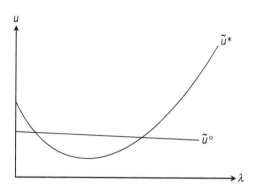

Figure 9.4 The equilibrium under complete lagging patent breadth and the social optimum.

quality have to wait for the benefits of the innovation until the next one arrives. This reduction of social welfare is represented by the second term. Finally, θ/r measures the average number of innovations per unit of time.

Let $\tilde{u}^o$ denote the minimum inventive step that maximizes the welfare in (9.9).

Lemma 9.6 (O'Donoghue et al., 1998, Lemma 2). $\tilde{u}^o(0) < \hat{u}$, and $\tilde{u}^o(\cdot)$ is decreasing.

Proposition 9.9 (O'Donoghue et al., 1998, Proposition 5). Suppose tastes are heterogeneous. There exists a λ^* such that $\tilde{u}^*(\lambda) > \tilde{u}^o(\lambda)$ for all $\lambda \geq \lambda^*$.

In Figure 9.4, it can be seen that $\tilde{u}^* > \tilde{u}^o$ when the arrival of ideas is sufficiently frequent, i.e. λ is high. Thus, the equilibrium minimum inventive step is too large as compared to the social optimum under complete lagging breadth without leading breadth. However, for low and medium values of λ, $\tilde{u}^*$ is smaller than the optimal value. Consequently, policy $\{u, 0, \infty\}$ may not only result in an innovation rate that is too low (large λ) but also in an innovation rate that is too high (small λ).

Finite leading breadth

As before, if an idea is infringing, i.e. $u \leq b_+$, the inventor has to negotiate a licence agreement with the market leader. Only non-infringing innovations supersede the current market leader. Different from the model of homogeneous consumers, however, the profits of the former market leader do not immediately terminate. Rather, the former high-quality good becomes the low-quality product. While being the market follower, new licence agreements are not struck since new ideas cannot infringe the follower's patent rights.

Similar to the model in the last section, a leading breadth $b_+ < \tilde{u}^*$ is inefficient for the same reasons as explained above. Thus, only policies with $b_+ \geq \tilde{u}^*$ need to be considered. In addition, it is presumed that λ is sufficiently high so that a policy without leading breadth generates too few innovations.

Since an infringing idea of size u cannot violate the follower's patent rights, it only contributes to the current market leader's profit. The expected market profit of an idea having made an inventive step u is

$$E \pi^b(u, b_+) = \frac{\pi_h u}{r + \theta(b_+)} - C.$$

Clearly, the current market leader will find it profitable to enter into licence negotiations with the firm having the idea u expected profits are positive.

For a given leading patent breadth b_+, the equilibrium is given by

$$\tilde{u}^b(b_+) = \begin{cases} b_+ & \text{if } E \pi^b(b_+, b_+) \leq 0 \\ u' & \text{if } E \pi^b(b_+, b_+) > 0, \quad E \pi^b(u', b_+) = 0 \end{cases}$$

Again, the equilibrium under leading breadth specifies a minimum inventive step u' that is smaller than b_+ and, thus infringing. Different from the model with homogeneous tastes, however, the equilibrium inventive step is not necessarily smaller than the $\tilde{u}^*$ under policy $\{u, 0, \infty\}$. This is a direct consequence of the natural oligopoly framework. Another difference is:

Proposition 9.10 (O'Donoghue et al., 1998, Proposition 6). Suppose tastes are heterogeneous.

1. $\tilde{u}^b(b_+) = \tilde{u}^*$ for all $b_+ \in [0, \tilde{u}^*]$.
2. There exists $b_+^* > \tilde{u}^*$ such that the rate of innovation and social welfare are strictly larger for $b_+ = 0$ than for any $b_+ \in (\tilde{u}^*, b_+^*)$.

The first result merely restates the observation that all leading breadths $b_+ < \tilde{u}^*$ are ineffective. The second result shows that a positive leading breadth may retard innovation as compared to a policy without leading breadth. With homogeneous tastes, the innovation rate with leading breadth was always larger than the one without leading breadth. Again, this result is a direct consequence of the natural oligopoly framework and is especially pronounced when $\tilde{u}^*(\lambda) < \tilde{u}^o(\lambda)$, i.e. when the innovation rate is suboptimally high under a policy without leading breadth.

Infinite leading breadth

A policy $\{0, \infty, T\}$ has a different inner logic than either a policy $\{0, b_+, \infty\}$ or a policy without leading breadth. Under $\{0, b, \infty\}$ and $\{u, 0, \infty\}$, a market leader is the firm that holds the non-infringing patent with the highest quality and the market follower is the firm that is the owner of the non-infringing patent with the second highest quality. Since patents last forever, the market follower's patent is still valid when it is superseded as the market leader.

Under a policy $\{0, \infty, T\}$, the market follower is the firm those patent has just expired. As every firm is able to offer a product based on the just expired patent, the market segment for the low-quality product should be perfectly competitively. However, O'Donoghue *et al.* (1998) assume that a random firm serves the low-quality market segment.

Since market leadership is terminated according to the same rules as in the model with homogeneous tastes and a new idea does not contribute to the randomly chosen market follower, the expected profit of a new idea is given by

$$E\pi^T(u, T, g) = \frac{\gamma(T)}{r}\pi_h u + L(T, g) - C,$$

$\gamma(T) = 1 - e^{rT}$. Again, investment occurs if the expected profit is positive.

An equilibrium under infinite leading breadth can be defined as

$$\tilde{u}^T(T, g) = \begin{cases} \tilde{u}' & \text{if } E\pi^T(\tilde{u}', T, g) = 0 \text{ and } \tilde{u}' > 0, \\ 0 & \text{if } E\pi^T(0, T, g) > 0 \end{cases}$$

so that all ideas $u \geq \tilde{u}^T$ become innovations for all histories $g \in G$.

Welfare effects

In the model with homogeneous tastes, the problem of static inefficiencies did not arise so that the (optimal) rate of innovation was used as a benchmark. Here, both policies $\{0, b_+, \infty\}$ and $\{0, \infty, T\}$ did raise the innovation rate as compared to a policy without leading breadth. However, infinite leading breadth could result in too many innovations as stated in Proposition 9.7. Infinite leading breadth does achieve the same innovation rate as finite leading breadth with a shorter patent term, but at the expense of higher total development costs.

When consumers have heterogeneous tastes, additional social costs arise as not all consumers benefit from new innovations immediately. As a consequence, a longer effective patent life delays the point in time when the consumers with low willingness to pay can enjoy the technical progress. Thus, although the development costs are lower under a policy with finite leading breadth even with heterogeneous consumers, the higher social costs arising under the same policy may counterbalance the lower development costs. The latter is confirmed by the following result:

Proposition 9.11 (O'Donoghue et al., 1998, Proposition 7). Suppose tastes are heterogeneous and that two policies $\{0, b_+, \infty\}$ and $\{0, \infty, T\}$ have the same rate of innovation. Then, $W^b(b_+) < W^T(T)$.

The functions $W^b(b_+)$ and $W^T(T)$ are the welfare excluding the development costs and evaluated at the equilibrium inventive steps under the policies with finite and infinite patent breadth respectively. A priori, it is however unclear whether infinite or finite leading breath does invoke the lower total social costs.

9.A Proofs to the lemmata and propositions

Proof to Lemma 9.4. If there are two firms in the market, the indifferent consumer has willingness to pay of $\tilde{\zeta} = (p_k - p_{k-1})/u_k$. Then, demand is given by

$$q_h = \zeta_u - \frac{p_k - p_{k-1}}{u_k},$$

$$q_l = \frac{p_k - p_{k-1}}{u_k} - \zeta_l.$$

Maximizing the profits for the quality leader and follower yields equilibrium prices of

$$p_h = \frac{u_k}{3}(2\zeta_u - \zeta_l),$$

$$p_l = \frac{u_k}{3}(\zeta_u - 2\zeta_l).$$

The rest of the variables are easily derived. $\square$

10　The non-obviousness standard

The patent system intends to correct the incentives to create inventions and innovations. By granting exclusive rights, the incentives usually increase since revenues rise by the ability to charge higher prices or to license the invention. Modern patent systems aim at protecting *true* inventions. Yet, a universal definition of what a *true* invention is does not exist. Together with the requirements of utility and novelty, the non-obviousness requirement is applied to ensure a minimum qualitative technical progress in the respective technology line. In this sense, the non-obviousness standard (NOS) constitutes the societies' definition of an invention.

In this way, trivial advances in the technology field such as the obvious combination of certain parts are not rewarded, and inventors that target higher inventive steps are encouraged. The NOS is especially important for cumulative innovations and bears certain similarities with patent breadth (cf *supra*). Since a patentee can be sure that small advances in the respective technology field are not patentable, slightly superior technologies cannot render the patent owner's technology obsolete. This usually increases the incentives to innovate.

A NOS that is too weak will certainly entail welfare losses. If small improvements over a previous invention are granted patent rights, the value of the first patent decreases. The first patent owner's profits drop, because he has to share the market with at least the one new competitor. In this situation the incentives to achieve (socially) more valuable inventions decrease since the expected profits may not cover the research costs. On the other hand, if NOSs are so strong that hardly any inventor can satisfy the requirement, incentives to undertake research may vanish altogether, because even *true* inventions do not receive patent protection.

The first section introduces the basic assumptions of the model. Here, the relation between the NOS and patent breadth are explained in greater detail. In the second section, the optimal research effort is characterized and the effects of a higher NOS on a firm's behaviour is explored. The subsequent section is concerned with the optimal NOS. Finally, the effects of certain industry-specific characteristics on the optimal NOS are derived.

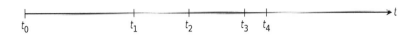

Figure 10.1 A sequence of patent races.

10.1 The basic framework of a model with an infinite sequence of patent races

The model is based on Hunt (1999a, 2002) and describes the following situation: a number of firms are competing in research and development (R&D) as well as prices.[1] Again, two sources of uncertainty associated with the research process are considered here. Firstly, although the completion date can be influenced, it essentially remains a chance event. Secondly, the invention's improvement over the prior art is a random variable.

By choosing a higher research effort, a firm reduces the expected development time of the invention. Given a certain firm has come up with an invention, the innovation size is a random variable drawn from an underlying distribution function common to all firms. If the invention's improvement over the prior art exceeds the NOS, property rights granting a temporary monopoly position are conferred to the inventor. In case the improvement is smaller than the NOS, the invention does not qualify for a patent and the associated information instantly becomes common knowledge. The rest of this section describes the assumptions in detail.

10.1.1 An infinite sequence of patent races

Time is considered to be a continuous variable, and the time horizon is infinite. In Figure 10.1, the dates t_k are regarded to be stochastic and mark the points in time when an invention is made.

The time span between two successive discoveries is a patent race.[2] Each patent race ends when a new invention has arisen upon which the next race starts. In Figure 10.1 e.g. the first patent race ends with the discovery of the first invention at t_1 so that the patent race covers a time of length $t_1 - t_0$. Since the inventions' arrival dates are stochastic, the actual duration of patent races varies and, hence, the economic patent life of the former invention.[3]

An infinite sequence of patent races can be modelled as follows. Let a Poisson process determine the duration τ_k, $k \in \mathbb{N}$, of the kth patent race.[4] Then, $\{\tau_k\}_{k=1}^{\infty}$ is a sequence of variables which are independently, identically distributed according to an exponential distribution with parameter λh_i for firm i, $i = \{1 \ldots n\}$ (Davis, 1993, 37). The parameter λ, $\lambda > 0$, is the innovation efficiency common to all firms and exogenously given. h_i denotes the research effort of firm i. The arrival times are then determined by $t_k := \sum_{j=1}^{k} \min\{\{\tau_{ji}\}_{i=1}^{n}\}$.

Further, note that a firm can be in one of two states z: being the incumbent (z^I) or a challenger (z^C). A firm is a challenger in the kth race if it was unsuccessful in creating a patentable invention in the previous patent race. In contrast, the

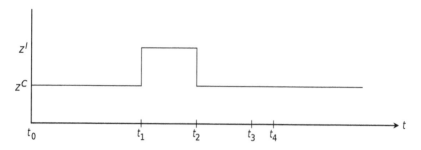

Figure 10.2 A sample path for firm *i*.

firm occupies the incumbency during the *k*th patent race if it made a patentable discovery in the last race.

The random variables $\tau_k \in \mathbb{R}_0$ and $z_k \in \{z^I, z^C\}$ together define a jump process, where $z_0 = z^C$ is additionally imposed. Hence, all firms are challengers before the first patent race has been concluded. Consequently, an infinite sequence of patent races can be described by a piecewise-deterministic-process (PDP) (Davis, 1993, ch. 24) associated by the jump process which is defined by $\{\tau_k, z_k\}$. A sample path for firm *i* is presented in Figure 10.2.

10.1.2 Patentability and the non-obviousness standard

The non-obviousness standard

Every patent race ends with a discovery. The first one creates a new technology or a new product. Every following invention improves the existing technology or product line so that inventions are cumulative.

As explained above, an invention has to be non-obvious to qualify for a patent. A discovery is considered to be non-obvious if the problem solved by the invention cannot be anticipated by an expert having ordinary skills in the respective field of technology. The NOS's function is to prevent patent rights being conferred for inventions that only slightly improve existing products or technology lines. The standard encourages inventors to pursue larger, (socially) more valuable improvements and protects them once a patent is granted.[5]

Assume the *k*th patent race ends with the appearance of the *k*th invention in the respective technology line. Let u_k denote the improvement of the *k*th invention over the $k-1$st invention. The improvement of the *k*th invention u_k is a random variable drawn from the interval $[0, \bar{u}]$ with the corresponding distribution and density functions $F[u_k]$ and $f[u_k]$.[6] The random variable u_k is exogenous and stationary in the sense that it is independent of a firm's research history, innovation effort and time. In particular, this means that a firm can only influence the expected development time of the current project, but not the size of the improvement.[7]

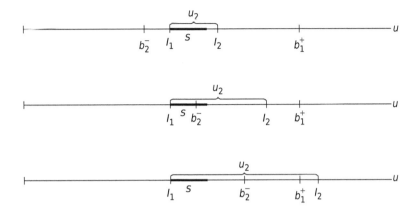

Figure 10.3 The relation between patentable inventions.

The NOS is a parameter s, $s \in [0, \bar{u}]$. Then, the kth invention qualifies for a patent only if $u_k \in [s, \bar{u}]$. Accordingly, a discovery with an improvement in the range of $[0, s)$ is not patentable. The probability that a given innovation satisfies the NOS is denoted by $\theta := 1 - F[s]$.

Patentability, infringement and licensing

Some additional assumptions on the relation between successive inventions are necessary. It is postulated that non-patentable discoveries immediately become common knowledge so that all firms are free to use the associated information.[8]
The question concerning the relation between patentable inventions is more difficult. The claims in a patent application define the patent's scope (cf *supra*). Since claims of path-breaking inventions are usually wide, the associated patent will be equally broad. In this situation, several constellations are possible. Firstly, a later invention, although patentable infringes on the first patent and vice versa. Then, neither inventor can practise their own invention without the consent of the other inventor: the patents block each other. This problem is usually overcome by cross-licence agreements. Secondly, only the later invention may infringe on the former one so that the second inventor must obtain a licence from the first inventor who is, however, free to exercise his invention without the consent of the second inventor (cf *supra*). Finally, there is the case where neither invention infringes on the other. Figure 10.3 illustrates the cases.
In Figure 10.3, there are two inventions I_1 and I_2, where the latter improves the former. In each representation, it has been postulated that the size of invention I_2 is sufficient to obtain a patent, i.e. $u_2 > s$. The topmost example illustrates the case of mutually blocking patents. Here, the second-generation invention I_2 infringes on the first patent since I_2 lies within the leading breadth, i.e. $I_2 < I_1 + b_1^+$. On the other hand, the first patent would violate the second inventor's rights since the

lagging breadth is so large as to encompass the first invention, i.e. $I_2 - b_2^- < I_1$. Observe that the improvement u_2 is smaller than both, leading breadth b_1^+ and lagging breadth b_2^-.

The picture in the centre presents the situation in which $b_1^+ > u_2 \geq b_2^-$. Thus, the second innovation infringes on the first invention, since $I_2 < I_1 + b_1^+$. Yet, the first invention does not violate the second inventor's patent rights as $I_1 < I_2 - b_2^-$. The last picture shows the case where $b_1^+ > b_2^- > u_2$ so that neither invention infringes on the other's rights.

In principle, the infringement problem of patentable inventions could be prevented either by applying a strong NOS or by restricting the leading and lagging breadth so that $s > \max\{b_1^+, b_2^-\}$ is always satisfied. Here, it is implicitly assumed that a policymaker decides on a leading and lagging breadth such that $s > \max\{b_{max}^+, b_{max}^-\}$ always holds and licensing is never necessary. For simplicity, it is assumed that upon the arrival of a new patentable invention the last can be used freely by all firms.

10.1.3 Demand and prices

Following Hunt (2002), demand is supposed to be completely inelastic and normalized to one. Consumers are identical, and their reservation price for each new generation of a product or technology is identical to the invention's improvement u_k.[9]

Firms are engaged in Bertrand competition and production takes place at no costs. Let U_{k+1}, $U_{k+1} := \sum_{l=1}^{k} u_l$ denote the cumulated improvements embodied in the latest technology. If the kth invention is patentable, the innovator is the only firm able to offer a product of quality U_{k+1}. Therefore, the incumbent of the $k+1$st patent race is able to charge the consumers' reservation price u_k for the product. Since all inventions prior to the kth invention can be freely used by all firms once the kth invention is made, all challengers can offer a product of quality U_k. As long as the number of firms exceeds three, Bertrand competition ensures that the challengers obtain zero gross profits, i.e. the price becomes zero.

In case the invention is unpatentable because it does not satisfy the NOS, the invention becomes common knowledge and can be used by all firms. In this situation, the firm having made the last *patentable* invention remains the incumbent. Note that the incumbent is the only firm that can draw an advantage from the unpatentable invention. In particular, it is assumed that the inventor of the last patentable discovery offers a product of quality U_{k+1}.

10.1.4 The expected profits

In order to increase the chances of winning the current patent race, firms may increase their research effort h_i, $h_i \in \mathbb{R}_0$, by investing $C(h_i)$ units per period. The usual assumptions of twice continuous differentiability and convexity are posed on the research cost function so that $\partial C(\cdot)/\partial h_i = C'(\cdot) > 0$, $\partial^2 C(\cdot)/\partial h_i^2 = C''(\cdot) > 0$, and $C(0) = 0$.

Owing to Bertrand competition, all challengers realize zero gross profits per period. Consequently, their net instantaneous profit is given by

$$\pi_i(z^C) := -C\big(h_i(z^C)\big) \tag{10.1}$$

which is negative. To facilitate notation, $\pi_i(z^C)$ and $h_i(z^C)$ are abbreviated by π_i^C and h_i^C respectively.

Since the consumers' reservation price is equal to the improvement of the product u_k and demand is normalized to one, the expected gross profit is identical to the expected price the incumbent is able to charge. The incumbent must have made a patentable discovery so that the expected price conditional on the invention being non–obvious is $\int_s^{\bar{u}} uf[u]\, du/\theta$. Then, the expected instantaneous net profit can be written as:

$$\pi_i(z^I) := \int_s^{\bar{u}} u\frac{f[u]}{\theta}\, du - C\big(h_i(z^I)\big). \tag{10.2}$$

Again, π_i^I and h_i^I stand for the more cumbersome $\pi_i(z^I)$ and $h_i(z^I)$ henceforth.

10.2 Firms and the optimal research effort

It has been assumed that the innovation efficiency λ and the average size of an improvement over a previous invention stay constant over time. An immediate consequence is that the second and all subsequent patent races are identical: a firm is either the incumbent or a challenger. The first patent race, however, differs from all others since all firms are identical, i.e. neither firm has gained the incumbency yet. Hence, the sequence of patent races can be divided into an ex-ante situation and an ex-post situation. The former refers to all points in time where the first patent race has not been concluded so that firms are identical. The latter comprises all points in time where the first patent race is over so that one firm occupies the monopoly position.

It can be expected that firms choose their research effort conditional on their position in the current patent race, i.e. the incumbent may invest less than a challenger.[10] Yet, all challengers will exert the same effort in the second and all subsequent patent races as they are indistinguishable.

In general, it may be optimal for firms to invest a different amount of effort in the first patent race. Accordingly, the analysis is undertaken separately for the ex-ante and the ex-post situation. Since the ex-post value functions are the main ingredients for the ex-ante one, the ex-post situation is considered first.

10.2.1 The ex-post value functions

After the first patent race has been concluded, the sequence of patent races constitutes a PDP so that the heuristic concept of the *Bellman principle of optimality* can be applied to study the firms' optimal behaviour (see e.g. Davis, 1993, ch. 4). Firms decide on their research effort so as to maximize their expected discounted stream of future profits. In doing so, they take the competitors' behaviour as given.

Let $V_{ik}(z_k)$ denote the value firm i assigns to be in position z_k during the kth patent race. Then, the generator of the PDP defined by $\{\tau_k, z_k\}$ is given by

$$\pi_i(z_k) + \mathfrak{h}_i(z_k)\big(V_{ik+1}(z \setminus z_k) - V_{ik+1}(z_k)\big) - rV_{ik}(z_k),$$

where r is the exogenous interest rate and $\mathfrak{h}_i(\cdot)$ is the hazard rate of the associated PDP. z_k denotes the state of a firm and $z \setminus z_k$ the opposite state of z_k.

Consumers' preferences and the distribution for the innovation size are stationary so that expected prices and expected profits remain constant over time as well. Accordingly, the value functions will be identical for all patent races, i.e. $V_{ik}(z_k) = V_{ik+1}(z_k)$ and the subscript k indicating the patent race can be dropped. In general, the Bellman principle of optimality requires the value functions to satisfy $\pi_i(z_k) + \mathfrak{h}_i(z_k)\big(V_i(z \setminus z_k) - V_i(z_k)\big) - rV_i(z_k) = 0$. In our specific example with two states z_k, the value functions have to satisfy the following system of equations

$$rV_i^I = \pi_i^I + \mathfrak{h}_i^I\big(V_i^C - V_i^I\big),$$
$$rV_i^C = \pi_i^C + \mathfrak{h}_i^C\big(V_i^I - V_i^C\big),$$

(10.3)

where V_i^l and $\mathfrak{h}_i^l$ are the shorter notations for $V_i(z^l)$ and $\mathfrak{h}_i(z^l)$, $l = I, C$.

The hazard rates $\mathfrak{h}_i^l$, $l = I, C$, define the average time $1/\mathfrak{h}_i^l$ that a firm will be in position l before a change occurs. For example, the average time before a challenger becomes the incumbent is $1/\mathfrak{h}_i^C$, whereas it takes the incumbent approximately $1/\mathfrak{h}_i^I$ to become a challenger. Obviously, the hazard rates are state dependent which reflects the fact that it is much harder to win a patent race than to lose the monopoly position.

If all inventions were patentable ($s = 0$) the hazard rate for a challenger would simply be $h_i^C \lambda$, i.e. the probability for firm i to make a discovery between t and $t + dt$. With a positive NOS, however, not every invention is patentable. Consequently, even if challenger i has created an invention, he remains in this position during the next patent race if the invention does not satisfy the NOS ($u_k < s$). Therefore, the hazard rate for a challenger has to be modified to $\mathfrak{h}_i^C := h_i^C \theta \lambda$.

Similarly, in the absence of an NOS, the hazard rate for the incumbent is defined by the probability that any of the challengers succeeds in inventing between t and $t + dt$, i.e. by $\sum_{j \neq i} h_j^C \lambda$. Again, since a patentable invention occurs with probability θ, the incumbent's hazard rate is given by $\mathfrak{h}_i^I := a_i^I \theta \lambda$ with $a_i^I := \sum_{j \neq i} h_j^C$.

Given the hazard rates, the system of Bellman equations (10.3) can be explicitly solved for the value functions:

$$V_i^I = \frac{\pi_i^C}{r} + \frac{r + h_i^C \theta \lambda}{\phi_i} \frac{\pi_i^I - \pi_i^C}{r},$$
$$V_i^C = \frac{\pi_i^C}{r} + \frac{h_i^C \theta \lambda}{\phi_i} \frac{\pi_i^I - \pi_i^C}{r},$$

(10.4)

where $\phi_i := r + (a_i^I + h_i^C)\theta\lambda$. A challenger's continuation value consists of two parts. The first one is the present value of a permanent income stream π_i^C. It constitutes the value function's infimum and would be realized if challengers had no chance to win a patent race in the future, i.e. if they were never to change their position. The expression $h_i^C\theta\lambda/\phi_i$ is the average time firm i spends as the incumbent in future. Thus, the second term of a challenger's continuation value is the expected present value of profits earned over and above the guaranteed profit π_i^C during times of incumbency.

A comparison with the incumbents' continuation value shows that the certain profit stream and the one received due to future monopoly positions are also part of the value of being the incumbent in the current patent race. However, the incumbents' continuation value has an additional part reflecting the fact that they occupy the monopoly position in the current race and, thus, earn extra profits of $\pi_i^I - \pi_i^C$ until the next patentable discovery arises.

From equations (10.4), certain general properties of the value functions can immediately be deduced.

Lemma 10.1. Ceteris paribus, the value functions have the following properties:

1. $\partial V_i^k/\partial \pi_i^l > 0, k, l = I, C.$
2. $\partial V_i^I/\partial\lambda < 0, \partial V_i^C/\partial\lambda > 0,$
   $\lim_{\lambda\to 0} V_i^l = \pi_i^l/r, \lim_{\lambda\to\infty} V_i^l = \left(a_i^l\pi_i^C + h_i^C\pi_i^l\right)/\left(r(a_i^l + h_i^C)\right), l = I, C.$
3. $\Delta V_i := V_i^I - V_i^C \geq 0$ if $\pi^I \geq \pi^C,$
   $\partial\Delta V_i/\partial\lambda < 0.$

According to the first property, both value functions are increasing functions of the challengers' and the incumbent's flow profits. Both effects are straightforward. First consider the case of the monopoly profit π_i^I. If it raises, e.g. because the upper limit to the innovation size $\bar{u}$ extends, the extra profit earned during future incumbency positions increases. Since the incumbent and a challenger have equal chances of holding the monopoly position in future, both continuation values increase. If a challenger's profit π_i^C increases, the continuation value is affected in two ways. On the one hand, it increases the present value as the permanent stream π_i^C/r rises. However, the extra profit $\pi_i^I - \pi_i^C$ earned during the spells of future incumbency declines. Yet, as long as all firms have a strictly positive probability of winning a patent race in future, i.e. $h_i^C\theta\lambda/\phi_i \in (0, 1)$, the effect on the permanent income dominates, and both continuation values increase.

The second property is concerned with the effect of the innovation efficiency on the continuation values. According to the lemma, the incumbent's value is a decreasing function and a challenger's value is an increasing function of the innovation productivity. Independent of a firm's position, the parameter λ has two effects on firms. Firstly, a larger λ means that the firm under consideration is more productive in generating discoveries. Thus, a higher innovation efficiency raises a firm's chances of winning future patent races, thereby increasing the expected future profits that can be earned in excess of π_i^C. Secondly, since every firm is becoming more productive, the patent races accelerate and thereby reduce the expected economic life of a patent. As a consequence, the time during which the extra profits can be earned becomes shorter. This negatively affects the expected profits and the continuation values. However, since $h_i^C \theta \lambda / \phi_i$ is an increasing function of the efficiency parameter, the average time spent as the incumbent increases indicating that firms occupy the monopoly position more often which over-compensates the shortened patent life for a firm presently being a challenger.

The same effects are present with firms currently being the incumbent. In addition, however, the present patent race is shortened by a general increase in the research efficiency which reduces the profits above π_i^C that can be earned during the current race. The lemma asserts that this negative effect dominates.

To gain further insight, the properties at the limit are given. Indeed, as λ approaches zero, firms generate fewer and fewer discoveries, and the patent races lengthen on average. At an extreme, firms do not change their states z_k at all; the incumbent keeps the monopoly position and the challengers remain in their state for ever. Consequently, the value functions approach π_i^I / r and π_i^C / r for the incumbent and a challenger, i.e. the initial position, becomes all-important.[11] In contrast, if λ approaches infinity, innovations arise so quickly that the position in the current patent race becomes insignificant, and the continuation values for both states become identical and equal to π_i^C / r.

The last property verifies that firms assign a higher value at being the incumbent than at being a challenger. Furthermore, it confirms that the importance of the position in the current patent race declines as patent races pick up speed.

10.2.2 The ex-ante value function

Given the optimal research effort for the second and all subsequent patent races, the ex-post versions of the continuation values only depend on parameters, i.e. they are independent of the firms' decisions for the first patent race. Then, firm i's ex-ante value function is given by

$$
\begin{aligned}
V_i^A &= \int_0^\infty e^{-(r+(a_i+h_i)\theta\lambda)t} \left(h_i \theta \lambda V^I + a_i \theta \lambda V^C - C(h_i) \right) dt, \\
&= \frac{h_i \theta \lambda V^I + a_i \theta \lambda V^C - C(h_i)}{r + (a_i + h_i)\theta\lambda},
\end{aligned}
\tag{10.5}
$$

where again, $a_i = \sum_{j \neq i} h_j$ is the cumulated research effort of all competitors. Since neither firm has made a discovery in the respective product or technology line, the ex-ante value function does not depend on a firm's position. It is the expected value of participating in the whole sequence of patent races.

10.2.3 The optimal research effort

As the ex-ante value function depends on the optimal research effort for the second and all subsequent patent races, we again commence by studying the ex-post situation.

The ex-post situation

The value functions in (10.4) are the only functions that satisfy the Bellman's principle of optimality. Hence, after the first patent race has been concluded, firms are constantly switching between the two states of being an incumbent or challengers (cf 10.2 *supra*). A firm in position z^l, $l = I, C$, will choose its research effort such that the continuation value V_i^l is maximized. Since the value functions are state-dependent, the optimal research efforts will be state-dependent as well. Therefore, we are seeking an asymmetric equilibrium $h^* = \{h^{I*}, h^{C*}\}$.

For the incumbent, the first-order condition reads

$$\frac{\partial V_i^I}{\partial h_i^I} = -\frac{r + a_i^I \theta \lambda}{r \phi_i^2} C'(h_i^I) \leq 0, \tag{10.6}$$

where the profit functions in (10.1) and (10.2) have been used. The inequality sign is due to the non-negativity constraint of the research effort. Evidently, the first-order condition can only be satisfied as an equation if the research costs are fixed, i.e. if they are independent of the effort level. However, if the research costs are increasing in the effort level, the first-order condition holds as strict inequality and the incumbent's optimal choice is $h^{I*} = 0$ and therefore refrains from any research activity. This result is well-known in the innovation literature (cf e.g. Grossman and Helpman, 1991). The incumbents' incentive to invest in research is lower than the challengers' one since they already occupy the monopoly position. They cannot expect to gain by winning the current patent race because the value functions are identical for all patent races and the innovation size depends neither on the effort level nor on the previous successes.[12] Instead, the incumbent sinks resources on an uncertain event as winning the current patent race is by no means certain. Consequently, the incumbent does not engage in research at all.

With the incumbent not participating in the current patent race, only the challengers compete for the monopoly position in the subsequent patent race. As all challengers are identical, the situation can be described by a symmetric $(n-1)$-player game. The following result immediately follows:

Proposition 10.1. Given $\theta, \lambda > 0$, there exists a unique symmetric equilibrium $h^{C*} > 0$ where h^{C*} satisfies

$$\theta \lambda \left(\pi^I + C(h^{C*}) \right) = \left(r + (n-1) h^{C*} \theta \lambda \right) C'(h^{C*}). \tag{10.7}$$

As usual, the expected benefits $\theta \lambda (\pi^I + C(h^{C*}))/\phi$ and the costs $C'(h^{C*})$ of the last invested unit of research effort balance at the equilibrium. Clearly, if the NOS takes its maximum ($\theta = 0$) or the innovation efficiency is low ($\lambda = 0$), the optimal research effort is zero. In the former case, firms are discouraged because it is nearly impossible to make a discovery having an improvement size of $u_k = s = \bar{u}$. Firms do not waste resources on trying to get a patentable invention if the likelihood of success is zero. In the latter case, i.e. when $\lambda = 0$, the firms do not invent and putting more effort in research does not change the situation. Then, the best the firms can do is not to invest at all.

Equation (10.7) defines the equilibrium effort for the $(n-1)$ challengers. The next result shows how changes in the environment affect the optimal research effort of the challengers.

Proposition 10.2.   Let $H := (n-1)h^C$ denote the aggregate equilibrium research effort.

1. The optimal research effort h^{C*} declines but the aggregate research effort H^* increases if the number of firms n rises.
2. The optimal research effort is an increasing function of the innovation efficiency λ.
3. The equilibrium research effort is an inversely U-shaped function of the NOS, i.e.

$$\frac{\partial h^{C*}}{\partial s} \gtreqless 0 \quad \Longleftrightarrow \quad s \lesseqgtr \bar{s},$$

with $\bar{s} := nh^{C*}C'(h^{C*}) - C(h^{C*})$.

The first result re-establishes the one developed by Loury (1979) for one patent race: if competition increases the individual research effort declines but the aggregate research effort H^* rises in equilibrium. In the present model, the expected gains from the last unit of research effort is given by $\theta\lambda(\pi^I + C(h^C))/\phi$, where $\theta\lambda/\phi$ measures the additional time spent as an incumbent in future. This additional time as a monopoly that can be achieved by an extra unit of effort is shorter if more firms enter the sequence of patent races. Consequently, the expected gains of the last unit h^{C*} are lower and each firm dedicates fewer resources to innovation projects in order to balance the marginal expected benefits and the marginal costs. However, the reduction of a challengers individual research effort is less than the additional effort of the new participants so that the industry as a whole invests more on research. An immediate consequence is that the expected duration of the races becomes shorter when more firms undertake innovation projects.

The second result states that firms invest more when their efficiency to generate inventions is higher. As explained in Lemma 10.1, an increase in the research efficiency λ has two opposing effects. On the one hand, it increases the probability of winning the next patent race for a given firm. Thus, firms tend to invest more. On the other hand, the competitors become more productive as well. This discourages firms to invest because the chance of winning becomes smaller. However, the direct effect on individual firms dominates as demonstrated in Lemma 10.1 so that firms invest in total more when they become more productive in innovating.

The last result shows the influence of the NOS. For a weak NOS, firms are encouraged to exert higher efforts if the NOS increases. In contrast, if the NOS is already strong, firms are discouraged by an even stricter NOS so that they invest less. In revealing the underlying mechanisms, it is convenient to note that $(\pi^I + C(h^C))/\phi = V^I - V^C$ so that the first-order condition in (10.7) becomes $\theta\lambda(V^I - V^C) = C'(h^C)$. Then, a change in the NOS affects the expected benefits from the last unit of effort according to

$$(V^I - V^C)\frac{\partial\theta}{\partial s} + \theta\lambda\left(\frac{\partial V^I}{\partial s} - \frac{\partial V^C}{\partial s}\right).$$

The first term is the static and the second one the dynamic effect. The static effect captures the change of the expected marginal benefits induced by the altered probability that a given invention is patentable. Clearly, increasing the NOS reduces the likelihood for a given discovery to be patentable so that the static effect is negative. The dynamic effect describes the variations in expected earnings induced by a higher NOS for a constant probability of the discovery being patentable. The dynamic effect is positive since a stronger NOS reduces the pace of patent races implying that the monopoly profit can be earned for longer time spans. Then, the last result of Proposition 10.2 states that the dynamic effect dominates the static one for weak NOS, i.e. a deceleration of the patent races stimulates investments. In contrast, when the NOS is already strong, the static effect dominates the dynamic one revealing that firms are discouraged by the decreased likelihood that a given invention is patentable.

The ex-ante situation

Firms may wish choose a different research effort in the first patent race. Given all participants behave rationally, i.e. they invest $h^* = \{0, h^{C*}\}$ in all succeeding races, the ex-post continuation values V^I and V^C are independent of the first patent race's research effort. Hence, firm i sets a h_i so that the ex-ante expected value of participating in the sequence of patent races V_i^A in (10.5) is maximized.
The following result ensues:

Proposition 10.3. For the first patent race, there exists a unique symmetric Nash equilibrium satisfying $h^{A*} = h^{C*}$.

Consequently, all firms choose the same research effort in the first patent race that they exert in all following races. As a direct consequence, it can be concluded that the industry investment is slightly higher in the first patent race than in the subsequent ones. The reason is that all n firms are challengers in the ex-ante situation and invest h^{C*}, while only $n - 1$ firms are in this position in an ex-post situation. Concerning other parameter variations, the following result can be obtained:

Corollary 10.1. The properties of the optimal research effort in Proposition 10.2 also apply for the equilibrium research effort for the ex-ante situation h^{A*}.

In particular this means that the research effort in the first patent race is a decreasing function of the number of firms n, an increasing function of the innovation productivity and is inverse U-shaped with respect to the NOS.

10.3 The optimal non-obviousness standard

This section draws attention to the principal question of the chapter: What will the optimal NOS be? The policymaker has to distinguish the ex-ante and the ex-post situation as well. Studying the ex-ante situation shows how future product and technology lines are affected by the NOS and parameter changes. In contrast, analysing the ex-post situation informs about the influence of parameter changes on existing industries.

It is assumed that the country's decision maker chooses the NOS so that the welfare is maximized. In general, the policymaker may differently decide when an industry is in an ex-ante or in an ex-post situation. Consequently, both situations are separately considered.

10.3.1 The ex-post version

The country's instantaneous welfare comprises the consumers' and the firms' surplus. The consumers' surplus is, however, zero since consumers are identical and the monopoly appropriates all rents.

In the ex-post situation, a firm is either the incumbent receiving π^I or a challenger earning π^C. The society's expected instantaneous welfare w is determined by $w := \pi^I + (n-1)\pi^C$. Different from individual firms, the society's expected welfare is independent of the identity of the incumbent. Hence, society faces a steady stream of instantaneous welfare w. As a consequence, the expected present value of welfare reads

$$W := \int_0^\infty e^{-rt}\, w\ \mathrm{d}t = \frac{1}{r}\Big[\pi^I - (n-1)C(h^{C^*})\Big], \tag{10.8}$$

where h^{C^*} has the properties stated in Proposition 10.2.

In an ex-post situation, the policymaker maximizes the social welfare in (10.8) by choosing a NOS $s \in [0, \bar{u}]$.

Proposition 10.4. When the first patent race has already been concluded, the decision-maker chooses a NOS $s^* = \tilde{s}$, where $\tilde{s} := \big\{ s \in [0, \bar{u}] : \theta\lambda\big(\pi^I + C(h^{C^*}(\cdot))\big) - \phi C'(h^{C^*}(\cdot)) = 0, h^{C^*}(s) = 0 \big\}$.

The validity of the result can easily be demonstrated graphically (cf Figure 10.4). According to (10.2), an incumbents' expected profit simplifies to $\pi^I = \int_s^{\bar{u}} uf[u]\ \mathrm{d}u/\theta$ since they do not actively participate in the current patent race. The expected profit π^I is an increasing function of the NOS s and attains its maximum at $s = \bar{u}$.[13]

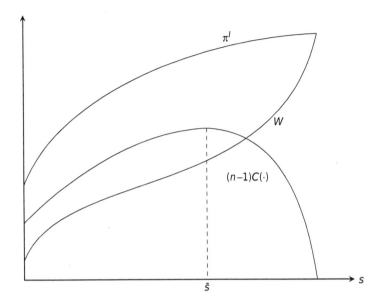

Figure 10.4 The ex-post welfare function.

The second component of the welfare function consists of the research expenses of the $n-1$ challengers. The innovation costs are positively correlated with the research effort, i.e. $C' > 0$. However, the research effort itself is an inversely U-shaped function of the NOS due to Proposition 10.2. In addition, there exists an NOS $\tilde{s} \leq \bar{u}$ so that the optimal research effort becomes zero. To see this, consider the challengers first-order condition in (10.7). Formally, the threshold value $\tilde{s}$ satisfies $\theta \lambda \pi^I - \phi C'(0) = 0$. In case the marginal costs of the first unit of research effort are negligible, i.e. if $C'(0) = 0$, the threshold value $\tilde{s}$ equals the maximal possible improvement size $\bar{u}$. In contrast, if the marginal costs of the first effort unit are strictly positive, $\tilde{s}$ will be strictly lower than the maximal innovation size. As a consequence, the aggregated research expenses $(n-1)C(h^{C^*})$ are inversely U-shaped as well and intersects the abscissa at $\tilde{s} \leq \bar{u}$. Accordingly, the welfare function attains its maximum at $s^* = \tilde{s}$.

Essentially, Proposition 10.4 implies that it is optimal for the policymaker to set the NOS such that the challengers have no incentive to engage in research in the ex-post situation. The result seems counter-intuitive and need to be interpreted with great care.

The model economy describes an industry where the incumbent is able to appropriate the entire consumers' surplus. After the first patent race has been concluded, one firm is always the incumbent earning the monopoly profit. However, the challengers are exerting effort to gain this position in future. From a social point of view, it is irrelevant which particular firm is the incumbent. In this sense, any research effort is socially wasteful so that a NOS of $\tilde{s}$ is socially optimal. Then, the incumbent keeps his position forever and research costs are at a minimum.

The practical significance of the result is limited by the assumptions. Most importantly, consumers do not draw any benefit from the improvement of existing products in the model economy. Clearly, this is a simplifying assumption which, however, drives the result. It can be expected that the result changes if consumers value increases in the quality of products and if the incumbent is not able to extract the entire consumers' surplus.

The next result describes how the optimal NOS varies with the innovation productivity in an ex-post situation:

Corollary 10.2.   The optimal NOS $\tilde{s}$ is an increasing function of the research efficiency λ.

Consequently, the more productive firms are in generating inventions, the higher is the optimal NOS. This result follows since a higher innovation efficiency encourages firms to exert more effort. This increases the industry research costs and accelerates the patent races. Then, firms only abandon research when the threshold level is higher. Consequently, the decision-maker would typically want to impose a higher NOS on industries having a higher innovation efficiency.

10.3.2 The ex-ante version

In an ex-ante situation, the first patent race has not been concluded yet. Hence, a new product or technology line is created in future. Owing to the fact that neither firm occupies incumbency yet, the industry accumulates only costs until the first patent race has been decided.

Dissimilar to an ex-post situation, the policymaker faces a trade-off in maximizing the discounted expected industry profit. On the one hand, setting the NOS equal to the threshold value $\tilde{s}$ minimizes the research expenses in the second and all subsequent patent races. Clearly, this policy maximizes the industry profit in an ex-post situation. On the other hand, choosing a weak NOS, i.e. $s \leq \tilde{s}$, accelerates patent races, especially the first one. Following this policy minimizes the research costs during the first patent race. However, it also implies that the expected stream of industry profits is lower.

This dilemma immediately leads to two related issues. Firstly, in an ex-ante situation, a policymaker's choice is subject to time inconsistency. Whenever the government announces one NOS to be imposed on a certain industry henceforth, it has incentives to revise its decision after the first patent race is over. Consequently, a single NOS that will be applied for the future is not credible unless the government commits itself to it, as e.g. by passing a law.[14] Secondly, the optimal set of NOSs is $s^{A*} = \{0, \tilde{s}\}$, i.e. the decision-maker chooses an NOS of zero for the first patent race and $\tilde{s}$ for all subsequent patent races.

For the remainder of this section, however, it is assumed that the policymaker has to commit to one single NOS that is imposed on the industry henceforth.

Under these circumstances, neither an NOS of zero nor $\tilde{s}$ will be optimal. In the former case, the expected time until the first discovery is made is minimized. However, this comes at the expense of effective patent terms that are too short. In addition, the total research costs in future are suboptimally high.

With a credible commitment, the decision-maker chooses an NOS such that the ex-ante welfare function is maximized. The latter is the discounted expected profit stream for the entire industry. Consequently, the ex-ante welfare function is defined as

$$W^A := nV^A = n\frac{h\theta\lambda V^I + a\theta\lambda V^C - C(h)}{r + (a+h)\theta\lambda} \tag{10.9}$$

Using the equilibrium versions of the continuation values in (10.4), and maximizing the ex-ante welfare function, the following result immediately ensues:

Proposition 10.5. Given $C''(\bar{h}) \geq C'(\bar{h})/\bar{h}$ for any $\bar{h} \in \mathbb{R}_0$, there exists a unique optimal NOS s^{A^*}, where $s^{A^*} := \{s \in [0, \bar{u}] : nh^{C^*}C'(h^{C^*}) - C(h^{C^*}) - s = 0\}$.

The restriction on the convexity of the investment cost function only ensures the uniqueness of the equilibrium. If the cost function is not sufficiently convex, one additional equilibrium may exist.

Three further points are worth mentioning here. Firstly, the optimal ex-ante NOS is strictly positive and strictly smaller than the threshold value $\tilde{s}$. Hence, the policymaker picks a NOS so that research continues to take place after the first patent race has been concluded. Secondly, the decision-maker chooses the NOS such that $\partial h^{C^*}/\partial s = 0$, i.e. a small increase in the NOS would not raise the individual and industry research effort (cf Proposition 10.2). Thirdly, at the optimal NOS, the average duration of a patent race is not minimal. To see this, note that the average duration of a patent race is $((a+h)\theta\lambda)^{-1}$. If the NOS were chosen so that the average duration of patent races is minimized, it has to satisfy the following condition

$$\frac{h^{C^*}f[s] - h^{C^*\prime}\theta}{(nh^{C^*}\theta\lambda)^2} = 0.$$

The NOS $s_{\min}$ minimizing the duration of patent races lies in the interval where $h^{C^*\prime} > 0$, i.e. where $s_{\min} < s^*$. Consequently, the optimal NOS, although allowing the patent races to have a finite expected duration, avoids the establishment of an over heated innovation climate.

The next result shows how the optimal NOS is affected by the number of firms and the invention efficiency:

Corollary 10.3. The optimal NOS s^* is an increasing function of the number of firms n and the innovation efficiency λ.

Typically, a policymaker would choose a higher ex-ante NOS when there are more firms in the market or when the industry is more productive in generating discoveries. Both results follow the same logic. A higher number of firms and a greater innovative capacity tend to accelerate the patent races. By setting a stronger NOS, firms are discouraged in their pursuit to make discoveries so that the patent races slow down. This especially protects inventions having a greater improvement and, thus, being of greater social value.

10.4 The ease of invention

Typically, one would expect small inventions to arise more frequently than larger ones. Thus, the cumulative distribution function $F[u]$ governing the size of inventions will be skewed.[15] One might expect that the properties of the cumulative distribution function's skewness is sector-specific. There may be industries where larger inventions on average occur more often than in other industries. The question addressed in this section is, therefore, whether differences in the likelihood to generate large inventions justifies sector-specific NOSs.

The analysis proceeds in two steps: Firstly, how different degrees of skewness affects the firms' decision concerning their optimal research effort is examined. Everything else being constant, i.e. in particular the same research cost function $C(\cdot)$ as well as an identical Poisson parameter λ and the degree of competition measured by the number of firms n in all industries, the analysis will reveal to which extent differences in the firms' and industries' research expenses are explained by differences in the ease of invention. Subsequently, the policymakers' choice of the optimal NOS is studied. The results will disclose whether a one-size-fits-all policy may be rejected when differences in the ease to invest persist between industries.

To simplify the analysis, it is assumed that differences in the skewness of the cumulative distribution function between industries can be captured by a single parameter α, $\alpha \in \mathbb{R}_0$. Then, $\alpha_i > \alpha_j$ means that a given invention is on average larger in industry j than another one in industry i.

The principal results are obtained without resorting to a specific class of cumulative distribution functions. However, the relevance of some conditions are more easily demonstrated by a specific function. Hence, one of the following assumptions are imposed:

Assumption 10.1.   The cumulative distribution function $F[\alpha, u]$

1. has the following properties: $F_\alpha := \partial F[\alpha, u]/\partial \alpha > 0$;
2. is given by

$$F[\alpha, u] := 1 - \left(\frac{\bar{u} - u}{\bar{u}}\right)^{1+\alpha}.$$

The firms' decision

Above, Proposition 10.1 and Proposition 10.3 prove the existence of an equilibrium in the firms' research effort under fairly general conditions. In particular, the equilibria exist without posing any regularity conditions on the cumulative distribution function. It immediately follows that an asymmetric and a symmetric equilibrium in the the firms' research effort exists in an ex-post and an ex-ante situation respectively for all $\alpha \in \mathbb{R}_0$, i.e. for an arbitrary skewness of the cumulative distribution function $F[\alpha, u]$.

Concerning the skewness parameter's effect on the optimal choice of the firm's effort, the following result arises:

Lemma 10.2. Under Assumption 10.1 (1), a sufficient condition for the challengers' optimal research effort being a decreasing function of the skewness parameter α is that $\partial \pi^I / \partial \alpha < 0$.

The lemma states that, if the invention size of a given industry becomes on average smaller (α increases), each challenger conducts less research under certain circumstances. Again, the skewness parameter α has an immediate (static) and a dynamic effect. The former exerts its influence through the probability of a given invention being patentable. Since larger values of the skewness parameter indicate that small inventions become more likely, the static effect is always negative for a given NOS.

The dynamic effect works through the present and future profits obtained when the firm occupies the incumbency position. Owing to the assumptions on the consumers' preferences and the market structure, the incumbent charges a price identical to the inventive step. Accordingly, a change in the skewness of the underlying cumulative distribution function affects the price and, hence, the profits that can be accrued. Intuition suggests that the dynamic effect has to be negative as well since smaller inventions resulting in lower profits arise on average more often. However, this judgement is at least a little rash. Figure 10.5 shows two cumulative distribution functions with $\alpha_1 > \alpha_2$.

It can easily be seen that $f[\alpha_1, u'] < f[\alpha_2, u']$, yet $f[\alpha_1, u''p] > f[\alpha_2, u''p]$. Thus, small inventions are more likely and large ones less probable under $F[\alpha_1, u]$ than under $F[\alpha_2, u]$. As the density function $f[\alpha, u]$ is an essential part of the incumbent's expected profit, it is by no means clear that the dynamic effect is indeed negative.

The sufficient condition in Lemma 10.2 simply requires the dynamic effect to be negative. With the static and the dynamic effect being negative, the above discussion shows that individual firms are inclined to spend less on research.[16]

Since the total number of firms is exogenous, it immediately follows that the amount of industry research declines as well when the distribution of the invention size becomes more skewed. Assuming that there exist two industries that are identical except for the skewness parameter α, Lemma 10.2 implies that the industry in which the innovation size is on average smaller is characterized by

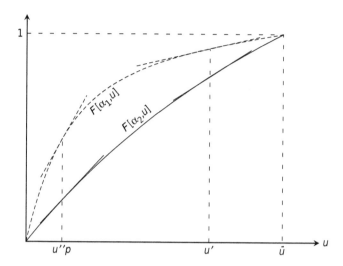

Figure 10.5 A parametrized cumulative distribution function and its properties.

lower individual and total research expenses as long as the dynamic effect is sufficiently small. Thus, in the absence of firm-specific expertise and a correlation between the research effort and the innovation size, firms are discouraged by a high probability of small innovations.

For the specific cumulative distribution function given above, we find the following result:

Lemma 10.3. Under Assumption 10.1 (2), the dynamic effect $\partial \pi^I / \partial \alpha$ is always negative.

Thus, for a particular convincing class of cumulative distribution functions, the dynamic effect is always negative so that the model predicts that firms in industries with a smaller average invention size engage less in research.

The government's decision

The previous discussion has revealed that the optimal NOS for existing product and technology lines is such that no further research activities take place in the ex-post situation.[17] Since this result has been derived without restrictions on the cumulative distribution function, it remains valid for all permissible values of the skewness parameter α. Accordingly, only the policymaker's choice for the ex-ante situation is examined here.

Again, since Proposition 10.5 has proven the existence of an optimal NOS without restrictions on the cumulative distribution function, the existence and uniqueness for an optimal ex-ante NOS is ensured for all $\alpha \in \mathbb{R}_0$ under Assumption 10.1.

Concerning the influence of the skewness parameter on the optimal ex-ante NOS, the following ensues:

Lemma 10.4. Under Assumption 10.1, the optimal NOS s^* is a decreasing function of the skewness parameter α when $\partial h^{C*}/\partial\alpha < 0$.

The lemma immediately leads to the principal result of this section:

Proposition 10.6. The optimal ex-ante NOS s^* is lower in industries, where the invention size is on average smaller as compared to other industries if $\partial\pi^I/\partial\alpha < 0$ under Assumption 10.1 (1) and under Assumption 10.1 (2) respectively.

In light of the previous discussion, the intuition for this result is straightforward. To make the illustration more accessible, assume again that there are two industries with skewness parameters $\alpha_1 > \alpha_2$ so that sector 1 on average achieves smaller inventions. For any given NOS, firms in industry 1 exert less research effort than firms in sector 2 as it is less probable that an invention can be protected by a patent. In an ex-ante situation, the expected development time of the base invention is longer in sector 1 than in sector 2. Consequently, firms of sector 1 not only suffer from lower expected profits, but research expenses have to be paid for a longer time span. Both effects have a negative influence on the welfare generated in this sector. On the other hand, a lower NOS encourages firms to invest more since the probability of obtaining a patent increases and, thus, the expected profit rises. Therefore, a policymaker would choose a lower NOS in industry 1 than in industry 2 to offset the detrimental consequences of a higher skewness on the challengers' optimal research effort.

10.A Proofs to the lemmata and propositions

Lemma 10.1. *Part I*: The derivatives of the value functions in equation (10.4) with respect to profits are given by:

$$\frac{\partial V_i^I}{\partial \pi_i^C} = \frac{a_i^I \theta \lambda}{r\phi_i} > 0, \qquad \frac{\partial V_i^I}{\partial \pi_i^I} = \frac{r + h_i^C \theta \lambda}{r\phi_i} > 0,$$

$$\frac{\partial V_i^C}{\partial \pi_i^C} = \frac{r + a_i^I \theta \lambda}{r\phi_i} > 0, \qquad \frac{\partial V_i^C}{\partial \pi_i^I} = \frac{h_i^C \theta \lambda}{r\phi_i} > 0.$$

Part II: The derivatives of the value function with respect to the research efficiency parameter read:

$$\frac{\partial V_i^I}{\partial \lambda} = -\frac{a_i^I \theta (\pi_i^I - \pi_i^C)}{\phi_i^2} < 0, \qquad \frac{\partial V_i^C}{\partial \lambda} = \frac{h_i^C \theta (\pi_i^I - \pi_i^C)}{\phi_i^2} < 0.$$

The result for $\lambda \to 0$ directly follows from (10.4) and the result for $\lambda \to \infty$ was derived by applying l'Hospitale's rule.

Part III: ΔV_i is determined with $(\pi_i^I - \pi_i^C)/\phi_i$. Then, the derivative is given by

$$\frac{\partial \Delta V_i}{\partial \lambda} = -\frac{\theta(a_i^I + h_i^C)(\pi_i^I - \pi_i^C)}{\phi_i^2} < 0. \qquad \Box$$

Proposition 10.1.   The proof proceeds in three steps. First, the existence of potentially multiple equilibria is established. Second, it is demonstrated that the equilibrium is unique and finally, it is shown that the equilibrium is symmetric.

Part 1: The first-order condition for challenger i reads

$$F_i(h_i^C, a_i^I) := \theta\lambda\big(\pi_i^I + C(h_i^C)\big) - \big(r + (a_i^I + h_i^C)\theta\lambda\big)C'(h_i^C) = 0. \qquad (10.10)$$

Given the cost function $C(\cdot)$ is an increasing function of the research effort h_i^C and the parameters θ and λ are strictly positive, $\mathrm{grad}_{a_i^I} F_i(\cdot)$ is non-singular so that $r_i(a_i^I) := \{h_i^C \in \mathbb{R}_0 : F(h_i^C, a_i^I) = 0\}$ is continuously differentiable in a_i^I by the implicit function theorem.

Following Vives (2000, 42), a solution to (10.10) exists if $R(a_i^I) := \sum_{i=1}^n r_i(a_i^I)$ has a fixed point. Observe that $\mathbb{R}_0$ is a complete lattice and $R(\cdot)$ is quasi-increasing as $r_i(\cdot)$ is continuously differentiable. Then, $R(\cdot)$ has a fixed point by Tarski's fixed point theorem; and a solution to (10.10) exists.

Part 2: By the index theory approach (cf Vives, 2000, 48), the equilibrium is unique if $\det \nabla(-F(\cdot)) > 0$ at $F_i(\cdot) = 0$. The partial derivatives are given by $\partial F_i/\partial h_i^C = -\phi_i C' p(h_i^C)$ and $\partial F_i/\partial h_j^C = -\theta\lambda C'(h_i^C) < 0$. Let $\alpha_i := \phi_i C''(h_i^C) - \theta\lambda C'(h_i^C)$ and $\beta_i := \theta\lambda C'(h_i^C)/\alpha_i$. Then,

$$\det \nabla(-F(\cdot)) = \prod_{i=1}^n \alpha_i \left(1 + \sum_{i=1}^n \beta_i\right).$$

Given the convexity of the cost function, $\alpha_i > 0$ and $\beta_i > 0$ so that $\det \nabla(-F(\cdot)) > 0$ and the equilibrium is unique.

Part 3: Since all challengers are identical, the equilibria are symmetric. $\qquad \Box$

Proposition 10.2.   *Part 1*: The first-order condition for a challenger i reads: $G := \theta\lambda(\pi^I + C(h_i^C)) - (r + (a_i^I + h_i^C)\theta\lambda)C'(h_i^C) = 0$. Since the second-order condition is satisfied at the equilibrium, the sign of the derivative $\partial G/\partial n$ determines the sign of $\partial h_i^{C*}/\partial n$. The latter is determined by

$$\frac{\partial G}{\partial n} = -h_j^{C*}\theta\lambda C(h_i^{C*}) < 0.$$

To evaluate the effect of additional competitors on the industry research effort can also be derived from the first-order condition. Since $H = (n-1)h_i^{C*}$, the first-order condition can also be written as $G := \theta\lambda\big(\pi^I + C(H/(n-1))\big)$

$-(r+H\theta\lambda)C'\big(H/(n-1)\big)=0$. Then, $\partial G/\partial n = H\big((r+H\theta\lambda)C''(\cdot)-\theta\lambda C'(\cdot)\big)$. Since $C''>C'/h$ for convex functions, $\partial G/\partial n > 0$.

Part 2: The reaction function $r_i(a_i^I)$ is positively sloped at the equilibrium, i.e. $\partial r(a^I)/\partial\lambda = r\theta C'/(\phi C'')>0$. Consequently, $R=nr$ is an increasing function of the research efficiency so that the $\partial h^{C^*}/\partial\lambda > 0$.

Part 3: The derivative of the reaction function with respect to the NOS is given by

$$\frac{\partial r_i(a_i^I)}{\partial s} = \frac{\lambda f[s]}{\phi_i C''}\Big[(a_i^I + h_i^C)C' - C - s\Big].$$

The sign of $\partial R/\partial s$ and is identical to the one of the reaction function r. It follows immediately that

$$\frac{\partial h^{C^*}}{\partial s} \gtreqless 0 \quad\Longleftrightarrow\quad s \lesseqgtr \bar{s},$$

with $\bar{s} := nh^{C^*}C'(h^{C^*}) - C(h^{C^*})$. □

Proposition 10.3. To prove the result, it is sufficient to show that h^{C^*} constitutes an equilibrium in the first patent race.

The first-order condition for firm i's problem is given by

$$\theta\lambda\big(G+C(h_i)\big) - \phi_i C'(h_i) = 0,$$

where $\phi_i = r+(a_i+h_i)\theta\lambda$ and $G := rV^I + a_i\theta\lambda(V^I-V^C)$. Replacing the ex-post value functions with the equilibrium versions of (10.4) yields

$$G = \frac{1}{r+nh^{C^*}\theta\lambda}\Big[\big(r+(a_i+h^{C^*})\theta\lambda\big)\pi^I + \big(a_i-(n-1)h^{C^*}\big)\theta\lambda C(h^{C^*})\Big].$$

At the point $a_i = (n-1)h^{C^*}$, the function G simplifies to $G = \pi^I$. Accordingly, the first-order condition for the first patent race reduces to the first-order condition for the second and all subsequent patent races.

Let $r_i^A(a_i)$ denote firm i's best response function for the first patent race and $r_i(a_i^I)$ the one in an ex-post situation. Then it becomes apparent that $r_i^A\big((n-1)h^{C^*}\big) = r_i\big((n-1)h^{C^*}\big)$: when the aggregated research effort of $n-1$ firms is $a_i = (n-1)h^{C^*}$, firm i's best response in the first patent race is to choose $r_i\big((n-1)h^{C^*}\big) = h^{C^*}$.

Since all firms are identical in the first patent race, the best response for $n-1$ firms is given by $R^A(a_i)=(n-1)\big(a_i+r_i^A(a_i)\big)/n$. At $a_i=(n-1)h^{C^*}$, the aggregated best response is $R^A\big((n-1)h^{C^*}\big) = h^{C^*}$. Consequently, the function $R^A(a_i)$ has a fixed point at $a_i = (n-1)h^{C^*}$ and $h^{A^*} = h^{C^*}$ is a Nash equilibrium.

The index theory approach only requires information at the candidate equilibrium to establish uniqueness. Since the first-order condition for the first and all subsequent patent races are identical at $h^{A^*} = h^{C^*}$, their derivatives are identical so that the equilibrium is unique. □

Corollary 10.1.   The result follows directly from Proposition 10.3.   □

Corollary 10.2.   The optimal NOS has to satisfy

$$\theta\lambda\pi^I - rC'(0) = 0$$

since the optimal research effort vanishes at this point. Differentiating this equation with respect to λ yields

$$\frac{\partial\tilde{s}}{\partial\lambda} = \frac{\theta\pi^I}{\lambda f[\tilde{s}]\tilde{s}} > 0.$$ □

Proposition 10.5.   Differentiating the ex-ante welfare function with respect to the NOS s leads to

$$\frac{\partial W^A}{\partial s} = -\frac{nh^{C^*}\lambda f[s]}{r\phi^2 C''(\cdot)}\left(nh^{C^*}C'(\cdot) - C(\cdot) - s\right)\left[(n-1)\theta C'(\cdot) - \phi C''(\cdot)\right],$$

where the first-order condition of the challengers' problem, $\theta\lambda(\pi^I + C(\cdot)) - \phi C'(\cdot) = 0$, and the effect of the NOS on the optimal research effort, i.e. $\partial h^{C^*}/\partial s = f[s]\lambda(nh^{C^*}C'(\cdot) - C(\cdot) - s)/(\phi C''(\cdot))$, has been used. This equation potentially has two zeros: (1) the NOS satisfying $s^* := \{s \in [0, \bar{u}] : nh^{C^*}C'(\cdot) - C(\cdot) - s = 0\}$ and (2) the NOS satisfying $(n-1)\theta\lambda C'(\cdot) - \phi C''(\cdot) = 0$. The second zero only appears if the cost function is convex, i.e. if $C''(\cdot) > 0$. However, if $C''(\bar{h}) > C'(\bar{h})/\bar{h}$ $\forall \bar{h} \in \mathbb{R}_0$, $(n-1)\theta\lambda C'(\cdot) - \phi C''(\cdot)$ is negative for all $h^{C^*} \in \mathbb{R}_0$ so that the second zero does not exist. Hence, under this condition, there exists a unique equilibrium.   □

Corollary 10.3.   Given the first-order condition for the decision-maker's problem, it is easy to see that

$$\frac{\partial s^*}{\partial\lambda} = C''(\cdot)\frac{\partial h^{C^*}}{\partial\lambda},$$

which is positive according to Proposition 10.2.

Similarly, it can be shown that

$$\frac{\partial s^*}{\partial n} = C'(\cdot)\frac{\partial H}{\partial n} - \left(HC''(\cdot) + C'(\cdot)\right)\frac{\partial h^{C^*}}{\partial n}.$$

According to Proposition 10.2 this derivative is positive as well.   □

Lemma 10.2.   According to Proposition 10.3, the optimal research effort in the ex-ante situation is identical to the one in an ex-post situation. Owing to

Proposition 10.1, the challengers' optimal research effort satisfies $\theta\lambda(\pi^I + C(h^{C^*})) = (r + nh^{C^*})C'(h^{C^*})$. Since only the cumulative distribution function depends on the skewness parameter α, the first-order condition can be written as $\theta(\alpha)\lambda(\pi^I(\alpha) + C(h^{C^*})) = (r + (a^I + h^{C^*})\theta(\alpha)\lambda)C'(h^{C^*})$. Then, the derivative $\partial h^{C^*}/\partial\alpha$ is given by

$$\frac{\partial h^{C^*}}{\partial\alpha} = -\frac{\theta_\alpha\lambda(\pi^I + C - nh^{C^*}C') + \theta\lambda\pi^I_\alpha}{-\phi C''},$$

where $\theta_\alpha := \partial\theta(\alpha)/\partial\alpha = -F_\alpha[\cdot] < 0$ and $\pi^I_\alpha := \partial\pi^I_\alpha(\alpha)/\partial\alpha$. From the first-order condition of the challengers' maximization problem follows that $\pi^I + C - nh^{C^*}C' = rC'/(\theta\lambda) > 0$. Accordingly, a sufficient condition for the derivative $\partial h^{C^*}/\partial\alpha$ to be negative is that $\pi^I_\alpha < 0$. □

Lemma 10.3. For the cumulative distribution function given in Assumption 10.1 (2), the incumbent's expected profit is given by

$$\pi^I = \frac{(1+\alpha)s + \bar{u}}{2+\alpha}.$$

Hence, the dynamic effect is determined with

$$\frac{\partial\pi^I}{\partial\alpha} = -\frac{\bar{u} - s}{(2+\alpha)^2},$$

which is unambiguously negative for all $\alpha \in \mathbb{R}_0$ as long as the NOS s is strictly smaller than the maximum invention size $\bar{u}$. □

Lemma 10.4. Let $g := nh^{C^*}C'(h^{C^*}) - C(h^{C^*})$. According to Proposition 10.5, the first-order condition for the optimal ex-ante NOS reads $g(h^{C^*}(\alpha, s^*)) - s^* = 0$. Then,

$$\frac{\partial s^*}{\partial\alpha} = \frac{\partial g}{\partial h^{C^*}}\frac{\partial h^{C^*}}{\partial\alpha}\left(1 - \frac{\partial g}{\partial h^{C^*}}\frac{\partial h^{C^*}}{\partial s^*}\right)^{-1}.$$

Note that $\partial h^{C^*}/\partial s = 0$ iff $g(\cdot) - s = 0$. Further $\partial g/\partial h^{C^*}$ is positive and finite since as the cost function is twice continuously differentiable. Consequently, sign $\partial s^*/\partial\alpha = $ sign $\partial h^{C^*}/\partial\alpha$. □

Proposition 10.6. This result is a direct consequence of Lemmata 10.2 through 10.4. □

Part III

Patent policy in an international framework

11 Introduction

With the exception of a very few authors, the vast majority of models describing the effects of patent policy instruments have been restricted to closed economies.[1] For several reasons, it is natural that patent policy instruments are first studied in a national framework. Firstly, patent law is national in reach, and it has immediate consequences for the domestic market structure and intensity of competition despite the fact that the patentee might be a foreigner. Although one country might exert a certain influence over other countries to change their patent laws, the process is usually slow and painstaking and the outcome is by no means certain.[2]

Secondly, closed economy models are structurally less complex at the outset so that they are ideal to develop an understanding of how policy instruments work. In addition, not every policy instrument has external effects on an international scale. However, cross-country profit flows associated with patents are sizeable. McCalman (2005) estimates that the United States (US) enjoy a net inflow of $US 1,277 million, whereas India suffers a net outflow of about the same size. Although this figure might be insufficient for the US to tailor their patent laws to maximize the net inflows of profits, the same might not be true for developing countries. Thus, studying patent policy instruments in an international framework might lead to new insights.

The third part of this book is dedicated to models that allow for international differences in patent policy. Two examples are presented: the case of patentable subject matters and the one of international differences in the non-obviousness standard.

Chapter 12 Is Concerned with patentable subject matters. This topic gains frequently even public interest, since decisions on whether or not patents are to be issued in newly arisen technology fields have to be made. The latest examples include biotechnology and nanotechnology. Since patent laws are national, it can be expected that not all countries decide simultaneously on the issue. In addition, it is by no means certain that all countries will eventually choose do expand the range of patentable subject matters as the example of the European Union's decision on computer-implemented inventions (cf *infra*) shows. The next chapter studies a very special scenario: one country already offers patents for a certain subject matter, and the domestic country decides on whether or not to expand its range of patentable subject matters. We derive conditions under which the domestic country will prefer to free-ride on the foreign country and when it will provide patent protection for the new technology field. Interestingly, it can be demonstrated that there are certain parameter constellations for which firms of both countries are better off when the domestic country does not extend patent protection.

Chapter 13 is the natural extension to Chapter 10 in which the non-obviousness standard was examined from a purely national point of view. Chapter 13 demonstrates that identical countries will not choose the same non-obviousness standard in an international framework, i.e. countries benefit from diversification. Contrary to what one might have expected, a decentralized solution will result in too little divergence in international non-obviousness standards to be optimal. However, the basic insights from Chapter 10 according to which countries with higher research abilities should set stronger non-obviousness standards are confirmed under certain conditions.

12 New patentable subject matters

Especially when new technology fields are created, the question arises of whether patents should be granted in this field.[1] For an economy in autarchy, the answer is rather simple: when social benefits exceed the social costs including the negative effects of the market power introduced by patents, protection should be offered in the new technology field. More interesting, however, is the problem in an international context where some countries already provide patent protection for inventions in the new field and others have to decide on the issue. A recent example includes the discussion on patents on computer-implemented inventions in the European Union (EU).

In 2003, the first reading of the 'Proposal for a Directive of the European Parliament and of the Council on the patentability of computer-implemented inventions' (European Commission, 2002) took place. Although *pure software* is explicitly excluded as a patentable subject matter according to the Art. 52(1) of the European Patent Agreement, numerous software patents have been issued by the European Patent Office (EPO) and national patent offices.[2] In addition, the praxis of granting patents have been different in the EU countries. While the German Patent Office was more generous in issuing patents for computer-implemented inventions, the patent office of the United Kingdom (UK) handled cases more strictly.

In the US, computer-implemented inventions as well as business methods are patentable. Consequently, European firms can obtain patents in the US which will result in cross-border profit flows into Europe if the European firms prove to be successful in the US market.

Given that the US market is large and already provides patent protection for *new* technology fields, the immediate question for the EU is whether it is really necessary to provide the same protection.[3] After all, firms can collect the profits to recoup their research expenses abroad and the domestic country could enjoy a market with less or no distortions owing to limited monopoly rights. This chapter explores the question in greater detail.

The first section introduces a simple model of two countries. In each country, there is one firm that participates in one global patent race. The second section provides an extension. Here, a sequence of global patent races is considered so that cross-border profit flows can change direction.

12.1 A simple model of new patentable subject matters

12.1.1 Two firms engaged in a single patent race

Consider two countries i, $i = A, B$. Whereas the foreign country A assigns patents to inventors of all nationalities for the subject matter in question, the home country B has to decide on the issue. For the sake of simplicity, it is assumed that there is a national champion j, $j = a, b$, in each country. Firm a (b) is exclusively owned by the citizens of country A (B) so that potential profits remain in the country and become capital income of the inhabitants.[4]

Both firms are direct competitors; they compete in the product market and in developing a new product, as e.g. a certain software package or the next generation of a computer chip. It is assumed that both firms actually develop their product, but only the firm which completed the invention first is granted a patent for T years. Accordingly, the second invention does not satisfy the patent requirements of novelty.[5] Since patents confer to the inventor the exclusive right of producing and marketing the product or process, the winner of the patent race in fact obtains a monopoly position for a limited time period.

Patents are by no means the only way to protect intellectual property. Trade secrecy and lead time are equally important.[6] In some industries, acquiring the knowledge embodied in the product by reverse-engineering is easier than in others. In such cases, the costs for imitating an inventor's product are only a small fraction of the total, initial development costs. In such industries, inventors will more heavily rely on patents to protect their intellectual property (cf *supra*). Here, it is assumed that imitation is possible at no additional costs. Then, the successful firm seeks patent protection in all countries offering it.

Formally, a three stage game is considered:

1. Nature chooses the winner of the patent race.
2. The home country B chooses between protection (p) and non-protection (n).
3. Firms start producing and receiving profits.

Nature's move is considered to be observable so that the winner's identity is common knowledge. The horizon of the last stage is infinite: in the first T years, the winner of the patent race occupies the monopoly position in all countries assigning patent rights for the subject matters in question. Subsequently, both firms compete in the markets.

Instead of specifying the demand and cost schedules, assumptions are directly imposed on the profit functions. As a consequence, the results are not restricted to a specific product market model but apply for a broad variety of demand and cost functions. The disadvantage of this approach is that some of the results could be specified by applying a particular product market model.

Here, it is assumed that firm j earns a flow profit of π_{ji}^m in market i while being a monopolist in this market. When both firms are active, firm j receives a flow profit of π_{ji}^d from market i. Since the duopoly profit cannot exceed the monopoly one, $\pi_{ji}^m \geq \pi_{ji}^d$ has to be satisfied.

Flow profits are assumed to be stationary, i.e. they are independent of time. Yet, the same firm may receive different profit levels from the foreign and the domestic market due to differences in the market size or the demand structure in this country. Allowing for differences in the efficiency, the foreign and the domestic firms' profit from a given market may differ as well. Finally, the flow profits of the patent race's loser have to be specified. As it was assumed that the products infringe on each other, the unsuccessful firm earns a zero flow profit in the country which grants a patent to the winner of the patent race.[7]

By directly imposing assumptions on the profits, it is not necessary to explicitly consider the last stage of the game. Since nature chooses the winner of the race and the home country decides on remaining in the status quo or on changing the patent law, four cases can be distinguished:

1. $\{a, n\}$, where the foreign firm (a) wins and the home country decides for the status quo,
2. $\{a, p\}$, where the foreign firm (a) is successful and the home country changes the patent law;
3. $\{b, n\}$, where the domestic firm (b) is the winner and the home country does not offer patent protection, and
4. $\{b, p\}$, where the domestic firm (b) is successful and both countries protect the subject matters in question.

By comparing these cases, the main results are obtained.

12.1.2 The domestic firm's disadvantage

Here, it is examined whether (i) the firms benefit from a change in the patent law and whether (ii) the domestic firms suffer a competitive disadvantage in the status quo. To address the second question, a distinction criterion is necessary:

Definition 12.1. A domestic firm is considered to have a competitive disadvantage vis à vis a foreign rival in the same position if its discounted present value is lower than the foreign competitor's one under non-protection and equal to the latter under protection.

First consider case $\{a, n\}$ for obtaining the present values V_i. Here, the foreign firm is the winner of the patent race, but it can only apply for a patent in the foreign country A. In the domestic market, firm a competes with the domestic competitor who can offer his own product owing to the absence of patent protection. During the patent life T, the foreign firm (a) earns total flow profits of $\pi_{aA}^m + \pi_{aB}^d$. Since the domestic firm cannot sell its product abroad, its only source of profits is the domestic market: π_{bB}^d. After the patent expires, both firms obtain profits of $\pi_{jA}^d + \pi_{jB}^d$. Let γ again be defined as $\gamma := 1 - e^{-rT}$ with r denoting the common discount rate. Then, the present value for the foreign firm is determined with:

$$
\begin{aligned}
V_a^{an} &= \int_0^T e^{-rt} \pi_{aA}^m \, dt + \int_T^\infty e^{-rt} \pi_{aA}^d \, dt + \int_0^\infty e^{-rt} \pi_{aB}^d \, dt, \\
&= \frac{1}{r} \left[\gamma \pi_{aA}^m + (1 - \gamma) \pi_{aA}^d + \pi_{aB}^d \right],
\end{aligned}
\tag{12.1}
$$

where the superscript *an* indicates the case $\{a, n\}$. Likewise, the present value for the domestic firm is derived by:

$$
V_b^{an} = \frac{1}{r} \left[(1 - \gamma) \pi_{bA}^d + \pi_{bB}^d \right].
\tag{12.2}
$$

Now consider case (2). Again, the foreign firm wins the patent race and is granted the monopoly position in the foreign country A. In addition, however, it also receives a patent in the domestic country B for T years so that the unsuccessful domestic firm (b) cannot offer its product in either market while the patent is active. During the first T years the foreign and domestic firms earn flow profits of $\pi_{aA}^m + \pi_{aB}^m$ and zero respectively. After the patent expired, both firms again realize $\pi_{jA}^d + \pi_{jB}^d$. In this situation, the firms' present values are given by

$$
\begin{aligned}
V_a^{ap} &= \frac{1}{r} \left[\gamma (\pi_{aA}^m + \pi_{aB}^m) + (1 - \gamma)(\pi_{aA}^d + \pi_{aB}^d) \right], \\
V_b^{ap} &= \frac{1 - \gamma}{r} \left[\pi_{bA}^d + \pi_{bB}^d \right].
\end{aligned}
\tag{12.3}
$$

Case (3) depicts the mirror image to case (1). The domestic country keeps the status quo, but the domestic firm (b) wins the patent race. It obtains the monopoly position in the foreign country (A) and faces competition by the foreign firm (a) in the domestic market. Consequently, the domestic firm b earns total flow profits of $\pi_{bA}^m + \pi_{bB}^d$ during the patent term and $\pi_{bA}^d + \pi_{bB}^d$ afterwards. In contrast, the foreign firm cannot compete in its domestic market A and can only offer his product in country B. The foreign firm's profit stream consists of π_{aB}^d during the patent life and $\pi_{aA}^d + \pi_{aB}^d$ afterwards. The firms' present values are given by

$$
\begin{aligned}
V_a^{bn} &= \frac{1}{r} \left[(1 - \gamma) \pi_{aA}^d + \pi_{aB}^d \right], \\
V_b^{bn} &= \frac{1}{r} \left[\gamma \pi_{bA}^m + (1 - \gamma) \pi_{bA}^d + \pi_{bB}^d \right].
\end{aligned}
\tag{12.4}
$$

Finally, case (4) is the counterpart to case (2): both countries protect the subject matter in question, but the domestic firm b is successful in innovating first.

Consequently, it becomes the sole producer of the invention in both markets for the first T years and earns $\pi_{bA}^m + \pi_{bB}^m$ and $\pi_{bA}^d + \pi_{bB}^d$ afterwards. The foreign firm having to stay inactive during the first T years receives $\pi_{aA}^d + \pi_{aB}^d$ after the patent expired. The present values read:

$$V_a^{bp} = \frac{1-\gamma}{r}\left[\pi_{aA}^d + \pi_{aB}^d\right],$$

$$V_b^{bp} = \frac{1}{r}\left[\gamma(\pi_{bA}^m + \pi_{bB}^m) + (1-\gamma)(\pi_{bA}^d + \pi_{bB}^d)\right].$$

(12.5)

Whether firms benefit from the expansion of patentable subject matters in the home country can be determined by comparing the cases $\{a,p\}$ and $\{a,n\}$ on the one hand and the cases $\{b,p\}$ and $\{b,n\}$ on the other hand. A firm is better off under patent protection if the difference $\Delta V_i^j := V_i^{jp} - V_i^{jn}, j = a, b$, is positive. Assuming that the foreign firm succeeds in winning the patent race, the appropriate differences ensue with

$$\Delta V_a^a = \frac{\gamma}{r}\left[\pi_{aB}^m - \pi_{aB}^d\right] > 0, \quad \Delta V_b^a = -\frac{\gamma}{r}\pi_{bB}^d < 0. \tag{12.6}$$

Since $\pi_{ji}^m >= .\pi_{ji}^d$, the successful foreign firm a always profits from the change in the domestic patent law. In contrast, the unsuccessful domestic firm's profits are lower when patent protection is introduced.

In the status quo, the winner and the loser of the patent race compete in the domestic market B. Hence, the unsuccessful firm can earn positive profits. In contrast, if the home country decides to protect the subject matters in question, the unsuccessful firm can only offer its product after the patent expired. Not providing intellectual property rights for certain subject matters therefore turns the home country B into a refuge for the unsuccessful domestic firm in which it can do business. By extending the patentable subject matters in the home country this refuge is destroyed. The unsuccessful domestic firm loses the opportunity to earn positive profits during the patent life; the domestic competitor is therefore worse off. Clearly, the successful foreign firm has the advantage of receiving the monopoly profit in country B which is higher than the duopoly one.

Now consider the case where the domestic firm wins and the foreign firm loses the patent race. The appropriate differences are determined with

$$\Delta V_a^b = -\frac{\gamma}{r}\pi_{aB}^d < 0, \quad \Delta V_b^b = \frac{\gamma}{r}\left[\pi_{bB}^m - \pi_{bB}^d\right] > 0. \tag{12.7}$$

Compared to (12.6), the firms change positions. The domestic firm wins and the foreign firm loses the patent race. In this situation, the home country provides a shelter for the unsuccessful foreign competitor in the status quo. Therefore, by changing the patent law, the destruction of the refuge makes the foreign firm worse off, and the advantage is on the domestic firm's side. The immediate conclusion is:

Proposition 12.1.   Extending the patentable subject matters on inventions for which protection can be obtained in the foreign country benefits the winner and hurts the loser of the patent race in an ex-post situation.

From (12.6) and (12.7) further conclusions can be drawn. First observe that the desirability of patent protection solely depends on the earning possibilities in the home country B, it does not depend on the profits earned in the foreign market. Scotchmer (2001) finds that smaller countries have a higher incentive to join an international treaty if the partner nation has a large market. This seems to contradict the result just derived.

However, Scotchmer studies a somewhat different setting. International treaties considered by her involve reciprocity, i.e. the foreign country A grants intellectual property rights only to individuals or firms from signatory states, i.e. National Treatment is conditional on reciprocity. The present model reflects the actual situation in which the US provide National Treatment for foreign inventors of all nationalities. Yet, in this situation, the change in the firms' earning possibilities in the US are independent of the home country's decision on the extension of patent protection. Consequently, a firm's incentive to support the domestic change of the patent law does not depend on the foreign country's market size.

Second, a longer patent life increases the advantage for the winner and the disadvantage for the loser of the patent race. This can directly be seen in (12.6) and (12.7) by noting that $(1 - \gamma)$ is a decreasing function of the patent term.

Finally, the winners' advantage and the loser's disadvantage depend on the competitive pressure in the domestic market in the status quo. A proxy for the density of competition is the difference between the monopoly profit and the duopoly profit.[8] Given the monopoly profit, the competitive pressure is solely reflected in the duopoly profit so that a lower duopoly profit is associated with a higher competitive pressure in the domestic market. From (12.6) and (12.7), it can be verified directly that the successful firm's gain from the introduction of patent protection for the subject matter in question increases with the competitive pressure in market B. In contrast, the unsuccessful firm's disadvantage from the change in patent law is the smaller the higher the competitive pressure in the home country is.

For the unsuccessful firm, the disadvantage of protecting the subject matters in question consists in depriving it of earning possibilities. Thus, the disadvantage is smaller under fierce competition since the latter is associated with lower earnings; not being able to earn small profits is better than not being able to realize large ones.

The winner's benefit from protecting the subject matter stems from the monopoly position gained in the domestic market. Since the duopoly profit obtained in an unprotected market is low when the competitive pressure is high, the inventor's gain, when being able to attain the monopoly profit due to a change in the domestic patent law, increases with the competitive pressure.

Proposition 12.1 suggests that the domestic firm suffers from a competitive disadvantage in the status quo if it is unsuccessful in the patent race. However, this conclusion is not valid because the firms compared find themselves in different positions. To address this question properly, firms' profits have to be compared when they are in the same position, i.e. when being the loser or the winner of the patent race.

According to the often mentioned hypothesis, the competitive disadvantage vanishes by introducing protection for subject matters that are patentable abroad. Consequently, the foreign and the domestic firm should receive the same profits under patent protection. Formally, $V_a^{ap} = V_b^{bp}$ and $V_a^{bp} = V_b^{ap}$ have to be satisfied. From (12.3) and (12.5) it can be seen that those conditions only hold true if $\pi_{ai}^d = \pi_{bi}^d$ and $\pi_{ai}^m = \pi_{bi}^m$, $i = A, B$, i.e. if firms are equally productive when creating an invention of similar size. Put differently, differences in the efficiency entirely explain the discrepancies in profits when both countries protect inventions in a certain technology line.

Owing to Definition 12.1, the domestic firm has a competitive disadvantage under non-protection if $V_a^{an} > V_b^{bn}$ and $V_a^{bn} > V_b^{an}$. From equations (12.1), (12.2) and (12.4) follows that

$$V_a^{an} - V_b^{bn} = \frac{1}{r}\left[\gamma\left(\pi_{aA}^m - \pi_{bA}^m\right) + (1 - \gamma)\left(\pi_{aA}^d - \pi_{bA}^d\right) + \left(\pi_{aB}^d - \pi_{bB}^d\right)\right]$$

$$V_a^{bn} - V_b^{an} = \frac{1}{r}\left[(1 - \gamma)\left(\pi_{aA}^d - \pi_{bA}^d\right) + \left(\pi_{aB}^d - \pi_{bB}^d\right)\right]$$

The first equation applies to the situation in which the domestic firm wins the patent race. As it can be seen, the foreign firm has a larger present value than the domestic competitor if $\pi_{ai}^m > \pi_{bi}^m$ and $\pi_{ai}^d > \pi_{bi}^d$, i.e. if the foreign rival produces his good that is based on a similar innovation more efficiently. Yet, the discrepancy in the profit streams is not caused by the non-existence of patent protection for the subject matters in question. The reason can exclusively be traced to differences in productivity. The same holds true for the second equation that compares the foreign and the domestic firm when losing the patent race. Hence, the present model does not support the hypothesis that the domestic firm experiences a competitive disadvantage in the status quo.

12.1.3 The home country's decision

Policymakers will change the patent law to include additional technology fields for patent protection if doing so increases welfare. In principle, an ex-post and an ex-ante situation could be distinguished. However, basing patent laws or the decision of patent authorities on ex-post considerations leads to an erratic policy (cf Chapter 10). Moreover, the principle of National Treatment of foreign applicants would not longer be satisfied. Consequently, we assume that the domestic policymaker chooses to extend the patentable subject matter if this leads to a higher ex-ante welfare, i.e. the government behaves as if the winner of the patent race is unknown. To determine the domestic country's welfare, an assumption concerning the consumers' surplus is necessary.

Let $S(2)$ and $S(1)$ denote the instantaneous consumers' surplus when there is a duopoly and a monopoly in the market. Since competition usually leads to lower prices, it is reasonable to assume $\Delta S := S(2) - S(1) \geq 0$. Then $-\Delta S$ measures the loss in the consumers' surplus when the domestic market becomes monopolized.

The probability that the domestic firm b wins the patent race is denoted by $\mathfrak{p}$ and $1 - \mathfrak{p}$ is the probability that the foreign firm a wins. Let $z_j, j = a, b$, stand for the relative duopoly profit in the domestic market B, i.e. $z_j := \pi_{jB}^d / \pi_{jB}^m, z_j \in [0, 1]$.

In the ex-ante situation, a firm's support for the change in patent law depends on the expected present values of future profits. Given country B does not protect the subject matters in question, the firms' expected present values are given by $EV_j^n = (1 - \mathfrak{p})V_j^{an} + \mathfrak{p}V_j^{bn}, j = a, b$. In case the home country changes the patent law, the corresponding expected present values read $EV_j^p = (1 - \mathfrak{p})V_j^{ap} + \mathfrak{p}V_j^{bp}$. Then, the benefits from the protection of additional subject matters for firms can be measured by

$$EV_a^p - EV_a^n = \frac{\gamma(T)}{r}\pi_{aB}^m\left[(1 - \mathfrak{p}) - z_a\right],$$

$$EV_b^p - EV_b^n = \frac{\gamma(T)}{r}\pi_{bB}^m(\mathfrak{p} - z_b).$$

(12.8)

Proposition 12.2. Let $\mathfrak{p}_a(z_a)$ and $\mathfrak{p}_b(z_b)$ be defined as $\mathfrak{p}_a(z_a) := 1 - z_a$ and $\mathfrak{p}_b(z_b) := z_b$. Given a subject matter is patentable in the foreign country, lifting the exclusion of the subject matter in the domestic country is beneficial for both firms if $\mathfrak{p} \in [\mathfrak{p}_b, \mathfrak{p}_a]$ (area I) and detrimental for both firms if $\mathfrak{p} \in [\mathfrak{p}_a, \mathfrak{p}_b]$ (area II).

The functions $\mathfrak{p}_j, j = a, b$, are the probabilities for which firm j is indifferent between the existence and the non-existence of patent protection for the subject matter in the domestic country. Firm j will support a change of patent law if $EV_j^p - EV_j^n$ is positive. From (12.8), it can be concluded that foreign firm a favours patent protection if $\mathfrak{p} \leq \mathfrak{p}_a(z_a)$, i.e. if the probability that the domestic firm wins the patent race is sufficiently low. In contrast, the domestic firm b supports the protection of additional subject matters if $\mathfrak{p} \geq \mathfrak{p}_b(z_b)$, i.e. if the probability is sufficiently large. The proposition follows immediately.

The situation is illustrated in Figure 12.1. The slopes of the functions $\mathfrak{p}_j(z_j)$ can be explained as follows. If the domestic market stays unprotected, the unsuccessful firm is guaranteed the positive duopoly profit during the patent life and afterwards in country B. In contrast, if the home country changes the patent law, the unsuccessful firm stays inactive during the patent life and earns zero profits. When the duopoly profit is relatively large, firms are reluctant to trade the certain but smaller profit against the uncertain monopoly profit. Given the relative duopoly profit z_j is high, a firm is only willing to support the protection of additional subject matters if the probability of winning the patent race is sufficiently high. Since $\mathfrak{p}_j$ is

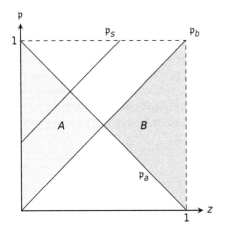

Figure 12.1 The effects of domestic protection for additional subject matters on firms.

the probability of the domestic firm to win for which firm j is indifferent between the existence and non-existence of patent protection for certain subject matters, $\mathfrak{p}_b$ is negatively sloped and $\mathfrak{p}_a$ is positively sloped in Figure 12.1.

Since the foreign firm supports the change in the domestic patent law when $\mathfrak{p} \leq \mathfrak{p}_a(z_a)$ and the domestic firm prefers the protection of additional subject matters when $\mathfrak{p} \geq \mathfrak{p}_b(z_b)$, the area A in Figure 12.1 marks $\{z, \mathfrak{p}\}$ combinations for which both firms are better off under the existence of protection, whereas the $\{z, \mathfrak{p}\}$ combinations forming region B indicate situations where both firms are worse off when patents are offered in the home country. Note that z is inversely related to the competitive pressure in the domestic market. Then, Figure 12.1 shows that the foreign and domestic firms benefit from extending the range of patentable subject matters if the competitive pressure is high, and they are reluctant to support the change of the patent law if the competition pressure is low.

When the identity of the patent race's winner is unknown to the domestic policymaker, the latter will aim at maximizing the expected social welfare stream. In case the domestic government does not offer additional protection, the expected future welfare flow is given by $EW_B^n = EV_b^n + S(2)$. If the decision-makers pass a new patent law, the expected welfare will be $EW_B^p = EV_b^p + S(1)$. Using the definitions of the appropriate expected value functions, the effect of protecting additional subject matters is determined with

$$EW_B^p - EW_B^n = \frac{\gamma(T)}{r}\left[(\mathfrak{p} - z_b)\pi_{bB}^m - \Delta S\right].\tag{12.9}$$

An immediate consequence is:

Proposition 12.3. Let $\mathfrak{p}_s$ be defined as $\mathfrak{p}_s(z_b) := \mathfrak{p}_b + \Delta S(z_b)/\pi_{bB}^m$. If patent protection for the subject matter in question is available in the foreign country, extending the patentable subject matter is beneficial for the home country if $p \geq p_s$.

p_s is the probability that the domestic firm wins the patent race for which the domestic policymaker is indifferent between not protecting and protecting additional subject matters. From the definition of p_s follows $p_s > p_b$. Consequently, the domestic firm would support the protection of additional subject matters for probabilities p for which the government is not willing to change the law. In fact, if $\Delta S(z_b)/\pi_{bB}^m$ exceeds one, the home country will never benefit by extending patent protection.

12.1.4 Shortcomings

The model presented in this section neglects some aspects. Firstly, it was assumed that there is only one firm in each country. Although there are industries where only a few internationally operating firms exist, as e.g. the aeroplane industry, we observe oligopolistic markets on the national level more frequently. When there is more than one firm operating in markets, it is reasonable to assume that the probability of winning a patent race decreases for an individual firm.

Secondly, it has been postulated that only one patent race takes place. Again, this might be plausible for specific industries but certainly not for industries related to computers.[9] The hardware and software industry is characterized by a sequence of patent races and more often than not, inventions are cumulative. When patent races are sequential, the statuary life of a patent may become irrelevant as the latest innovation may render the older ones obsolete before patents expire. One of the prominent examples is the computer-chip industry. Here, every twelve to eighteen months a new computer chip becomes available which almost immediately drives the demand for the older ones to zero. When the innovation process is stochastic, the economic life of a patent, i.e. the time during which positive profits can be obtained, is stochastic as well (cf *supra*).

The next section extends the model so that the question of whether or not a society should protect additional subject matters given protection is offered abroad can be answered in a broader context.

12.2 New patentable subject matters and endogenous research effort

In this section, the advantages and disadvantages of protecting additional subject matters is studied in a framework of sequential patent races and oligopolistic structures on the national product market. The model to be developed here, is based on the variant introduced in Chapter 10. It is also an extension of the previous version since two countries have to be considered. Consequently, some changes in the assumptions are necessary.

12.2.1 Basic assumptions

The international structure

Again, two countries, $i = A, B$, are considered. The foreign country A already offers patents for the subject matter in question, whereas the home country B has to decide on the issue. Different from the model in the previous section, there is a number of firms in each country capable of undertaking research, i.e. there are n_i, $n_i \geq 1$, firms in market i. As before, country i firms are exclusively owned by residents of country i so that total profits earned by i-firms increases welfare in country i independent of the market from which they stem.

Domestic as well as foreign firms participate in an infinite sequence of global patent races. Both countries may differ with respect to the market size measured by the number of firms or, alternatively, by the profit earned when the market is monopolized. Furthermore, although all firms within a country have the same research abilities, the latter may differ across firms of different countries.

Sequential patent races on a global scale

Essentially, we use the same approach to model an infinite sequence of patent races as laid out in Chapter 10. In particular, this means that an ex-ante and an ex-post situation has to be distinguished. Different from the version in Chapter 10, the patent races are global in nature, so that the n_A foreign and n_B domestic firms participate in the patent races.

When focussing on industrialized countries, it seems appropriate to postulate that all firms have access to the same innovation technology so that the innovation efficiency parameter λ is identical for domestic and foreign firms. However, when including developing countries into consideration, this supposition cannot be upheld. Thus, it is assumed that the research efficiency is country specific, i.e. country i firms innovate at a rate of λ_i, $i = A, B$. This extension does not alter the general description of a patent race. Accordingly, the infinite sequence of patent races still forms a piecewise-deterministic process (PDP) defined by the pair $\{\tau_k, z_k\}$.

Inventions and intellectual property rights

As described in Chapter 10, every patent race ends with a discovery. Similar to the model above, it is also assumed that new inventions do not infringe on their predecessors, i.e. to produce the latest product or to employ the latest technology, it is not necessary to obtain licences on older products or technologies. In addition, previous products or technologies can be freely used by every firm once a new product or technology has been discovered.

In the two-country version of the model, additional factors have to be considered. Firstly, to keep the analysis as simple as possible, the NOS s is regarded to be zero, i.e. every invention qualifies for a patent.[10] Next a situation is examined in which the foreign country A offers patent protection for the subject matter in question and the home country B assesses whether or not to extend protection for this branch of technology. In general, the foreign country – and the home country after amending the law – may restrict patent protection to citizens or firms residing in the country.[11] However, for signatory states of the Agreement of Trade Related Aspects of Intellectual Property (TRIPs Agreement), this is no longer an option. Rather, each member is required to treat national and foreign inventors alike (*National Treatment*). Accordingly, all firms irrespective of their domicile are eligible for patent protection in all countries offering the protection for the subject matter in question. Hence, even if the home country does not extend the patentable subject matters, domestic firms are free to seek protection in the foreign country. Since a patent application does not entail any costs in the present model, a firm will always file for a patent in every country protecting the subject matter in question.

Firms and the product market

Similar to the model discussed in Chapter 10, firms have to exert some research effort h, $h \in \mathbb{R}_0$, in order to actively participate in the patent races. Concerning the research technology, one of the following assumptions is maintained:

Assumption 12.1. The research cost function is

1. either convex, i.e. $C'(h) > 0$, $C''(h) > 0$, $C(0) = 0$;
2. or linear, i.e. $C(h) = Ch$.

In particular, it is assumed that domestic and foreign firms share the same research cost function and the same production technology. This assumption seems rather strong when the question of extending patentable subject matters is not restricted to industrialized countries but rather includes developing countries as well. Firms in less developed countries will frequently face a very different innovation cost function. However, the research technology consists of two components here: the input and the output. Since the developing countries are postulated to have a lower innovation efficiency λ_i, imposing identical cost functions does not restrict generality.

The winner of the kth patent race is granted a monopoly position in all countries offering this protection for the technology line under scrutiny. During the following patent race the successful firm receives a monopoly profit π_i^m, $i = A, B$, until the race ends whereupon its product or technology becomes commonly available. Differences in the monopoly profit across countries may reflect different price elasticities, but also differences in the market size.

Since reverse-engineering is possible at no additional costs, all firms can offer the latest innovation at the domestic market in case the home country does not protect the subject matter in question. Then, the incumbent as well as the challengers of both countries earn profits of π_B^C. Evidently, $\pi_i^m \geq \pi_B^C$ must hold true. Otherwise no firm would find it worthwhile to engage in a patent race.

Here, the competition profit π_B^C is independent of the number of competitors in the domestic market so that it freely varies in the interval $[0, \pi_B^m]$. This is due to the fact that a particular product market model is not incorporated. Every product market model renders a characteristic functional relationship between the competition profit attainable and the total number of firms n. Once this relationship is obtained, some of the derived results can be specified.

12.2.2 The firms' value functions

Again, we commence by deriving the general forms of the firms' value functions and studying their properties.

The general form of the value functions

THE EX-POST SITUATION

Recall that the ex-post situation comprises all points in time where the first patent race has been concluded. Consequently, both states are occupied. Let $\pi_{ji}(z)$, $j \in \{1, \ldots, n_i\}$, $i = A, B$, stand for the profit firm j from country i can earn in both countries while being in state z. As before, $V_{ji}(z^C)$ and $V_{ji}(z^I)$ denote the value of being a challenger and the incumbent respectively to a firm j from country i. According to the Bellman principle of optimality, the value functions have to satisfy the following system of equations:

$$rV_{ji}(z^C) = \pi_{ji}(z^C) + \mathfrak{h}_{ji}(z^C)\big(V_{ji}(z^I) - V_{ji}(z^C)\big),$$

$$rV_{ji}(z^I) = \pi_{ji}(z^I) + \mathfrak{h}_{ji}(z^I)\big(V_{ji}(z^C) - V_{ji}(z^I)\big),$$

where r is the exogenously given interest rate, and the functions $\mathfrak{h}_{ji}(z)$ are the hazard rates of the underlying Poisson process.

From Chapter 10, it is clear that the hazard rates are independent of the value functions. The same holds true for the instantaneous profits π_{ji} so that the system of equations can be solved for the value functions:

$$V_{ji}(z^C) = \frac{\pi_{ji}(z^C)}{r} + \frac{\mathfrak{h}_{ji}(z^C)}{r\big(r + \mathfrak{h}_{ji}(z^C) + \mathfrak{h}_{ji}(z^I)\big)}\big(\pi_{ji}(z^I) - \pi_{ji}(z^C)\big),$$

$$V_{ji}(z^I) = \frac{\pi_{ji}(z^C)}{r} + \frac{r + \mathfrak{h}_{ji}(z^C)}{r\big(r + \mathfrak{h}_{ji}(z^C) + \mathfrak{h}_{ji}(z^I)\big)}\big(\pi_{ji}(z^I) - \pi_{ji}(z^C)\big).$$

$$(12.10)$$

The familiar characteristics of the general value functions can be recognized. A challengers profit $\pi_{ji}(z^C)$ serves as the permanent income of a firm independent of its situation in the current patent race. Therefore, $\pi_{ji}(z^C)/r$ is the minimum which the value of being a challenger and the incumbent can attain.

Since the profit earned while being the incumbent exceeds the one while being a challenger, the expected profits from obtaining the monopoly position in future is part of the continuation values provided the challenger has a strictly positive probability of winning the next patent race. The last component is the expected compensation a successful firm receives until its incumbency ends and is unique to the value of being the incumbent. As can be seen, the continuation value for the incumbent is always larger than that for the challengers independent of the specific forms of the profit functions $\pi_{ji}(z)$ and the hazard rates $\mathfrak{h}_{ji}(z)$.

To obtain the general form of the continuation values, the hazard rates have to be determined. Keeping in mind that foreign and domestic firms participate at the global patent races, the hazard rates differ from those introduced in Chapter 10. Take the hazard rate $\mathfrak{h}_{ji}(z^C)$. It measures the instantaneous probability that a challenger changes its position and becomes the incumbent in all countries offering patent protection. Furthermore, let $a_i^I := \sum_{k \neq j} h_{ki}(z^C)$ and $H_i := \sum_{k=1}^{n_i} h_{ki}(z^C)$. Hence, H_i are the expenditures spend by country i firms when country i does not host the incumbent. Likewise, a_i^I denotes the aggregated research effort of country i when the incumbent has its research laboratory in country i. Then, the overall chances that any of the foreign or domestic firms discovers an invention between t and $t + dt$ is $\lambda_i (a_i^I + h_{ji}(z^I)) + \lambda_l H_l, i, l = A, B$. To obtain the probability of winning the next race for country i firm the overall probability has to be adjusted by the weight of the individual firm in the total set of firms. Therefore, the hazard rate for a firm j of country i to become an incumbent reads

$$\mathfrak{h}_{ji}(z^C) := \frac{\lambda_i h_{ji}(z^C)}{\lambda_i (a_i^I + h_{ki}(z^I)) + \lambda_l H_l} \left[\lambda_i (a_i^I + h_{ki}(z^I)) + \lambda_l H_l \right]$$

$$= \lambda_i h_{ji}(z^C).$$

(12.11)

By analogy, the hazard rate for the incumbent to become a challenger can be determined with

$$\mathfrak{h}_{ji}(z^I) := \lambda_i a_i^I + \lambda_l H_l, \quad i, l = A, B.$$

(12.12)

As usual, the hazard rates are state dependent, and it is far more likely to lose an incumbency than to obtain this position.

Apart from this, it can also be seen that the hazard rate for the incumbent of becoming a challenger is independent of the own research effort. If the firms were not able to choose their research effort freely, but rather were bound to spend e.g. one unit, $\mathfrak{h}_{ji}(z^C) \geq \mathfrak{h}_{jl}(z^C)$ and $\mathfrak{h}_{jl}(z^I) \geq \mathfrak{h}_{ji}(z^I)$ if and only if $\lambda_i \geq \lambda_l$. A challenger domiciled in the high innovation country would have better chances to become the incumbent than a competitor in the same situation that resides in the low innovation country. On the other hand, a high innovation incumbent would have a better chance of keeping his position as compared to a low innovation incumbent.

However, since the firms' research effort is not fixed, firms having a low innovation productivity can counterbalance their disadvantage by exerting a higher effort. Yet, the low productivity firms will typically not choose to fully compensate their disadvantage since the higher research effort is associated with additional costs.

Using the hazard rates defined in (12.11) and (12.12), the general forms of the continuation values read

$$
V_{ji}(z^C) = \frac{\pi_{ji}(z^C)}{r} + \frac{\lambda_i h_{ji}^C}{r\phi_i} \left(\pi_{ji}(z^I) - \pi_{ji}(z^C) \right),
$$

$$
V_{ji}(z^I) = \frac{\pi_{ji}(z^C)}{r} + \frac{r + \lambda_i h_{ji}^C}{r\phi_i} \left(\pi_{ji}(z^I) - \pi_{ji}(z^C) \right),
$$

(12.13)

where $\phi_i := r + \lambda_i (a_i^I + h_{ji}^C) + \lambda_l H_l$.

THE EX-ANTE SITUATION

In the ex-ante situation, the first invention that creates a new product or technology line has not yet arisen. Accordingly, all firms are identical as far as their positions in the patent race are concerned: they are challengers and the incumbency position is vacant.

Firms behave rationally and anticipate the ex-post situation and their decisions. Consequently, firms foresee their ex-post equilibrium choices $\{h_i^{I*}, h_i^{C*}\}$ presented in Proposition 12.4 below. This implies that the ex-post continuation values are independent of the effort levels chosen for the first patent race (cf Chapter 10). Recalling that the invention date is governed by a Poisson process, the ex-ante value of participating at the infinite sequence of global patent races can be determined with (cf Loury, 1979)

$$
V_{ji}(z^0) = \int_0^\infty e^{-\phi^0 t} \Big[\phi^0 V_{ji}^*(z^C)
$$

$$
+ \mathfrak{h}_{ji}(z^C)\left(V_{ji}^*(z^I) - V_{ji}^*(z^C)\right) - C(h_{ji}^0) \Big] dt,
$$

where the superscript 0 marks values specific for the ex-ante situation and the asterisk signifies the equilibrium versions of the ex-post continuation values. The variable ϕ^0 is defined as $\phi^0 := r + \lambda_i H_i + \lambda_l H_l$. Since neither of the ex-post continuation values depends on a firm's ex-ante decision, ex-ante value function can be expressed in an explicit form:

$$
V_{ji}(z^0) = \frac{1}{\phi^0} \Big[\left(\lambda_i H_i + \lambda_l H_l\right) V_{ji}^*(z^C)
$$

$$
+ \lambda_i h_{ji}^0 \left(V_{ji}^*(z^I) - V_{ji}^*(z^C)\right) - C(h_{ji}^0) \Big].
$$

(12.14)

The expected value from participating at the global patent races consists of the value of being a challenger $V_{ji}^*(z^C)$ all the time less the expected research costs

$C(h_{ji}^0)$ accumulated until the first patent race ends. These two components form the infimum of $V_{ji}^0(z^0)$. In case the firm has a strictly positive probability of winning the first race because its research efficiency λ_i is strictly positive and the cost of exerting the first unit of effort are not too high, the ex-ante value exceeds its infimum. The premium is equivalent to the difference between the value of being an incumbent and a challenger earned during the spells of incumbency in future.

No patent protection in country B

Suppose the home country B does not protect the subject matter in question, i.e. we consider the status quo. Since an unprotected discovery immediately becomes common knowledge and can be imitated freely and costlessly, all firms are able to offer the latest inventor's product in market B and earn $\pi_{ji}(z^C) := \pi_B^c - C(h_{ji}^c)$, where h_{ji}^c is short for $h_{ji}(z^C)$. However, the foreign country A grants patents to firms of all nations so that foreign as well as domestic firms may obtain the monopoly position in market A. The incumbent receives a flow profit of $\pi_{ji}(z^I) := \pi_A^m + \pi_B^c - C(h_{ji}^I)$. Using the definitions of the profits under non-protection and the ones for the hazard rates in the general form of the continuation values (12.10) yields

$$
\begin{aligned}
V_{ji}^n(z^C) &= \frac{\pi_B^C - C(h_{ji}^C)}{r} + \frac{\lambda_i h_{ji}^C}{r\phi_i}\left(\pi_A^m - C(h_{ji}^I) + C(h_{ji}^C)\right), \\
V_{ji}^n(z^I) &= \frac{\pi_B^C - C(h_{ji}^C)}{r} + \frac{r + \lambda_i h_{ji}^C}{r\phi_i}\left(\pi_A^m - C(h_{ji}^I) + C(h_{ji}^C)\right),
\end{aligned}
\tag{12.15}
$$

where $\phi_i := r + \lambda_i(a_i^I + h_{ji}^C) + \lambda_I H_I$, and the superscript n means *no patent protection*.

Firstly, note that the firm index j can be dropped since all firms within a country are identical and, therefore, the value functions are the same. Secondly, for any given equilibrium configuration of the research efforts $\{h_i^{I*}, h_i^{C*}\}$, the value of being the incumbent exceeds the one of being a challenger. This is due to the fact that the incumbent presently earns the higher monopoly profit and has equal chances to obtain the incumbency again in future. Lastly, a firm from a developing country does not necessarily have lower continuation values. However, if firms in a particular country do not have any innovation ability, i.e. $\lambda_i = 0$, the continuation values are certainly lower than the ones for the high innovation country.

Patent protection in the home country

The protection regime differs from the non-protection regime solely in the firms' payoffs. The probabilities governing success and failure of a research project remain unchanged.

Consider the case of the incumbent when the home country B protects the subject matter in question. The inventor occupies the monopoly position in both countries and earns $\pi_i(z^I) = \pi_A^m + \pi_B^m - C(h_i^I)$. However, the challengers are not able to offer an imitation of the latest invention in either market so that they have to restrict themselves to research. Then, their profit is given by $\pi_i(z^C) = -C(h_i^C)$.

Using the specified profit functions in the general continuation values yields:

$$V_i^p(z^C) = -\frac{C(h_i^C)}{r} + \frac{\lambda_i h_i^C}{r\phi_i}\left[\pi_A^m + \pi_B^m - C(h_i^I) + C(h_i^C)\right],$$

$$V_i^p(z^I) = -\frac{C(h_i^C)}{r} + \frac{r + \lambda_i h_i^C}{r\phi_i}\left[\pi_A^m + \pi_B^m - C(h_i^I) + C(h_i^C)\right],$$

(12.16)

where the superscript p stands for *protection*. Again, the firm index has been dropped since firms residing in the same country only differ with respect to their position in the current patent race, but not concerning their income in the same position.

Comparing the continuation values in the protection regime (12.16) with the appropriate ones in the non-protection regime (12.15) shows the differences quite clearly. Since the challengers have no *secure* refuge, the formerly permanent income would turn into permanent costs when the home country were to extend the patentable subject matters. As a compensation for the *lost income* source, the expected profits from current and future incumbency rise for given levels of research effort.

12.2.3 The firms' optimal choice

As explained in Chapter 10, the distinction between ex-ante and ex-post situations is not a result of pure analytical necessity. It coincides with different development stages of an industry. In studying the effects of changes in policy variables, it is instructive to allow firms to respond differently in an ex-ante and an ex-post situation. This defines the approach towards the optimal research effort in an ex-post situation.

For an ex-ante situation, however, there are two options. Either, firms that compete in creating a new technology line set a uniform research effort for the first and all succeeding patent races. Alternatively, one may argue that firms wish to change their research plans after the first patent race has ended. Then, firms may exert a higher or a lower effort during the first patent race as compared to subsequent races in which they are challengers. Since the latter alternative is the more general approach allowing for the possibility that identical efforts in all patent races while being a challenger, it is pursued here.

The non-protection regime

THE EX-POST SITUATION

In an ex-post situation, firms have two distinguishing characteristics: their position in the current patent race, i.e. incumbent or challenger, and their domicile.

The firms' optimal research effort will depend on both characteristics. Formally, a country i firm in position z^k, $i = A, B$ and $k = I, C$, will choose an effort level h_i^k so that the ex-post continuation value $V_i(z^k)$ is maximized. Since all $n := n_A + n_B$ firms decide simultaneously, we have a non-cooperative game with n players. Therefore, a Nash equilibrium of the game is a list of effort levels $\{h_i^k\}_{\substack{i=A,B \\ k=I,C}}$. In the remainder of the section we will frequently use the abbreviation **h** defined as $\mathbf{h} := \{h_i^I, h_i^C\}_{i=A,B}$. The following result is derived:

Proposition 12.4. Under Assumption 12.1 there exists a unique equilibrium $\mathbf{h}^n = \{0, h_i^{C*}\}$ where h_i^{C*} solves

$$\lambda_i\left(\pi_A^m + C(h_i^C)\right) - \phi C'(h_i^C) \leq 0, \tag{12.17}$$

$i = A, B$.

As expected, the incumbent never invests into the improvement of a product or technology line. Challengers of both countries might also decide not to innovate if the cost of the first unit of effort is too large, i.e. if (12.17) holds as strict inequality for all $h_i^C \in \mathbb{R}_+$. Given $C'(0) > 0$, there always exists a strictly positive research productivity $\bar{\lambda}_i^n$ such that (12.17) holds as strict inequality for all $\lambda_i < \bar{\lambda}_i^n$. This becomes especially relevant for developing countries for which it can be assumed that λ_i is rather small compared to the innovation efficiency of industrialized countries. Hence, if $C'(0) > 0$ it can be expected that challengers of a developing country will never invest. Note also that if $C'(0) = 0$ the equilibrium effort is always positive provided the innovation productivity is strictly positive. This result is independent of the aggregated innovation expenditures of the other country.

As to the properties of the equilibrium effort, we find the following:

Proposition 12.5. Given $C''(h) > C'(h)/h$ and under Assumption 12.1 (1),

1. the research effort rises with the own innovation efficiency and decreases when the research efficiency of the other country's challengers is increasing, i.e. $\partial h_i^{C*}/\partial \lambda_i > 0$ and $\partial h_i^{C*}/\partial \lambda_l < 0$;
2. the optimal effort is negatively correlated to the number of firms in either country, i.e. $\partial h_i^{C*}/\partial n_i < 0$, $\partial h_i^{C*}/\partial n_l < 0$;
3. firms that are more productive in generating inventions exert the higher effort, i.e. $h_i^{C*} \geq h_l^{C*}$ if $\lambda_i \geq \lambda_l$.
4. In case $C'(0) = 0$, the research effort increases with the monopoly profit given the innovation productivity of both countries is not too dissimilar, i.e. $\partial h_i^{C*}/\partial \pi_A^m > 0$.

Firstly, observe that the results are not applicable for linear innovation cost functions because they fail to satisfy the condition $C''(h) > C'(h)/h$. The first property states that the challengers invest more when they are more productive in generating innovations. The same result has been derived in Proposition 10.2 (2). As explained in Chapter 10, there are two opposing effects. The direct effect describes the fact that a given challenger's probability of winning the next race increases as their own innovation efficiency rises so that unsuccessful firms are willing to invest more. The indirect effect is negative and works through the rival challengers. An increase in λ_i makes the other country i's challengers also more productive so that the probability of winning the next race declines and challengers are less inclined to invest in research and development. The proposition confirms that the direct effect dominates the indirect one.

The first property also states that country i challengers are discouraged when country l challengers on average create more inventions. Since a variation in λ_l does not have a direct and thus positive effect on country i challengers, the latter will always reduce their research effort.

The first part of the second result is also well known and confirms the validity of the corresponding result in Proposition 10.2 (1) for an open economy. If more firms compete in a patent race, each individual firm exerts less research effort. With a global competition in research, it is not surprising that a larger number of country l firms negatively affects the research effort of country i challengers. Although the patent races accelerate when the number of firms in either country rises, the individual chances of winning a patent race drop. Consequently, the expected profits from a future incumbency decline and challengers will respond by downsizing their research projects.

The third property states that firms in countries that have higher research abilities will spend more on research. The rational for this result is straightforward. A higher innovation efficiency λ_i is associated with a greater chance of obtaining an incumbency in future and therefore leads to larger expected profits. Thus, firms having a larger λ_i find it profitable to invest more. Applied to the context of industrialized and developing countries, the finding certainly confirms everyday experience.[12] However, this seems to cement the worldwide pattern of economic development: the leaders remain on top, whereas the followers seem to have no chance to catch up. Yet, the model leaves learning and spill-over effects out of consideration so that the innovation productivity is considered to be constant in both countries. Actually, the innovation efficiency may depend on a number of factors as e.g. the general level of human capital, special abilities of researchers to transform a solution to a problem (invention) into a marketable product (innovation), and the ease to raise funds (cf Chapter 3). To the extent to which developing countries are able to improve conditions for the underlying determinants of the innovation efficiency, the latter may rise faster than the innovation productivity in industrialized countries.

Finally, the last property shows that an increase in the market size of the country offering patent protection has a positive effect on the research effort under reasonable circumstances. The proof to this part shows that challengers that are less productive in generating inventions always increase their research expenditures when π_A^m increases. This result appears because a larger monopoly profit increases expected returns on achieving the monopoly position in future. Hence, exerting a greater effort is appropriate. In contrast, the same reaction for challengers domiciled in the industrialized country can only be demonstrated if firms from a less advanced country are not too far behind. Accordingly, more efficient firms race to keep their superiority. In case the differences in the innovation efficiency are huge, more productive firms may or may not increase their research effort.

In the remainder of this chapter, the following assumption is frequently used:

Assumption 12.2.   Let the innovation efficiencies λ_i, $i = A, B$ be such that the equilibrium research effort of both countries' challengers is an increasing function of the foreign country's market size π_A^m.

THE EX-ANTE SITUATION

Before the first patent race, firms decide on the optimal research effort anticipating their optimal choices for the second and all subsequent races. Thus, firm j chooses the effort h_{ji}^0 that maximizes the value function given in (12.14) conditional on $\mathbf{h}^n$ defined in Proposition 12.4.

Different from the ex-post situation, firms find themselves all in the same position. However, they still reside in different countries so that the decision on the research budget is again a simultaneous-move, n-player game with heterogeneous agents. The equilibrium is a list of effort levels $\{h_i^0\}_{i=A,B}$.

Proposition 12.6.   Under Assumption 12.1,

1. a unique equilibrium exists.
2. If $\pi_B^c = 0$, then $\{h_i^{0*}\}_{i=A,B} = \{h_i^{C*}\}_{i=A,B}$.
3. If $\pi_B^c > 0$, then $\{h_i^{0*}\}_{i=A,B} > \{h_i^{C*}\}_{i=A,B}$ under Assumption 12.1 (1) and $\{h_i^{0*}\}_{I=A,B} < \{h_i^{C*}\}_{i=A,B}$ under Assumption 12.1 (2).

The proposition verifies that there is a pair of research efforts $\{h_A^{0*}, h_B^{0*}\}$ that maximize the expected value from participating at the infinite sequence of patent races. Similar to the ex-post situation, the optimal research effort might be zero if the first unit of effort is too costly. Once again, however, we find that the equilibrium ex-ante research effort is strictly positive if $C'(0) = 0$.

The proposition also states some properties of the equilibrium. In case the competition is fierce in country B, i.e. $\pi_B^c = 0$, firms choose identical research efforts in the ex-ante and the ex-post situation. At the first glance, this results seems to diverge from the corresponding one in Proposition 10.3 in that it is conditional on an efficient market in B. In Chapter 10, however, the demand structure is slightly richer as compared to the present model. In fact, the gross profits of the investment expenditures are zero in the approach of Chapter 10 as well. Thus, the result remains unchanged in an international framework.

The result that firms use the same effort level in the ex-ante and the ex-post situation when market B is efficient serves as a useful benchmark case. When firms earn strictly positive profits even without patent protection in country B the ex-ante effort level will generally differ from the ex-post one. Here, it is important to keep in mind that no revenues (or gross profits) are easing the burden of research expenditures in the first patent race since the path-breaking invention has not been created yet. Clearly, after the first patent race is over, firms earn either the monopoly or the competition profit. Consequently, the first patent race is different from all other races. If market B is efficient, however, firms receive nothing in the first race and challengers earn nothing in every subsequent patent race. The distinction between the first and the following patent races as a challenger vanishes for $\pi_B^c = 0$.

If the competition profit is strictly positive, the expected value of participating at the sequence of patent races increases. According to Proposition 12.6, firms having a convex research cost function spend more as compared to the benchmark case. By doing so, they increase their individual probability of winning the race and, therefore, accelerate it. Thus, larger expenditures are met for a shorter expected time. In contrast, if firms have a linear cost function, they spend less than in the reference scenario. Here, the first patent race is prolonged, and lower costs have to be borne for a longer expected time.

The protection regime

THE EX-POST SITUATION

Again, foreign and domestic firms find themselves in an n-player game, where the objective is to maximize their continuation value given in equation (12.16) with respect to the research effort. The following result ensues:

Proposition 12.7. Under Assumption 12.1, there exists a unique equilibrium $\mathbf{h}^p = \{0, h_i^{C*}\}$, where h_i^{C*} solves

$$\lambda_i\left(\pi_A^m + \pi_B^m + C(h_i^C)\right) - \phi C'(h_i^C) \leq 0, \tag{12.18}$$

$i = A, B.$

This result is the counterpart to Proposition 12.4 for the non-protection regime so that the discussion following the latter also applies here. Since the optimality conditions (12.17) and (12.18) are structurally identical, the optimal research effort in the protection regime has the same properties as stated in Proposition 12.5 for the non-protection regime.

Assumption 12.2 ensures that the optimal research effort of a challenger is an increasing function of the monopoly profit π_A^m (Proposition 12.5 (4)). The next result is derived immediately.

Corollary 12.1.   Under Assumptions 12.1 (1) and 12.2, $\mathbf{h}^p \geq \mathbf{h}^n$.

The expectation of acquiring the monopoly position in both markets induces firms to exert a higher research effort in the protection regime as compared to the non-protection regime.

Here, an environment is considered in which a number of firms strive to come up with a basic technology defining an entirely new product or technology line that is patentable in both countries. Consequently, in the first and all subsequent patent races, only the successful firms earn positive profits. Again firms anticipate their behaviour in subsequent patent races when deciding on the research effort of the first one.

Proposition 12.8.   Under Assumption 12.1, a unique equilibrium exists, where $\mathbf{h}^{0p} = \mathbf{h}^p$.

Different from the non-protection regime counterpart, firms in the ex-ante situation always choose the same level of research effort as in all subsequent patent races. This is simply the consequence of patent protection. The challengers earn nothing when inventions are patentable. This situation corresponds to Proposition 12.6 (2).

12.2.4   The effect on firms

In the last section, the existence of a solution to the firms' problem has been established for the non-protection and protection regime. Here, it is examined how the extension of patentable subject matters affects firms. Therefore, the firms' continuation value for a certain state in the non-protection and protection regime are compared.

Challengers choose different levels of the research effort in the non-protection and protection regime. Unfortunately, the firms' optimal effort need not to be a monotone function of the monopoly profit so that firms may invest more or invest less in the protection regime as compared to the non-protection one. Only if the research productivity of foreign and domestic firms are sufficiently similar will firms exert a larger effort when protection is granted. The following result applies only to those circumstances in the ex-post situation.

Proposition 12.9.   Under Assumptions 12.1 and 12.2 there exist $\underline{\pi}_i$ and $\overline{\pi}_i$ with $0 \leq \underline{\pi}_i < \overline{\pi}_i < \pi_B^m$ so that

-   for $\pi_B^c \in [0, \underline{\pi}_i)$ both challengers and the incumbent of country i benefit from patent protection,

–   for $\pi_B^c \in [\underline{\pi}_i, \overline{\pi}_i)$ only the incumbent of country i is better off if protection is introduced and

–   for $\pi_B^c \in [\overline{\pi}_i, \pi_B^m]$ neither challengers nor the incumbent of i wishes the extension of patentable subject matters.

Whether or not firms welcome the extension of patentable subject matters depends on the market structure in the unprotected domestic market. Again, the role of an unprotected market as a refuge for unsuccessful firms of a patent race in which they are able to earn (potentially) positive profits is highlighted (cf Section 12.1).

Take the example of an extremely weak competition, i.e. when $\pi_B^c = \pi_B^m$ which may e.g. arise if the degree of product differentiation takes its maximum. Then, all challengers as well as the incumbent earn the monopoly profit even if inventions cannot be protected by patents. In contrast, only the incumbent is able to receive the monopoly profit and the challengers earn nothing if patent protection is introduced for the subject matters in question. By introducing the protection of new subject matters, the challengers' shelter is destroyed. In this extreme case, not even the incumbent would support such changes since he earns the monopoly profit with certainty in the non-protection regime. To the contrary, the successful firm has incentives to lobby actively against the extension of patentable subject matters. As it is not making an effort to develop a new invention during its incumbency, the firm is certain to be a challenger and, therefore earn nothing, in the subsequent patent race in the protection regime.

The other variant is the one of extremely fierce competition, i.e. $\pi_B^c = 0$, that may arise when there is only one homogeneous good and price competition. Here, the challengers earn zero profits in the non-protection and the protection regime. However, as long as there is a positive probability for every previously unsuccessful firm to win the current patent race, the continuation value is larger in the protection regime as compared to the non-protection regime because it obtains the monopoly position in two markets. Since the continuation value of the incumbent is always larger than the one of the challengers, firms in both states will support the introduction of patent protection for new subject matters.

Owing to the fact that the incumbent's continuation value is larger than that of a challenger, there must exist a range of competition intensities for which the incumbent prefers the extension of patentable subject matters but the challenger does not.

Unfortunately, no clear conclusion can be drawn for the ex-ante situation. In the non-protection regime, the effort level in the first and all subsequent patent races are equal only if the competition profit is zero. In this special case, the value of participating at the sequence of patent races must increase when patent protection is introduced for new subject matters because the ex-ante value function is a linear combination of the ex-post ones. However, if the competition profit is strictly positive, the research effort for the first patent race can be larger or smaller than that in all subsequent ones depending on the type of the cost function. Hence, the ex-ante value function might increase or decrease when patentable subject matters are extended.

12.2.5 The home country's welfare functions

Policymakers in the home country B are faced with the question of whether or not a subject matter that is already patentable abroad should also be protected in the domestic market. It is assumed that the sole decision criterion is society's welfare.

The society's and the firms' point of view have common and distinguishing features. Since firms' profits are part of society's instantaneous welfare, the ex-ante and ex-post situation with their respective states have also to be distinguished for the society. Different from the firms' position, however, it is only important whether or not a *domestic* firm is the incumbent for the society, i.e. the society is indifferent to the particular identity of the successful firm.

The analysis follows similar steps as the ones for the firm's problem. Hence, the general form of the welfare functions are derived first.

The general form of the welfare functions

THE EX-POST SITUATION

Here, each firm is either the incumbent or one of the challengers. Since society is only interested in whether a domestic or foreign firm is the incumbent in the present patent race, society's states have a slightly different interpretation. The state y^I means that one of the domestic firms holds the monopoly position abroad (and at home in the protection regime), whereas y^C denotes the fact that all domestic firms are challengers. Let $w(y)$ be the home country's instantaneous welfare while being in state y in the current patent race. The state-dependent welfare functions are denoted by $W(y)$, and the society's hazard rates are $\mathfrak{w}(y)$. Then, the welfare functions have to satisfy the following system of equations:

$$W(y^C) = w(y^C) + \mathfrak{w}(y^C)\left(W(y^I) - W(y^C)\right),$$
$$W(y^I) = w(y^I) + \mathfrak{w}(y^I)\left(W(y^C) - W(y^I)\right).$$

Again, the system can be solved with respect to the welfare functions which yields the now familiar forms of:

$$W(y^C) = \frac{w(y^C)}{r} + \frac{\mathfrak{w}(y^C)}{r\left(r + \mathfrak{w}(y^C) + \mathfrak{w}(y^I)\right)}\left(w(y^I) - w(y^C)\right),$$

$$W(y^I) = \frac{w(y^C)}{r} + \frac{r + \mathfrak{w}(y^C)}{r\left(r + \mathfrak{w}(y^C) + \mathfrak{w}(y^I)\right)}\left(w(y^I) - w(y^C)\right).$$

(12.19)

The functions bear the usual meaning.

To derive the general forms, the hazard rates $\mathfrak{w}$ have to be specified. When being in state y^C, the hazard rate gives the probability that one of the domestic firms wins the current patent race between t and $t + dt$. Since a foreign firm is the incumbent in the present patent race and does not engage in research, the overall hazard rate that any challenger, foreign or domestic, achieves an innovation within the next instant is $\lambda_A(n_A - 1)h_A^{C*} + \lambda_B n_B h_B^{C*}$. The probability that the successful firm is a domestic one is given by $\lambda_B n_B h_B^{C*}/(\lambda_A(n_A - 1)h_A^{C*} + \lambda_B n_B h_B^{C*})$, so that the hazard rate ensues with

$$\mathfrak{w}(y^C) = \lambda_B n_B h_B^{C*}.$$

State y^I means that a domestic firm occupies the monopoly position in the current patent race. Hence, the hazard rate $\mathfrak{w}(y^I)$ denotes the probability that a foreign firm wins the patent race within the next moment. Observe that a domestic firm succeeding another domestic firm as the monopoly does not change the society's state, although it changes the involved firms' states. By analogy to the above hazard rate, it follows that

$$\mathfrak{w}(y^I) = \lambda_A n_A h_A^{C*}.$$

Using the hazard rates in (12.19) yields the general form of the welfare functions:

$$W(y^C) = \frac{w(y^C)}{r} + \frac{n_B \lambda_B h_B^{C*}}{r\phi}\left(w(y^I) - w(y^C)\right),$$

$$W(y^I) = \frac{w(y^C)}{r} + \frac{r + n_B \lambda_B h_B^{C*}}{r\phi}\left(w(y^I) - w(y^C)\right). \tag{12.20}$$

The welfare functions specific for the protection and non-protection regime are obtained once the instantaneous welfare is determined.

THE EX-ANTE SITUATION

The welfare consequences of making additional subject matters patentable on future product and technology lines are assessed by the ex-ante welfare function. The latter is the expected value over the welfare when a domestic or a foreign firm wins the first patent race and can be written as

$$W(z^0) = \frac{1}{\phi^0}\left[n_B \lambda_B h_B^{0*} W(z^I) + n_A \lambda_A h_A^{0*} W(z^C)\right]. \tag{12.21}$$

The non-protection regime

When the home country does not confer patent rights for the subject matter in question, all firms including the incumbent are able to earn π_B^c in the domestic market. Let $S(n, \pi_B^c)$ denote the associated consumers' surplus. It is natural to assume that the consumers' surplus increases with the number of firms $n := n_A + n_B$ in the market and decreases with an increasing competition profit π_B^c. To facilitate notation, the consumers' surplus per domestic firm $\bar{S}(\cdot)$, $\bar{S}(\cdot) := S(\cdot)/n_B$ is introduced.

In case a foreign firm is the present incumbent, the firms' surplus is sum of the domestic firms profits $n_B(\pi_B^c - C(h_B^{C*}))$ so that the instantaneous welfare amounts to $\mathfrak{w}(y^C) = n_B[S(n, \pi_B^c) + \pi_B^c - C(h_B^{C*})]$. When a domestic firm has won the last patent race, it holds the monopoly position abroad, and the instantaneous welfare is $\mathfrak{w}(y^I) = \mathfrak{w}(y^C) + \pi_A^m + C(h_B^{C*})$. With the instantaneous welfare functions at hand, the welfare under non-protection are determined by

$$W^n(z^C) = \frac{n_B[\bar{S}(\cdot) + \pi_B^c - C(h_B^{C*})]}{r} + \frac{n_B \lambda_B h_B^{C*}}{r\phi}(\pi_A^m + C(h_B^{C*})),$$

$$W^n(z^I) = \frac{n_B[\bar{S}(\cdot) + \pi_B^c - C(h_B^{C*})]}{r} + \frac{r + n_B \lambda_B h_B^{C*}}{r\phi}(\pi_A^m + C(h_B^{C*})). \tag{12.22}$$

The ex-ante welfare function is readily available from (12.21) so that it is not presented here.

The protection regime

Here, the situation is considered, where the subject matter in question is patentable in the home country. In the ex-post situation, the foreign and the domestic market are monopolized. The consumers' surplus given by $S(1, \pi_B^m)$ will be lower as compared to the one under the non-protection regime owing to the market power conferred by patent rights, i.e. $S(1, \pi_B^m) < S(n, \pi_B^c)$.

When all domestic firms are challengers, they earn zero profits, but have to bear the research expenditures so that the instantaneous welfare is $\mathfrak{w}(z^C) = n_B[\bar{S}(1, \pi_B^m) - C(h_B^{C*})]$, where again $\bar{S}(1, \pi_B^m) := S(1, \pi_B^m)/n_B$ is the consumers' surplus per domestic firm. In case a domestic firm is the present incumbent, it occupies the monopoly position in both markets. Then, the instantaneous welfare amounts to $\mathfrak{w}(z^I) = \mathfrak{w}(z^C) + \pi_A^m + \pi_B^m + C(h_B^{C*})$.

Using this information, the welfare functions specific for the protection regime read

$$W^p(z^C) = \frac{n_B[\bar{S}(\cdot) - C(h_B^{C*})]}{r} + \frac{n_B \lambda_B h_B^{C*}}{r\phi}(\pi_A^m + \pi_B^m + C(h_B^{C*})),$$

$$W^p(z^I) = \frac{n_B[\bar{S}(\cdot) - C(h_B^{C*})]}{r} + \frac{r + n_B \lambda_B h_B^{C*}}{r\phi}(\pi_A^m + \pi_B^m + C(h_B^{C*})). \tag{12.23}$$

Again, the ex-ante welfare function is readily determined using (12.21).

12.2.6 Welfare considerations

After determining the welfare functions for the non-protection and protection regime, the effects of extending patentable subject matters on the society as a whole can be studied. Comparing the appropriate welfare functions yields the following result:

Proposition 12.10.   If the consumers' surplus drops as a result of the proposed change in the patent law, society benefits for smaller ranges of the competition profit in the respective state and is potentially always worse off as domestic firms are.

Society takes the drop in the consumers' surplus following the introduction of new patentable subject matters into account. As a consequence, a policymaker would never consider to extend the patentable subject matter when the incumbent does not support (or lobby for) the proposed change, i.e. when $\pi_B^C \in [\overline{\pi}_B, \pi_B^m]$. Different to the firms' point of view, however, there is no guarantee that changing the patent law raises the society's welfare when competition is fierce in the non-protection regime.

Since the social desirability of introducing new patentable subject matters cannot be established for the ex-post situation, nothing can be said about the ex-ante one.

12.A Proofs to the lemmata and propositions

Proposition 12.4.   The proof proceeds in three steps: (1) it is demonstrated that $h_A^{I*} = h_B^{I*} = 0$; (2) it is established that at least one equilibrium configuration $h_i^{C*} \geq 0$ exists and; (3) it is verified that there is only one pair $\{h_A^{C*}, h_B^{C*}\}$ qualifying for an equilibrium.

Part (1): The first derivative of $V_i^n(z^I)$ reads

$$\frac{\partial V_i^n(z^I)}{\partial h_i^I} = -\frac{r + \lambda_i h_i^C}{r\phi}$$

which is obviously strictly negative for all values of $h_i^I \in \mathbb{R}_0$. Consequently, $h_A^{I*} = h_B^{I*} = 0$.

Part (2): Since $h_i^{I*} = 0$, then a challenger's first-order condition reads $G_i^n :=$ $\lambda_i(\pi_A^m + C(h_i^C)) - \phi C'(h_i^C) \leq 0$, where $\phi = r + n_A \lambda_A h_A^C + n_B \lambda_B h_B^C$ since all challengers within a country are identical. Let $\hat{H}$ be defined as $\hat{H} = n_A \lambda_A h_A^C + n_B \lambda_B h_B^C$. Then, a country i challengers' reaction function can be written as

$$r_i(\hat{H}) := \begin{cases} 0 & \text{if } G_i^n < 0 \,\forall h_i^C \in \mathbb{R}_+, \\ \{h_i^C \in \mathbb{R}_+ : G_i^n = 0\} & \text{else} \end{cases}$$

Define R as $R := n_A \lambda_A r_A(\hat{H}) + n_B \lambda_B r_B(\hat{H})$. Since $\partial r_i(\hat{H})/\partial \hat{H} \leq 0$, $\partial R/\partial \hat{H} \leq 0$. Owing to Assumption 12.1, $r_i(\cdot)$ is continuously differentiable so that R is continuously differentiable as well. Then, by Tarski's fixed point theorem, the set of equilibrium values $\mathbf{H}^* := \{\hat{H} \in \mathbb{R}_0 : \hat{H} = R(\hat{H})\}$ is non-empty. The pair of equilibrium values $\{h_A^{C*}, h_B^{C*}\}$ associated to an equilibrium value $\hat{H} \in \mathbf{H}^*$ are determined by $r_i(\hat{H}^*)$.

Part (3): Note that r_i is continuously differentiable, a decreasing function of $\hat{H}$ and $r_i(0) > 0$. Since R shares these properties, uniqueness of an equilibrium in $\hat{H}$ is ensured. Furthermore, as $r_i(\hat{H})$ is one-to-one under Assumption 12.1, the mapping $\hat{H}^* \longrightarrow \{h_A^{C*}, h_B^{C*}\}$ is also unique. $\qquad\square$

Proposition 12.5.   Since all firms within a country are identical, $a_i^I = (n_i - 1)h_i^C$ and $H_i = n_i h_i^C$. Then, the first-order conditions can be written as $\lambda_i(\pi_A^m + C(h_i^C)) - (r + n_A \lambda_A h_A^C + n_B \lambda_B h_B^C)C'(h_i^C) = 0$. The corresponding Jacobian is given by

$$
J := \begin{bmatrix} (n_A - 1)\lambda_A C'(h_A^C) + \phi C''(h_A^C) & n_B \lambda_B C'(h_A^C) \\ n_A \lambda_A C'(h_B^C) & (n_B - 1)\lambda_B C'(h_B^C) + \phi C''(h_B^C) \end{bmatrix}.
$$

Note that the determinant of the Jacobian is unambiguously positive.

Part 1: The challengers' research effort changes with the innovation productivity according to

$$
\frac{\partial h_i^{C*}}{\partial \lambda_i} = \frac{1}{\det J}\left[(\phi C''(h_i^{C*}) - \lambda_i C'(h_i^{C*}))\frac{r + n_l \lambda_l h_l^{C*}}{\lambda_l}C'(h_i^{C*}) \right.
$$

$$
\left. + n_l \lambda_l C'(h_i^{C*})(\pi_A^m + C(h_i^{C*})) \right] > 0,
$$

$$
\frac{\partial h_i^{C*}}{\partial \lambda_l} = \frac{-n_l C(h_i^{C*})}{\det J}\left[\lambda_l(\pi_A^m + C(h_i^{C*})) + h_l^{C*}(\phi C''(h_i^{C*}) - \lambda_l C'(h_i^{C*})) \right] < 0.
$$

Part 2: Similarly, we find changes of the number of firms:

$$
\frac{\partial h_i^{C*}}{\partial n_i} = -\frac{1}{\det J}\lambda_i h_i^{C*}C'(h_i^{C*})\left[\phi C''(h_i^{C*}) - \lambda_l C'(h_i^{C*}) \right] < 0,
$$

$$
\frac{\partial h_i^{C*}}{\partial n_l} = -\frac{1}{\det J}\lambda_i h_i^{C*}C'(h_i^{C*})\left[\phi C''(h_i^{C*}) - \lambda_l C'(h_i^{C*}) \right] < 0.
$$

Part 3: Note that if $C'(0) = 0$, a challenger's optimal research effort is strictly positive as long as the own innovation productivity is strictly positive as well. Only if $\lambda_i = 0$ is it optimal for a challenger to abstain from research. Next, if $\lambda_i = \lambda_l$ then $h_i^{C*} = h_l^{C*}$. Then, $h_i^{C*} > h_l^{C*}$ if $\lambda_i > \lambda_l$ directly follows from part 1.

Part 4: The optimal effort changes with variations in the monopoly profit in market A according to

$$\frac{\partial h_i^{C*}}{\partial \pi_A^m} = \frac{1}{\det J}\left[\lambda_i\big(\phi C''(h_i^{C*}) - \lambda_l C'(h_i^{C*})\big) + n_l \lambda_i \lambda_l^2\left(\frac{C'(h_l^{C*})}{\lambda_l} - \frac{C'(h_i^{C*})}{\lambda_i}\right)\right].$$

Observe that the derivative simplifies to

$$\frac{\partial h_i^{C*}}{\partial \pi_A^m} = \frac{\lambda}{\phi C''(h^{C*}) + (n_i + n_l - 1)\lambda C'(h^{C*})} > 0$$

if $\lambda_i = \lambda_l = \lambda$. Owing to the first-order condition, $\pi_A^m + C(h_i^{C*}) = \phi C'(h_i^{C*})/\lambda_i$. Assume that $\lambda_l > \lambda_i$. Then $\pi_A^m + C(h_i^{C*}) = \phi C'(h_i^{C*})/\lambda_l > \phi C'(h_i^{C*})/\lambda_i = \pi_A^m + C(h_i^{C*})$, so that $\partial h_i^{C*}/\partial \pi_A^m > 0$. Now suppose that $\lambda_i > \lambda_l$. Then $C'(h_i^{C*})/\lambda_l - C'(h_i^{C*})/\lambda_i < 0$ and the derivative potentially becomes negative. However, as long as the difference between the innovation productivity is not too large, this term is dominated by the first which is unambiguously positive. $\square$

Proposition 12.6. *Existence*: Let $\hat{H}_i := (n_i - 1)\lambda_i h_i^0 + n_l \lambda_l h_l^0$. Firm i's first-order condition is given by $G_i^{n0} := \lambda_i(rV_i^{I*} + C(h_i^0)) + \lambda_i \hat{H}_i(V_i^{I*} - V_i^{C*}) - \phi^0 C'(h_i^0) \leq 0$. The corresponding reaction function is defined by

$$r_i^0(\hat{H}_i) = \begin{cases} 0 & \text{if } G_i^{n0} < 0 \;\forall h_i^0 \in \mathbb{R}_+, \\ \{h_i^0 \in \mathbb{R}_+ : G_i^{n0} = 0\}. \end{cases}$$

Define R^0 as $R^0 := (n_i - 1)\lambda_i r_i^0(\hat{H}_i) + n_l \lambda_l r_l^0(\hat{H}_i)$. Under Assumption 12.1(1), the regular part of the reaction function is continuously differentiable so that R^0 also is continuously differentiable. Applying again Tarski's Fixed Point Theorem, the set of equilibrium values $\mathbf{H}^{n*} := \big\{\hat{H}_i \in \mathbb{R}_+ : \hat{H}_i = R^0(\hat{H}_i)\big\}_{i=A,B}$ is ensured. For linear cost functions, the system of first-order conditions can be solved directly.

Uniqueness: Observe that the regular part of the reaction function is negatively sloped. Since $G_i^{n0} > 0$ at $\hat{H}_i = 0$ for at least some values of h_i^0, the equilibrium is unique.

Fierce competition: In the ex-post situation, the first-order condition is given by $G^n = \lambda_i(\pi_A^m + C(h_i^{C*})) - \phi^* C'(h_i^{C*}) = 0$. Using this equation and the definitions of the continuation functions in G_i^{n0} yields:

$$G_i^{n0} = \lambda_i \pi_B^c + \lambda_i\big(C(h_i^0) - C(h_i^{C*})\big) - \phi^0\big(C'(h_i^0) - C'(h_i^{C*})\big) + \phi^0 G^n/\phi^* = 0.$$

Given that π_B^c vanishes in efficient markets and $G^n = 0$ by definition, $h_i^0 = h_i^{C*}$ ensues.

Moderate competition and cost functions: Since G^n vanishes per definition, $\lambda_i\big(C(h_i^0) - C(h_i^{C*})\big) - \phi^0\big(C'(h_i^0) - C'(h_i^{C*})\big)$ has to be negative when the competition profit π_B^c is positive. If the cost function is linear, the condition reduces to

$C(h_i^0) < C(h_i^{C*})$ which is satisfied as long as $h_i^{C*} > h_i^0$. When the cost function is convex, the condition can only hold if the reverse is true. □

Proposition 12.7.   Let $\bar{\pi} := \pi_A^m + \pi_B^m$. Since Proposition 12.4 has been proven for arbitrary values of the monopoly profit in A, the Proposition 12.4 must hold as well when the incumbent's profit is $\bar{\pi}$. □

Proposition 12.8.   The proof of existence and uniqueness follows the steps laid out in the proof of Proposition 12.6.

The first-order condition is given by $G_i^p = \lambda_i(\pi_A^m + \pi_B^m + C(h_i^{C*})) - \phi^* C'(h_i^{C*}) = 0$. The function G_i^{p0} is analogously defined as G_i^{n0} in the proof of Proposition 12.6. Using the definitions of the continuation values in the protection regime yields:

$$G_i^{p0} = \lambda_i\big(C(h_i^0) - C(h_i^{C*})\big) - \phi^0\big(C'(h_i^0) - C'(h_i^{C*})\big) + \phi^0 G^p/\phi^* = 0.$$

Since $G^p = 0$, it must be true that $h_i^{0*} = h_i^{C*}$ in the protection regime and, thus $\mathbf{h}^0 = \mathbf{h}^p$. □

Proposition 12.9.   The first-order condition for the non-protection regime is given by $\lambda_i(\pi_A^m + C_i^n) = \phi^n C_i^{n\prime}$ so that $\pi_A^m + C_i^n = \phi^n C_i^{n\prime}/\lambda_i$, where C_i^n is short for $C(h_i^{Cn*})$. Likewise it can be found that $\pi_A^m + \pi_B^m + C_i^p = \phi^p C_i^{n\prime}/\lambda_i$ for the protection regime. Replacing those expressions in the challenger's continuation values in (12.15) and (12.16) and noting that h_i^I is zero in both cases, $\Delta V_i^C := V_i^p(z^C) - V_i^n(z^C)$ is given by

$$\Delta V_i^C = \frac{1}{r}\Big[\big(h_i^p C_i^{p\prime} - C_i^p\big) - \big(h_i^n C_i^{n\prime} - C_i^n\big) - \pi_B^c\Big].$$

According to Assumption 12.1 the cost function is convex, so that $hC' - C$ is increasing in the research effort. Owing to Assumption 12.2, $\mathbf{h}^p > \mathbf{h}^n$. Now, let $\underline{\pi}_i := \{\pi_B^c \in [0, \pi_B^m] : \Delta V_i^C = 0\}$. Then, $\Delta V_i^C > 0$ for all $\pi_B^c \le \underline{\pi}_i$.

Consider now the incumbent. By analogy, we find

$$\Delta V_i^I = \Delta V_i^C + \frac{1}{r\lambda_i}(C_i^{p\prime} - C_i^{n\prime}).$$

Let $\bar{\pi}_i := \{\pi_B^c \in [0, \pi_B^m] : \Delta V_i^I = 0\}$. Clearly, $\underline{\pi}_i < \bar{\pi}_i$ and $\Delta V_i^I > 0$ for all $\pi_B^c \le \bar{\pi}_i$. □

Proposition 12.10.   Let ΔW^C and ΔW^I be defined as $\Delta W^C := W^p(y^C) - W^n(y^C)$ and $\Delta W^I := W^p(y^I) - W^n(y^I)$. Using the appropriate welfare functions from (12.22) and (12.23), they are determined with

$$\Delta W^C = \frac{n_B}{r}\Big[\big(h_B^p C_B^{p\prime} - C_B^p\big) - \big(h_B^n C_B^{n\prime} - C_B^n\big) - \pi_B^c - \Delta\bar{s}\Big],$$

$$\Delta W^I = \Delta W^C + \frac{n_B}{r\lambda_B}\big(C_B^{p\prime} - C_B^{n\prime}\big),$$

where $\Delta \bar{S} := \bar{S}(n, \pi_B^c) - \bar{S}(1, \pi_B^m)$ is the decline in the consumers' surplus when the domestic market becomes monopolized. Let $\underline{\pi}_B^S := \left\{ \pi_B^c \in (-\infty, \pi_B^m] : \Delta W^C = 0 \right\}$ and $\overline{\pi}_B^S := \{ \pi_B^c \in (-\infty, \pi_B^m] : \Delta W^I = 0 \}$ with $\underline{\pi}_B^S < \overline{\pi}_B^S$. It is easy to see that $\underline{\pi}_B^S = \underline{\pi}_B - \Delta \bar{S}$ and $\overline{\pi}_B^S = \overline{\pi}_B - \Delta \bar{S}$. Since $\overline{\pi}_B^S$ might be negative depending on the size of the change in the consumers' surplus, it might never be worthwhile to introduce the proposed change in patent law. $\qquad \square$

13 Different non-obviousness standards

The Agreement of Trade Related Aspects of Intellectual Property (TRIPs Agreement) sets a minimum standard that has to be complied with by every signatory member of the World Trade Organization (cf *supra*). Despite the TRIPs Agreement, patent systems are far from harmonized. In an international framework, such discrepancies in policy instruments may have welfare effects. This chapter extends the model introduced in Chapter 10 so that welfare effects of differences in the non-obviousness standard (NOS) can be examined.

The results obtained in Chapter 10 suggest that countries whose firms are more efficient in generating inventions choose stricter NOSs. Consequently, one would expect industrialized countries to set stronger NOSs than developing countries. In addition it is natural to assume that identical countries will set the same NOS. In particular, this means that industrialized countries should harmonize the NOSs.

The present chapter however shows that differentiation is welfare enhancing for all countries. The result arises because larger inventions contribute more to social welfare than small ones. A uniform NOS cannot differentiate between the various social values of inventions. If NOSs are different across countries, larger inventions receive a higher reward in countries with strong NOSs where small inventions fail to receive a patent.

The first section introduces the additional assumptions necessary to extend the model in Chapter 10. Subsequently, the effect of different NOSs on the firms in both countries is studied. The third section characterizes the optimal NOS and derives the main results. Finally, some considerations on patent policy are presented.

13.1 The basic framework

The model to be presented in this section is a combination of the ones introduced in Chapters 10 and 12. Hence, the principal assumptions are maintained and only minor alterations are necessary.

Again, two countries i, $i = A, B$, are considered. Both countries are alike in that they grant patent rights for the subject matter in question. They differ in their firms' ability λ_i to generate inventions, in the number n_i of firms participating in patent races and in the applied NOS s_i. Hence, in contrast to the model in Chapter 12 and in accordance with the one in Chapter 10, not every invention qualifies for a patent. Rather, an invention is only patentable in country i if it meets the NOS s_i of the respective country.

13.1.1 Patentability and the non-obviousness standard

As explained in Chapter 10, the NOS prevents patent rights to be granted for trivial improvements over former inventions so that inventors are encouraged to pursue larger, (socially) more valuable discoveries.[1] The assumptions introduced in Chapter 10 are maintained here, and only two additional assumptions have to be introduced. Firstly, firms of both countries draw the inventive step of an invention from a common distribution $F[u_k]$. In particular, this means that the properties of the distribution depend on the product or technology line rather than on the innovator's origin or expertise.[2]

Secondly, both countries independently decide on the NOS s_i. Therefore, the NOSs might differ across countries. Judging from the results obtained in Chapter 10, one would expect that the country whose firms are more productive in generating inventions choose the higher NOS.

Since invention k is only patentable in country i if $u_k \geq s_i$, an invention of a given size may be eligible for a patent in one country, but not in the other. Without loss of generality, consider the case of $s_A < s_B$, i.e. the NOS in country B is higher than that in country A. Then, the probability that a given invention is patentable in country i is given by $\theta_i := 1 - F[s_i]$. Since it is assumed that country B invokes the stronger NOS ($s_A < s_B$), it is true that $\theta_A > \theta_B$. Accordingly, three cases can be distinguished: (i) $u_k < s_A < s_B$ so that the invention is not patentable in either country. This event occurs with probability $1 - \theta_A$. (ii) $s_A \leq u_k < s_B$ so that the discovery qualifies for a patent in country A but not in country B. For any given innovation, the corresponding probability is $\theta_A - \theta_B$. (iii) If $s_A < s_B \leq u_k \leq \bar{u}$, the discovery is patentable in both countries. The event occurs with probability θ_B. Analogous considerations apply for a situation in which $s_A > s_B$.

In case the countries set a uniform NOS, i.e. if $s_A = s_B$, markets become indistinguishable as far as patents are concerned: a given invention is either patentable or unpatentable in both countries. Here, the probability that the discovery is patentable is $\theta_A = \theta_B$.

It is instructive to compare the case in which countries decide for a uniform NOS and the one in which the NOSs are diverging. When the NOSs are identical in both countries, they protect the same inventions. In contrast, if the NOSs are different, the country applying the stricter NOS issues fewer, but (socially) more valuable patents. The other country grants more patents, but for inventions that have a lower average value. Thus, markets become distinct when the NOSs differ. Since larger inventions arise on average less frequently, the country setting the higher NOS protects them not only against imitation, but also guarantees on average a longer patent life and, thus, higher returns. As every inventor will apply for a patent in all countries where the invention meets the NOS, cross-border profit flows will be observed.[3]

13.1.2 Demand and prices

Again, the main assumptions concerning the preference structure and the firms' price setting behaviour introduced in Chapter 10 are upheld. In particular, it is postulated that consumers have identical preferences in both countries, i.e. they have a reservation price of u_k, where u_k denotes the improvement size of the invention concluding the kth patent race over the previous invention.

As before, firms of both countries are engaged in Bertrand competition in each market. The product markets of country A and B are of equal size in the sense that the total demand in each countries is normalized to one. Accordingly, a firm occupying the monopoly position in both countries faces total demand of two units.

13.1.3 The firms' position in an ex-post situation

Suppose that the countries have chosen different NOSs, i.e. $s_A \neq s_B$. Then, there are some inventions that are only patentable in the country having the weaker NOS. In this situation, a firm can be in four positions z^d, $d \in \{B, S, W, N\}$.

z^B: The firm is the incumbent in both markets.
z^S: The firm holds the monopoly position in the country imposing the stricter NOS.
z^W: The firm holds the monopoly position in the country applying the weaker NOS.
z^N: The firm is a challenger in both markets.

Clearly, a firm in position z^B has made a large innovation that meets the stronger NOS during the last patent race so that it holds the incumbency in both markets. In contrast, positions z^S and z^W refer to situation in which firms occupy the monopoly position in only one market. The position z^W is reached when the firm made a small invention that only meets the weaker NOS, but not the stricter condition. In contrast, position z^S is only accessible through position z^B. The firm must previously have made a large invention so that it held the monopoly position in both countries, i.e. it was in state z^B. The last invention, however, was made by another firm that achieved only a small improvement, so that the second firm could only apply for a patent in the country with the weaker NOS. Consequently, the first firm loses the incumbency in that country, but keeps the monopoly position in the one with the stricter NOS. Obviously, this position can only be reached after the second patent race.

In case the countries set a uniform NOS, i.e. $s_A = s_B$, inventions are either patentable or unpatentable in both countries. Accordingly, only two positions are relevant: z^I signifying that the firm is the incumbent in both markets or z^C showing the the firm is a challenger in both markets.

13.1.4 The expected profits

Since domestic and foreign firms only differ in their innovation efficiency and not in their production efficiency, two firms having made an invention of identical size will earn the same profit in a given market irrespective of their origin. Consequently, the country index for profits can be dropped. Let C denote the constant research costs per period. The function $\bar{\pi}^d(\bar{u}, s_A, s_B)$ is the profit gross of investment costs that a firm in position z^d can expect to earn. Then, the function $\pi^d(\bar{u}, s_A, s_B) := \bar{\pi}^d(\cdot) - C$ is the corresponding expected net profit. To facilitate notation $\pi^d(\bar{u}, s_A, s_B)$ is frequently abbreviated by π^d. In addition, let ψ and ρ be defined as $\psi := \max\{s_A, s_B\}$ and $\rho := \min\{s_A, s_B\}$. Obviously, the countries set a uniform NOS if $\psi = \rho$.

First, consider the position z^N. A firm in this position is a challenger in both markets. Owing to patent protection, the firm cannot offer a product based on the latest technology so that it receives no positive revenues. A challenger's profit is given by

$$\pi^N = \pi^C = -C, \quad \text{for } \psi \geq \rho. \tag{13.1}$$

Next, take the case of position z^B. The firm has made a large invention and occupies the monopoly position in both countries. It charges a price equal to the invention's inventive step. The expected price conditional on the invention being a large one, i.e. of $u_k \geq \psi$, is given by $\int_\psi^{\bar{u}} u_k f[u_k] \, du_k / (1 - F[\psi])$. Since the range of the improvement size is stationary over all patent races, and the firms face a unit demand in both countries, the expected instantaneous profit reads

$$\pi^B = \pi^I = 2 \int_\psi^{\bar{u}} u_k \frac{f[u_k]}{1 - F[\psi]} \, du_k - C, \quad \text{for } \psi \geq \rho. \tag{13.2}$$

Now turn to position z^W indicating that the firm holds the monopoly position in the country imposing the weaker NOS. Thus, the firm has made a small invention that does not qualify for a patent in the country applying the stricter NOS. Then, the expected price conditional on the invention being small is $\int_\rho^\psi u_k f[u_k] \, du_k / (F[\psi] - F[\rho])$. In case the NOSs are identical in both countries, i.e. when $\psi = \rho$, any invention that meets the NOS qualifies for a patent in both countries so that the inventor starts the next patent race as the incumbent in both countries. The expected instantaneous profits associated with this situation are determined with

$$\pi^W = \begin{cases} \int_\rho^\psi u_k \dfrac{f[u_k]}{F[\psi] - F[\rho]} \, du_k - C & \text{for } \psi > \rho, \\[3mm] 2 \int_\psi^{\bar{u}} u_k \dfrac{f[u_k]}{1 - F[\psi]} \, du_k - C & \text{for } \psi = \rho. \end{cases} \tag{13.3}$$

Finally, consider a firm in position z^S. Here, the firm is the sole supplier in the market imposing the stricter NOS, but a challenger in the one applying the weaker NOS. Consequently, the expected price charged by the firm can be written as $\int_\psi^{\bar{u}} u_k f[u_k]\, du_k / (1 - F[\psi])$. In case the countries choose a uniform NOS, i.e. if $\psi = \rho$, the firm finds itself in the position of a challenger since its invention becomes either obsolete in both countries or in neither of the two. Thus, the expected profit ensues with

$$\pi^S = \begin{cases} \displaystyle\int_\psi^{\bar{u}} u_k \frac{f[u_k]}{1 - F[\psi]}\, du_k - C & \text{for } \psi > \rho, \\ -C & \text{for } \psi = \rho. \end{cases} \qquad (13.4)$$

From the definition of the expected profits in (13.1)–(13.4), certain relations among the profit functions can be derived:

Lemma 13.1. The following conditions can directly be verified from the functions in (13.1)–(13.4):

1. If $\psi = \rho$, then

$$\pi^B = \pi^W = \pi^I, \quad \pi^N = \pi^S = \pi^C \quad \text{and} \quad \pi^I > \pi^C.$$

2. If $\psi > \rho$, then

$$\pi^B > \pi^S > \pi^W > \pi^N, \quad \pi^I > \pi^W.$$

For illustrative purpose, take the home country B's point of view according to which the foreign NOS s_A is given. The first result verifies that markets become indistinguishable when the home country applies the same NOS as the foreign country. Consequently, z^B and z^W as well as z^S and z^N collapse.

The second result applies when the domestic NOS differs from the foreign one. It states that being an incumbent in either market is more profitable than being a challenger in both markets ($\pi^W > \pi^N$). In addition, being the monopolist in the market with the stricter NOS yields a larger expected profit than the same position in the market with the weaker NOS ($\pi^S > \pi^W$). Finally, the expected profits from being an incumbent in both markets is always higher than the expected earnings received from only one market ($\pi^B > \pi^S$).

The results are a consequence of the assumptions concerning the consumers' preferences and Bertrand competition. With a completely inelastic demand there is always a positive relationship between the expected price and the expected profit. Since products using larger inventions can be sold at higher prices, profits that are earned in the country enforcing the stricter NOS are on average larger than the ones received in the other country.

It is worth noting that while the functions π^B and π^N are continuous, the functions π^L and π^S are not. Both functions are discontinuous at $\psi = \rho$.

13.2 Differences in the non-obviousness standard and their effect on firms

13.2.1 The value functions

The ex-post situation

Assume that the countries have chosen different NOSs, i.e. $\psi > \rho$. Then, a firm is in one of the four positions z^d, $d \in \{B, S, W, N\}$, after the first patent race has been concluded. Each position is associated with a continuation value V_i^d. Together, they have to satisfy the following system of Bellman equations:

$$rV_i^B = \pi^B + \mathfrak{h}_i^l \Big[\theta_\psi (V_i^N - V_i^B) + \Delta\theta (V_i^S - V_i^B) \Big],$$

$$rV_i^S = \pi^S + \mathfrak{h}_i^l \theta_\psi (V_i^N - V_i^S) + \mathfrak{h}_i^w \theta_\rho (V_i^B - V_i^S),$$

$$rV_i^W = \pi^W + \mathfrak{h}_i^l \theta_\rho (V_i^N - V_i^W) + \mathfrak{h}_i^w \theta_\psi (V_i^B - V_i^W), \tag{13.5}$$

$$rV_i^N = \pi^N + \mathfrak{h}_i^w \Big[\theta_\psi (V_i^B - V_i^N) + \Delta\theta (V_i^W - V_i^N) \Big],$$

where the subscript i refers to the firms' country of residence. The parameters θ_ψ, θ_ρ and $\Delta\theta$ are defined as $\theta_\psi := 1 - F[\psi]$, $\theta_\rho := 1 - F[\rho]$ and $\Delta\theta := \theta_\rho - \theta_\psi$. They denote the probability that an innovation meets the stricter NOS, the weaker NOS and the weaker but not the stricter one.

Here, $\mathfrak{h}_i^l$ and $\mathfrak{h}_i^w$ are the hazard rates at which the firm under consideration loses and wins the current patent race. As in the previous chapter, they are given by $\mathfrak{h}_i^l := (n_i - 1)\lambda_i + n_j\lambda_j$ and $\mathfrak{h}_i^w := \lambda_i$. The hazard rates yield information about the chances that the patent race ends between t and $t + dt$ owing to the occurrence of an invention in general, but they tell nothing about whether the invention will be patentable. Yet, only patentable inventions bring about changes in the firms' positions.[4] Therefore, the hazard rates have to be extended.

Take the example of a firm in position z^B (cf first equation in 13.5). The firm receives an instantaneous profit of π^B until the current patent race ends. The chances that a competitor makes a discovery first is $\mathfrak{h}_i^l$, and the probability that a given invention is a large one is θ_ψ. Hence, the combined probability that the firm loses the monopoly position in both markets between t and $t + dt$ is $\mathfrak{h}_i^l \theta_\psi$. In this situation, the firm starts the subsequent patent race as a challenger (z^N) in both markets so that the expected loss amounts to $\mathfrak{h}_i^l \theta_\psi (V_i^N - V_i^B)$.

However, a competitor's invention need not to be a large one. With probability $\Delta\theta$, it will be a small invention that is patentable in the country with the weak NOS although unpatentable in the other country. The probability that a firm in position z^B loses its dominance in the *low-quality* market, but not in the *high-quality* market is given by $\mathfrak{h}_i^l \Delta\theta$. In this case, the firm will be in position z^S during the next patent race and the expected loss equals $\mathfrak{h}_i^l \Delta\theta (V_i^S - V_i^B)$. Finally, if a competitor's invention is unpatentable (with overall probability $\mathfrak{h}_i^l \theta_\rho$) or succeeds in developing the next invention first (with probability $\mathfrak{h}_i^w$) a change in positions does not take place so that the firm remains the incumbent in both markets. By analogy, the other Bellman equations can be derived.

The system of Bellman equations possesses two characteristics worth mentioning here. Firstly, domestic and foreign firms may differ in their innovation efficiency λ_i and in turn in their hazard rates. A firm from a developing country (say B) will have a smaller chance of making a discovery, i.e. $\mathfrak{h}_B^w = \lambda_B < \lambda_A = \mathfrak{h}_A^w$. Therefore, the hazard rates are country specific. A direct consequence is that the continuation values depend on the firms' domicile as well. Secondly, from a firm's point of view, countries are interchangeable as far as the NOSs are concerned, i.e. continuation values depend solely on the level of the NOSs, but not on which particular country enforces them. This property follows from the assumption that firms are equally efficient in production despite differences in their research ability.

Before presenting the solution to the system (13.5), two variables are introduced to facilitate notation. Let ϕ_v be defined as $\phi_v := r + \theta_v(\mathfrak{h}_i^w + \mathfrak{h}_i^l)$, $v = \psi, \rho$ and $i = A, B$.[5] In addition, a *core value* $\bar{V}_i$ is introduced with $\bar{V}_i := [\theta_\psi(\mathfrak{h}_i^w V_i^B + \mathfrak{h}_i^l V_i^N) + \Delta\theta(\mathfrak{h}_i^w V_i^W + \mathfrak{h}_i^l V_i^N)]/\phi_\rho$. This core value measures the discounted expected value of having created a patentable invention independent of the position in the current patent race and is equivalent to

$$\bar{V}_i = \frac{1}{r\phi_\psi\phi_\rho}\left[\mathfrak{h}_i^w\theta_\psi\phi_\psi(\pi^B - \pi^W) + \phi_\psi\theta_\rho(\mathfrak{h}_i^w\pi^W + \mathfrak{h}_i^l\pi^N)\right.$$
$$\left. + \Delta\theta\left(\theta_\psi\mathfrak{h}_i^l\mathfrak{h}_i^w(\pi^S - \pi^N) + \mathfrak{h}_i^{w2}\theta_\psi(\pi^B - \pi^W)\right)\right].$$

Then, the value functions V_i^d satisfying the system of Bellman equations (13.5) are given by

$$V_i^d = \bar{V}_i + v_i^d, \quad d \in \{B, S, W, N\}, \text{ where}$$

$$v_i^B = \frac{\pi^B}{\phi_\rho} + \frac{\Delta\theta}{\phi_\psi\phi_\rho}\left[\mathfrak{h}_i^w(\pi^B - \pi^W) + \mathfrak{h}_i^l(\pi^S - \pi^N)\right],$$

$$v_i^S = \frac{\pi^S}{\phi_\rho} + \frac{\Delta\theta}{\phi_\psi\phi_\rho}\left[\mathfrak{h}_i^w(\pi^B - \pi^W) + \mathfrak{h}_i^l(\pi^S - \pi^N)\right],$$

$$v_i^W = \frac{\pi^W}{\phi_\rho}, \qquad\qquad\qquad\qquad\qquad\qquad\qquad (13.6)$$

$$v_i^N = \frac{\pi^N}{\phi_\rho}.$$

It can be seen that the core value is the principal component of all continuation values. Recalling its interpretation as the discounted expected value of a patentable invention, this is not surprising. The functions v_i^d are the position-specific parts of the value functions. The first term of v_i^d denotes the profit stream that a firm in position z^d can expect to earn over and above the value of a patentable invention until the next small invention arises.[6] Consequently, the second term of v_i^B and v_i^S measures the profit stream a firm in the respective position is able to receive until the next large invention is made.

Observe that the instantaneous profit of a firm in any position will be negative if the research costs C are (prohibitively) large. For sufficiently small values of C, only the instantaneous profit of a challenger, i.e. a firm in position z^N, is negative as it consists entirely of research expenses. However, owing to the forward-looking nature of the continuation values, the core value will be positive. As long as the core value is larger than the discounted profits earned until the next small inventions arises, the continuation value V_i^N is non-negative. To ensure that a firm currently being a challenger in both markets has incentives to participate in the current patent race, it is henceforth assumed that V_i^N is non-negative.

The corresponding continuation values for the case of a uniform NOS can be obtained as special cases of V_i^N and V_i^B, where $\psi = \rho$.

The equations in (13.6) and Lemma 13.1 directly imply:

Lemma 13.2. The value functions have the same properties as the profit functions, i.e.

1. if $\psi = \rho$, then

$$V_i^B = V_i^W = V_i^I, \quad V_i^N = V_i^S = V_i^C, \text{ with } V_i^I > V_i^C.$$

2. If $\psi > \rho$, then

$$V_i^B > V_i^S > V_i^W > V_i^N, \quad V_i^I > V_i^W.$$

The next result shows how the continuation values are affected by changes in the probability that a competitor achieves a discovery within the next instant.

Lemma 13.3. All value functions V_i^d, $d \in \{B, S, W, N, I, C\}$, are decreasing in $\mathfrak{h}_i^l$.

An increase of the hazard rate $\mathfrak{h}_i^l$ exerts its influence on the continuation values in two ways. Firstly, they increase the rivals' chances of winning the current and all future patent races. Secondly, a patent race becomes on average shorter so that the economic patent life decreases. In Section 12.2, both channels were summarized as the global effect which is negative. The individual effect also described in Section 12.2 is not triggered by changes in $\mathfrak{h}_i^l$ so that the overall effect of $\mathfrak{h}_i^l$ is negative.

Recall that the hazard rate $\mathfrak{h}_i^l$ is an increasing function of the number of firms and their research efficiencies in both countries. In contrast, $\mathfrak{h}_i^w$ solely consists of the own research ability λ_i. Consequently, Lemma 13.3 summarizes the individual effects exerted by changes in the research efficiency of a foreign firm λ_j and the number of firms in either country.

The ex-ante version

In order to study the effects of diverging NOSs on future production and technology lines, the ex-ante value function has to be derived. Since a firm cannot reach position z^S after the first patent race, the ex-ante value function for a firm i can be defined as $V_i^0 := \mathfrak{h}_i^w \left[\theta_\psi V_i^B + \Delta \theta V_i^W + (1 - \theta_\rho) V_i^N \right] + \mathfrak{h}_i^l V_i^N$. Using the definition of the core value function $\bar{V}_i$, the ex-ante version can be written as

$$V_i^0 = \phi_\rho \bar{V}_i + (1 - \theta_\rho)(\mathfrak{h}_i^w + \mathfrak{h}_i^l)\bar{V}_i + v_i^N. \tag{13.7}$$

Again, the corresponding ex-ante value function for the case of a uniform NOS can be derived by imposing $\psi = \rho$ which implies $\theta_\psi = \theta_\rho$.

13.2.2 The effect of a diverging domestic non-obviousness standard on firms

The ex-post situation

For expositional reasons, it is assumed that the foreign NOS s_j is exogenously given. Then, the domestic NOS can be smaller than ($\psi = s_j$), larger than ($\psi = s_i$), or equal to ($\psi = s_j = \rho$) to the foreign NOS s_j. When the whole range for the domestic NOSs $[0, \bar{u}]$ is considered, the value functions V_i^S and V_i^W are discontinuous at $s_i = s_j$. Whereas V_i^S jumps downwards, V_i^W jumps upwards at this point. Hence, to evaluate the situation of internationally diverging NOSs against a uniform NOS, marginal analysis cannot be used. Instead, the value functions at some NOS $s_i', s_i' \neq s_j$, have to be compared directly to the corresponding value functions at $s_i = s_j$.

Let $\Delta \bar{V}_i$ and ΔV_i^d be defined as $\Delta \bar{V}_i := \bar{V}_i|_{\psi \neq \rho} - \bar{V}_i|_{\psi = \rho}$ and $\Delta V_i^d := V_i^d|_{\psi \neq \rho} - V_i^d|_{\psi = \rho}$. The functions measure the advantage or disadvantage of a diverging domestic NOS over a situation of a uniform NOS. Clearly, a firm in position z^d benefits from an international differentiation in the NOSs if ΔV_i^d is positive.

Proposition 13.1.   If $s_i > s_j$ and $\{s_i, s_j\}$ are such that $G := \theta_i \mathfrak{h}_i^w (\bar{\pi}^B - \bar{\pi}^W) - (r + \theta_i \mathfrak{h}_i^l)\bar{\pi}^W > 0$, $i, l = A, B$, then ΔV_i^B, ΔV_i^S and ΔV_i^N are positive.

As Figure 13.1 shows for a numerical example, the restriction G tends to be satisfied for small values of the foreign NOS s_j. Then, the proposition states that there exist some combinations of a stronger domestic and a weaker foreign NOS so that firms in positions z^B, z^S and z^N gain by this international differentiation of NOSs.

A stronger domestic NOS affects the value functions V_i^d in two ways: through earning possibilities in future patent races and the expected profits from the

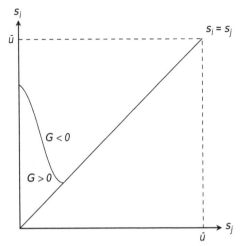

The restriction is calculated for a cumulative distribution function of $F[u] = 1-(\bar{u}-u)^2/\bar{u}^2$

Figure 13.1 Restriction.

current one. When there is a uniform NOS, both markets grant patents for the same inventions so that a firm is always the incumbent or a challenger in both markets. Every invention, even large ones, faces the same risk of becoming obsolete in the near future. This fact changes when countries set different NOSs. Then, there is a *high*-quality and a *low*-quality market. Whereas a large invention still leads to patent rights in both countries, a small invention does not. Since larger inventions arise less frequently, a firm holding the monopoly position in both markets now faces different risks of becoming a challenger in the two countries. The expected incumbency term in the low-quality market is shorter compared to the one in the high-quality market. As a consequence, the expected profits in the high-quality market and, thus, the value of being in position z^B or z^S increases. As every firm (even one in position z^W) has a positive probability of making a large invention in future, the continuation values tend to be larger when the NOSs are differentiated.

The effect of differentiated NOSs on future earning possibilities is the only channel by which a firm in position z^N is affected. Firms in positions z^B or z^S gain even in the current patent race since the expected economic patent life in the high-quality market is longer. In contrast, a firm in position z^W will on average experience a shorter economic patent life for its invention in the low-quality market. Accordingly, the expected profits during the current patent race are lower for a firm in position z^W. If the effect of a stronger domestic NOS on the future earning possibilities is larger than that on the current ones, even a firm in position z^W will gain from internationally differentiated NOSs.

Finally, observe that Proposition 13.1 holds for domestic and foreign firms alike. Unfortunately, an equivalent result cannot be obtained for the case of a weaker domestic NOS.

The ex-ante situation

When future product and technology lines are concerned, the ex-ante value function V_l^0 has to be used. Denoting by ΔV_l^0 a country l firm's advantage or disadvantage of internationally differentiated NOSs, we find:

Proposition 13.2.   If $G := \theta_\psi \mathfrak{h}_l^w (\bar{\pi}^B - \bar{\pi}^W) - (r + \theta_\psi \mathfrak{h}_l')\bar{\pi}^W > 0$, $l = A, B$, a firm in an ex-ante situation benefits from diverging NOSs irrespective of which country enforces the stricter one.

For a situation in which the domestic NOS is stricter than the foreign one, the result is a natural consequence of Proposition 13.1, especially since a firm in position z^W need not to be worse off as compared to a situation with a uniform NOS. Observe that Proposition 13.2 holds also for the case in which the domestic NOS is weaker than the foreign one. A similar result cannot be obtained for the ex-post situation. Consequently, if all firms are on an equal footing and do not know which position they will occupy in the next patent race, there are combinations $\{s_i, s_j\}$ for which firms strictly prefer the NOSs to diverge.

13.3 The optimal non-obviousness standard

In this section, the home and the foreign country's decision on the optimal level of the NOS is studied. It is assumed that governments make their choices independently. In a first step, the optimal NOS is determined for a given NOS of the other country. In the second step, both countries set their NOS simultaneously.

Owing to the stochastic nature of the innovation process, countries also switch between different positions after the first patent race has taken place, and the countries will experience position-specific welfare streams. In general, the policymakers' decision can be examined separately for the ex-post and the ex-ante situation. However, as the countries move continuously between different states in an ex-post situation, the optimal choice would be time inconsistent: the policymaker would wish to change the optimal NOS whenever the country's position changes. Clearly, such behaviour does not establish an economic framework in which private enterprises may reliably undertake research. Consequently, it is assumed that governments of both countries are far-sighted and base their decisions on the ex-ante welfare function.

13.3.1 The general forms of the social welfare functions

A country's position

Owing to the fact that a policymaker will take the firm's as well as the consumer's surplus into account, the country's and the firm's point-of-view differs. This manifests itself also in the states. Assume that $\psi > \rho$. Then, the four positions of a firm z^d, $d \in \{B, S, W, N\}$ are mutually excluding for a firm; it can only be in one of those states. However, if there are two or more firms in a country, there may arise situations in which two firms of the same country occupy the incumbency in different markets. Thus, a country may be in five different states:

y^{B_1}: One firm is the incumbent in both markets and the $(n_i - 1)$ remaining firms are challengers;

y^{B_2}: One of the firms in country i is the incumbent in market A, another country i firm holds the monopoly position in country B and $(n_i - 2)$ firms are challengers;

y^S: One firm is the incumbent in the high-quality market and $(n_i - 1)$ firms are challengers;

y^W: One firm holds the monopoly position in the low-quality market and $(n_i - 1)$ firms are challengers;

y^N: All n_i firms are challengers.

As before, the case of a uniform NOS can be treated as a special case where $\psi = \rho$. Then, the states y^{B_1}, y^{B_2} and y^W on the one hand and y^S and y^N on the other hand collapse into y^I and y^C respectively.

The country's instantaneous welfare

As usual, a country's welfare comprises the consumer's and the firm's surplus. Owing to the specific demand and market structure presumed here, the incumbent is always able to appropriate the entire consumer's surplus. Thus, a country's instantaneous welfare just equals the sum of the domestic firm's profits:

$$\omega_i^{B_1} = \pi^B + (n_i - 1)\pi^N,$$
$$\omega_i^{B_2} = \pi^S + \pi^W + (n_i - 2)\pi^N,$$
$$\omega_i^S = \pi^S + (n_i - 1)\pi^N, \qquad (13.8)$$
$$\omega_i^W = \pi^W + (n_i - 1)\pi^N,$$
$$\omega_i^N = n_i\pi^N,$$

where ω_i^d is short for $\omega_i(y^d)$.

Again, the now familiar pattern can be found for the instantaneous welfare:

Lemma 13.4. By the definition of a country's state and the profit functions (13.1)–(13.4), it immediately follows that:

1. if $\psi = \rho$

$$\omega_i^{B_1} = \omega_i^{B_2} = \omega_i^W = \omega_i^I, \quad \omega_i^N = \omega_i^S = \omega_i^C, \quad \omega_i^I > \omega_i^C.$$

2. If $\psi \neq \rho$

$$\omega_i^{B_1} > \omega_i^{B_2} > \omega_i^{S} > \omega_i^{W} > \omega_i^{N}, \quad \omega_i^{I} > \omega_i^{W}.$$

The lemma verifies that the situation of a uniform NOS across countries is a special case of a situation of internationally diverging NOSs when a country's position collapses. For the case of internationally differing NOSs, we find that having one firm that occupies a monopoly position is better as compared to a situation where all domestic firms are challengers ($\omega_i^{W} > \omega_i^{N}$). Given one firm is the incumbent, society prefers the firm to be the monopoly in the high-quality market because the expected profits are higher ($\omega_i^{S} > \omega_i^{W}$). Naturally, still higher profits can be earned when both markets are served by domestic firms ($\omega_i^{B_2} > \omega_i^{S}$). The fact that society prefers one firm as incumbent over two firms holding the monopoly position ($\omega_i^{B_1} > \omega_i^{B_2}$) arises because in y^{B_1} the *world-wide* monopoly has made a large invention and, therefore, receives on average higher profits than two firms in situation y^{B_2}.

Note also that states y^{B_1}, y^{B_2} and y^{N} necessarily involve cross-border profit flows which are directed either inwards (y^{B_1} or y^{B_2}) or outwards (y^{N}). In contrast, in positions y^{S} and y^{W}, cross-country profit flows can only be observed if domestic firms hold the monopoly position in the foreign market. In those situations, inflows and outflows of profits occur simultaneously, where the country whose firm is the incumbent in the market imposing the stricter NOS experiences net inflows.

The social welfare functions

In an ex-post situation, a country's discounted expected welfare stream depends on its position during the current patent race. Let W_i^d denote the social welfare function. Then they have to satisfy the following system of equations:

$$rW_i^{B_1} = \omega_i^{B_1} + \mathfrak{k}_i^{l}\theta_\psi(W_i^{N} - W_i^{B_1}) + \mathfrak{k}_i^{w}\Delta\theta(W_i^{B_2} - W_i^{B_1}),$$

$$rW_i^{B_2} = \omega_i^{B_2} + \mathfrak{k}_i^{l}\left[\theta_\psi(W_i^{N} - W_i^{B_2}) + \Delta\theta(W_i^{S} - W_i^{B_2})\right]$$
$$+ \mathfrak{k}_i^{w}\theta_\psi(W_i^{B_1} - W_i^{B_2}),$$

$$rW_i^{S} = \omega_i^{S} + \mathfrak{k}_i^{l}\theta_\psi(W_i^{N} - W_i^{S})$$
$$+ \mathfrak{k}_i^{w}\left[\theta_\psi(W_i^{B_1} - W_i^{S}) + \Delta\theta(W_i^{B_2} - W_i^{S})\right], \tag{13.9}$$

$$rW_i^{W} = \omega_i^{W} + \mathfrak{k}_i^{l}\theta_\rho(W_i^{N} - W_i^{W}) + \mathfrak{k}_i^{w}\theta_\psi(W_i^{B_1} - W_i^{W}),$$

$$rW_i^{N} = \omega_i^{N} + \mathfrak{k}_i^{w}\left[\theta_\psi(W_i^{B_1} - W_i^{N}) + \Delta\theta(W_i^{W} - W_i^{N})\right].$$

Here, the hazard rates $\mathfrak{k}_i^{w}$ and $\mathfrak{k}_i^{l}$ are defined by $\mathfrak{k}_i^{w} := n_i\lambda_i$ and $\mathfrak{k}_i^{l} := n_j\lambda_j$ respectively.

Explicit expressions of the social continuation values are obtained by solving the system above. To express the social welfare functions in an convenient way, additional variables are introduced. Let $\phi_{\rho\psi}$ be $\phi_{\rho\psi} := r + \theta_\psi \mathfrak{k}_i^l + \theta_\rho \mathfrak{k}_i^w$. The function $\bar{W}_i$ denotes the *core value* of the social welfare functions and is defined as $\bar{W}_i := [\theta_\psi(\mathfrak{k}_i^w W_i^{B1} + \mathfrak{k}_i^l W_i^N) + \Delta\theta(\mathfrak{k}_i^w W_i^W + \mathfrak{k}_i^l W_i^N)]/\phi_\rho$. This core value $\bar{W}_i$ is the society's equivalent to a firm's core value and measures the social welfare of a patentable invention independent of the position in the current patent race. The social core value can be expressed as:

$$
\bar{W}_i = \frac{1}{r\phi_\psi\phi_\rho\phi_{\rho\psi}} \left\{ \phi_{\rho\psi} \left[\theta_\psi \mathfrak{k}_i^w(\omega_i^{B1} - \omega_i^W) + \theta_\rho\phi_\rho(\mathfrak{k}_i w\omega_i^W + \mathfrak{k}_i^l\omega_i^N) \right] \right.
$$
$$
+ \Delta\theta\theta_\psi \mathfrak{k}_i^w \left[\theta_{\rho\psi} \mathfrak{k}_i^w(\omega_i^{B2} - \omega_i^W) + \phi_\psi \mathfrak{k}_i^l(\omega_i^W - \omega_i^N) \quad (13.10)
$$
$$
\left. + \Delta\theta \mathfrak{k}_i^l \mathfrak{k}_i^w(\omega_i^S - \omega_i^N) \right] \right\}.
$$

Then, the social welfare functions satisfying system (13.9) are given by:

$$
W_i^d = \bar{W}_i + w_i^d, \quad d \in \{B_1, B_2, S, W, N\},
$$

$$
w_i^{B_1} = \frac{\omega_i^{B_1}}{\phi_\rho} + \frac{\Delta\theta}{\phi_\psi\phi_\rho\phi_{\rho\psi}} \left[\mathfrak{k}_i^l\phi_\rho(\omega_i^{B_1} - \omega_i^W) + \mathfrak{k}_i^w\phi_{\rho\psi}(\omega_i^{B_2} - \omega_i^N) \right.
$$
$$
\left. + \Delta\theta \mathfrak{k}_i^l \mathfrak{k}_i^w(\omega_i^S - \omega_i^N) \right]
$$

$$
w_i^{B_2} = \frac{\omega_i^{B_2}}{\phi_\rho} + \frac{\Delta\theta}{\phi_\psi\phi_\rho} \left[\mathfrak{k}_i^w(\omega_i^{B_2} - \omega_i^W) + \mathfrak{k}_i^l(\omega_i^S - \omega_i^N) \right] \qquad (13.11)
$$

$$
w_i^S = \frac{\omega_i^S}{\phi_\rho} + \frac{\Delta\theta}{\phi_\psi\phi_\rho} \left[\mathfrak{k}_i^w(\omega_i^{B_2} - \omega_i^W) + \mathfrak{k}_i^l(\omega_i^S - \omega_i^N) \right]
$$

$$
w_i^W = \frac{\omega_i^W}{\phi_\rho},
$$

$$
w_i^N = \frac{\omega_i^N}{\phi_\rho}.
$$

The structural similarity of the social continuation values to the firm's value functions is obvious. The society's social welfare consists of the state-independent core value $\bar{W}_i$ measuring the value of a patentable invention and the position-specific parts. The latter comprise the welfare accumulated during the current patent race, i.e. the first term of w_i^d, and the part of the social welfare that can only be accrued if the NOSs differ across countries, i.e. the second term of $w_i^{B_1}$, $w_i^{B_2}$ and w_i^S.

Again, the corresponding welfare functions for a uniform NOS are derived as the special case of $\psi = \rho$ which is confirmed by the following result:

Lemma 13.5. The social continuation values have the same properties as the instantaneous welfare functions, i.e.

1. if $\psi = \rho$

$$W_i^{B_1} = W_i^{B_2} = W_i^W = W_i^I, \quad W_i^N = W_i^S = W_i^C, \quad W_i^I > W_i^C.$$

2. If $\psi > \rho$

$$W_i^{B_1} > W_i^{B_2} > W_i^S > W_i^W > W_i^N, \quad W_i^I > W_i^W.$$

The policymaker's objective function in determining the NOS, however, is the ex-ante social welfare function. Given the definitions of a country's position in an ongoing patent race, it can be defined as $W_i^0 := \ell_i^w [\phi_\psi W_i^{B_1} + \Delta\theta W_i^S + (1 - \phi_\rho)W_i^N] + \ell_i^l W_i^N$. Using the core value, the ex-ante social welfare function can be simplified to:

$$W_i^0 = \phi_\rho \bar{W}_i + (1 - \theta_\rho)(\ell_i^l + \ell_i^w)W_i^N. \tag{13.12}$$

13.3.2 The society's unilateral decision

When considering the government's decision problem, two situations arise: (1) policymaker's in both countries simultaneously choose the NOS, or (2) only one of the countries wishes to adjust the NOS. In this section the latter situation is examined.

A government may unilaterally set the NOS, e.g. because it extended the patentable subject matters and some NOS has to be imposed or because domestic firms improved their research abilities so that an adjustment becomes necessary. In either case, the foreign country's NOS s_j is regarded to be exogenously given. Then, the domestic policymaker's decision problem consists in setting a NOS s_i so that the ex-ante social welfare function W_i^0 is maximized. As it can be seen from equation (13.12), the ex-ante welfare function consists of two parts: (a) where $s_i \in [s_j, \bar{u}]$ and (b) where $s_i \in [0, s_j)$.

Lemma 13.6. Concerning the properties of the ex-ante welfare function, we find:

1. For $\ell_i^w = n_i = 0$, W_i^0 equals zero.
2. For $\ell_i^w, \ell_i^l > 0$, W_i^0 is continuous at $s_i = s_j$.
3. For $\ell_i^w, \ell_i^l > 0$, W_i^0 has decreasing differences at $s_i = s_j$.

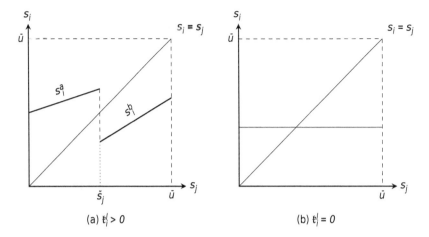

Figure 13.2 The optimal non-obviousness standard for the domestic country.

A situation as described in Lemma 13.6.1 resembles that of a developing country: firms have no research ability, i.e. $\lambda_i = 0$ and, consequently, there are no firms that could participate in global patent races, i.e. $n_i = 0$.[7] The lemma asserts that a developing country is indifferent towards a patent system if its domestic firms have no chance to win a future patent race. The consumer's surplus generated by the introduction of new products or processes is completely appropriated by the foreign inventors. As a consequence, a developing country is also indifferent to the NOS it introduces.[8]

Proposition 13.3. If a country unilaterally decides on the optimal NOS, an equilibrium is ensured:

1. If $t_i^w = n_i = 0$, any NOS in the range of $[0, \bar{u}]$ is optimal.
2. If $t_i^w > 0$ there exists a unique $s_i^* \in [0, \bar{u}]$ that maximizes equation (13.12) for any $s_j \in [0, \bar{u}]$.

Concerning the properties of the optimal NOS, the following can be discerned:

Proposition 13.4. For $t_i^w > 0$, Figure 13.2 shows the optimal NOS as a function of the foreign NOS s_j.

A direct consequence of the proposition is that the domestic (industrialized) country will never choose the same level of NOS as the foreign country no matter how similar or dissimilar the countries are. To understand the rationale behind the tendency for differentiation, it is important to note that society's welfare depends on both the level of the instantaneous profits and the duration (effective patent term) over which they can be earned. Increasing the level of instantaneous profits can be achieved by raising the domestic NOS. Since larger inventions occur less frequently, this policy also prolongs the effective patent term. With global patent races and national patent policy, however, patent policy instruments are a two-edged knife as long as both countries have research abilities. Then, a stronger domestic NOS has positive effects on domestic *as well as* foreign welfare.

While the foreign NOS s_j is small, larger inventions are still frequently enough so that choosing a higher domestic NOS pays, i.e. the positive effects on the domestic welfare dominate. When s_j becomes large, setting a still larger domestic NOS implies that eligible inventions become rare. Although this policy increases the instantaneous profits as well as the effective patent term and, therefore, may still be optimal for national patent races, it has a severe disadvantage too: it prolongs the average time until a domestic firm makes a patentable invention when the market is currently monopolized by a foreign firm. Hence, cross-border profit flows directed abroad are higher *and* occur longer. Consequently, as the foreign NOS increases, the domestic country is more and more reluctant to set a higher domestic NOS until the disadvantage of raising foreign welfare along with the domestic one dominates.

In Chapter 10, Corollary 10.3 establishes a positive relationship between the research efficiency and the number of firms on the one hand and the NOS on the other hand. For the international framework considered here, a comparable result cannot be obtained. Yet, the reverse cannot be proved either. Thus, the optimal domestic NOS might still be an increasing function of the domestic hazard rate ℓ_i^w, i.e. the domestic research efficiency and the domestic number of firms, for certain or even all parameter values.

The reason for the potential breakdown of the intuitive result that a larger domestic hazard rate calls for a stronger domestic NOS lies also in the incongruity of national patent laws and global patent races. To see this, it is expedient to restate the rational behind Corollary 10.3. Whenever the society's hazard rate increases either because the firms are more productive in generating inventions or because there are more firms participating in the patent races, the pace of the patent races accelerates. As a consequence, the expected time during which inventors are able to collect their reward becomes shorter and the expected return on investment shrinks. This is true for all inventions, i.e. for small and large ones. Although society does not care about the identity of the current incumbent, firms' profits are part of the social welfare. Hence, society as a whole is affected if a small invention renders a large one irrelevant. Therefore, society is better off counterbalancing the acceleration of patent races by increasing the NOS to guarantee a minimum reward for large contributions.

This rationale still holds true in an international setting, which explains why the findings in Corollary 10.3 cannot be disproved for the international framework. However, since firms in country i are exclusively owned by citizens of this country, a higher NOS not only protects larger inventions achieved by domestic firms but also those generated by foreign ones. Yet, foreign firms' profits do not contribute to domestic welfare. By strengthening the domestic NOS to counteract the effects of a higher domestic hazard rate, the drain of profits earned in the domestic market increases as well. This effect could only be neutralized if the cross-border profit flows into the domestic country increase by the same amount.

Although the isolated increase of the domestic hazard rate also puts domestic firms in a better position than their foreign competitors abroad so that the inflows of profits will also rise, it is a chance event that inflows and outflows exactly balance. Therefore, it can at least be expected that the positive relationship between the domestic NOS and the domestic hazard rate is weaker as compared to a purely national framework.

13.3.3 Simultaneous decision

We now turn to situations in which both countries simultaneously choose their NOSs. Although Congress and to a certain degree the Supreme Court can effect larger changes in the NOS, they seldom do. Surely, those rare events are best represented by a unilateral decision on the NOS. Patent law is, however, largely shaped by the numerous decisions on single cases. Hence, continual and sometimes hardly perceptible changes are made on a day-to-day basis. Those decisions are, perhaps, better represented by a simultaneous choice of the NOSs.

The result on the simultaneous choice of the NOSs follows immediately from Proposition 13.4 and in particular from Figure 13.2:

Proposition 13.5.

1. For $\ell_i^w > 0$, $\ell_j^w = n_j = 0$, a continuum of equilibria exist with $s_i^* \in (0, \bar{u})$ and s_j^* taking any value on $[0, \bar{u}]$.
2. For $\ell_i^w, \ell_j^w > 0$, existence and uniqueness of a pure strategy equilibrium is not ensured.

Again, the first case refers to a situation where country i is an industrialized country while country j is a developing country with no research abilities. The findings merely confirm the previous results derived on a unilateral decision that the developing country is indifferent concerning the domestic NOS.

Unfortunately, the fact that the ex-ante welfare function has decreasing differences at the point $s_i = s_j$ leads to the second result, i.e. that for some parameter constellations a pure strategy equilibrium need not exist (cf Figure 13.3). Although a mixed strategy equilibrium will exist even under those parameter constellations, it raises the usual concerns: mixed strategy equilibria do not possess a neat interpretation.[9] In addition, since the effect of the society's hazard rates on the policymaker's decision is ambiguous, it seems that one cannot verify the intuitive notion that the country having the larger hazard rate of winning future patent races also tends to set the stronger NOS.

The complexity of the model does leave us, however, not quite destitute. Consider the special case of an industrialized (home) country i and a developing

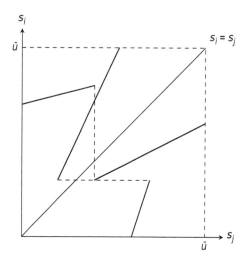

Figure 13.3 Non-existence of a pure strategy equilibrium.

(foreign) country j which, however, has some small research ability, i.e. $n_j > 0$ and $\ell_j^w = \ell_i^l$ is small but positive. Then, we find:

Proposition 13.6. If $\ell_i^w > \ell_j^w$ with ℓ_j^w small but positive, a unique equilibrium exists with $s_i^* > s_j^* > 0$. Figure 13.4 illustrates the situation.

The proposition asserts that a unique equilibrium exists if there are huge differences in the development level of the countries. In addition, the proposition and especially Figure 13.4 show that the country those firms are more productive in generating inventions will set the stronger NOS.

13.4 Policy implications

The previous analysis yielded some interesting points that allow suggestions towards international negotiations on intellectual property rights. Firstly, it has been demonstrated that transition countries will set lower NOSs as compared to industrialized countries.[10] Probably, they will find it optimal to raise the NOS as their research abilities grow.

Secondly, the poorest countries are indifferent to a patent system or the level of the NOS. However, as the present analysis is a partial one, important pros and cons have been neglected. In case those countries do establish a patent system, they should be allowed a considerable discretion in shaping it.

Lastly, although some of the results obtained in Chapter 10 have been re-established at least in a weaker form, it has been demonstrated that policymakers' of identical countries will generally not find it optimal to choose the same NOS.

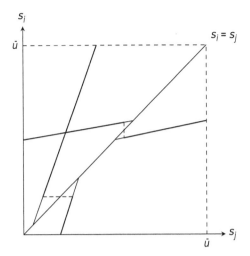

Figure 13.4 The optimal non-obviousness standard for a developed and a developing
country.

Hence, in an increasingly globalized world, international aspects have to be
considered when shaping national policy.

The fact that even identical countries will differentiate NOSs may seem
unconvincing at the first glance, especially because cross-border profit flows are
on average balanced when a uniform NOS is applied. However, this leaves the
important merits of differentiated NOSs out of account. Since larger inventions
occur less frequently, the country setting the stronger NOS shelters larger
inventions against being rendered irrelevant by medium-sized inventions without
denying protection for the latter altogether. On the other hand, the country
setting the weaker NOS ensures that medium-sized inventions receive protection,
but denying patents for trivial, small inventions. Accordingly, an international
differentiation of NOSs ensures that large inventions receive higher rewards
than medium-sized ones, and small inventions get no reward. As long as both
countries have a strictly positive hazard rate so that one of the domestic firms
may generate a (large) invention, this arrangement works to the benefit of both
countries.

From an overall perspective, however, it may be suspected that this international
differentiation of NOSs is too low since countries are negatively affected by the
outflow of profits earned by foreign firms. A first-best solution could only be
achieved if there was an international compensation system that recognizes the
positive externality of setting a higher NOS. Although conceivable from a theoretic
point of view, it would be impossible to try a practical application. First and
foremost, the uncertainty of the value of an invention deprives us from the sole
basis on which such a system could possibly work. Secondly, even though the
information were readily available, the administration of such a system would be

rather costly. In the absence of the means to implement the first-best solution, a further harmonization of NOSs should not be undertaken: the flexibility of the system is also its strength.

13.A Proofs to the lemmata and propositions

Lemma 13.3. The first derivative of the value function V_i^d with respect to the hazard rate $\mathfrak{h}_i^l$ is given by $\partial V_i^d / \partial \mathfrak{h}_i^l = \partial \bar{V}_i / \partial \mathfrak{h}_i^l + \partial v_i^d / \partial \mathfrak{h}_i^l$. The core value's derivative can be determined with

$$
\frac{\partial \bar{V}_i}{\partial \mathfrak{h}_i^l} = \frac{1}{r\phi_\psi^2 \phi_\rho^2} \Big[\theta_\rho \phi_\psi^2 (r + \mathfrak{h}_i^w \theta_\rho \pi^N) - \mathfrak{h}_i^w \theta_\rho^2 \phi_\psi^2 \pi^W
$$
$$
- \mathfrak{h}_i^w \mathfrak{h}_i^{l^2} \theta_\rho \theta_\psi^2 \Delta\theta (\pi^S - \pi^N) - \mathfrak{h}_i^w \theta_\psi (\alpha_1 + \alpha_2) \Big],
$$

where $\alpha_1 := \theta_\psi \big[(r + \mathfrak{h}_i^w \theta_\rho)(\phi_\rho + \mathfrak{h}_i^l \theta_\rho) + \mathfrak{h}_i^{l^2} \theta_\rho \theta_\psi \big] (\pi^B - \pi^W)$ and $\alpha_2 := \Delta\theta (r + \mathfrak{h}_i^w \theta_\psi)(r + \mathfrak{h}_i^w \theta_\rho)(\pi^B - \pi^W - \pi^S + \pi^N)$. The profit π^N is negative so that the first term of the derivative is negative as well. By Lemma 13.1, α_1 is positive. Lemma 13.1 together with the definitions of the profit functions imply that $\pi^B - \pi^W - \pi^S + \pi^N > 0$ so that α_2 is positive as well. Consequently, the derivative of the core value is negative. The fact that $\partial v_i^d / \partial \mathfrak{h}_i^l < 0$ can easily be verified from the definition of the position specific parts of the value functions. Therefore, $\partial V_i^d / \partial \mathfrak{h}_i^l < 0$. □

Proposition 13.1. The proof proceeds in two steps: Firstly it is demonstrated that $\Delta \bar{V}_i$ is positive if $s_i > s_j$ and $G > 0$. Secondly, it is shown that the position specific parts Δv_i^B, Δv_i^S and Δv_i^N are non-negative under the above conditions.

Part I: The function $\Delta \bar{V}_i$ can be determined with

$$
\Delta \bar{V}_l = \frac{\mathfrak{h}_l^w}{r\phi_\psi \phi_\rho} \Big\{ \Delta\theta \big[\theta_\psi \mathfrak{h}_l^w (\bar{\pi}^B - \bar{\pi}^W) + \mathfrak{h}_i^s \bar{\pi}^S + \phi_\psi \bar{\pi}^W \big] + \phi_\psi \big[\theta_\psi \bar{\pi}^B - \theta_\rho \bar{\pi}^I \big] \Big\},
$$

where $i, l = A, B$. Using the definition of π^B and π^I, it follows that $\theta_\psi \bar{\pi}^B - \theta_\rho \bar{\pi}^I = -2\Delta\theta \bar{\pi}^W$. Then, the function $\Delta \bar{V}_i$ can be written as

$$
\Delta \bar{V}_l = \frac{\Delta\theta \mathfrak{h}_l^w}{r\phi_\psi \phi_\rho} \Big[\theta_\psi \underbrace{(\mathfrak{h}_l^l \bar{\pi}^S - \mathfrak{h}_l^w \bar{\pi}^W)}_{\alpha_1} + \underbrace{\theta_\psi \mathfrak{h}_l^w \bar{\pi}^B - \phi_\psi \bar{\pi}^W}_{G} \Big].
$$

Note that α_1 is always positive since $\mathfrak{h}_l^l > \mathfrak{h}_l^w$. Consequently, $G > 0$ is a sufficient condition for $\Delta \bar{V}_i$ to be positive.

Part II: The position specific parts are obtained with

$$\Delta v_i^B = \frac{1}{\phi_\psi \phi_\rho} \left[\Delta \theta \left[\mathfrak{h}_i^l(\pi^S - \pi^N) + \mathfrak{h}_i^w(\pi^B - \pi^W) \right] + \phi_\psi(\pi^B - \pi^I) \right],$$

$$\Delta v_i^S = \frac{1}{\phi_\psi \phi_\rho} \left[\Delta \theta \left[\mathfrak{h}_i^l(\pi^S - \pi^N) + \mathfrak{h}_i^w(\pi^B - \pi^S) \right] + \phi_\psi(\pi^B - \pi^N) \right],$$

$$\Delta v_i^N = 0.$$

By Lemma 13.2, Δv_i^B and Δv_i^S are positive so that ΔV_i^B, ΔV_i^S and ΔV_i^N are positive as long as $s_i > s_j$ and $G > 0$. □

Proposition 13.2. By noting that $\theta_\psi \bar{\pi}^B - \theta_\rho \bar{\pi}^I = -2\Delta\theta\bar{\pi}^W$, the ex-ante value function can be obtained with

$$\Delta V_i^0 = \frac{(r + \mathfrak{h}_i^l + \mathfrak{h}_i^w)\Delta\theta\mathfrak{h}_i^w}{r\phi_\psi \phi_\rho} \left[\theta_\psi(\mathfrak{h}_i^l \bar{\pi}^S - \mathfrak{h}_i^w \bar{\pi}^W) + G \right],$$

with $G := \theta_\psi \mathfrak{h}_i^w(\bar{\pi}^B - \bar{\pi}^W) - (r + \theta_\psi \mathfrak{h}_i^l)\bar{\pi}^W > 0$. Since $\mathfrak{h}_i^l > \mathfrak{h}_i^w$, the proposition follows immediately. □

Lemma 13.6. **Part 1**: It is easy to see that the core value $\bar{W}_i$ as well as W_i^N become zero when $\mathfrak{k}_i^w = n_i = 0$.
Part 2: Evaluating the parts of the ex-ante welfare function at the point $s_i = s_j$ shows that both parts approach the value

$$\frac{1}{r} \left[\frac{2\mathfrak{k}_i^w \theta(r + \mathfrak{k}_i^w + \mathfrak{k}_i^w)}{\phi} \bar{\pi}^S - C(\mathfrak{k}_i^w + \mathfrak{k}_i^l n_i) \right]$$

so that the ex-ante welfare function must be continuous at that point.
Part 3: A function has decreasing differences if $\partial W_i^0(s_i, s_j'')/\partial s_i - \partial W_i^0(s_i, s_j')/\partial s_i < 0$ with $s_j' < s_j''$. Since

$$\lim_{\mu \to 0} \frac{\partial W_i^0(s_i, s_i + \mu)}{\partial s_i} - \frac{\partial W_i^0(s_i, s_i - \mu)}{\partial s_i} =$$

$$- \frac{2f[s_i]\mathfrak{k}_i^l \mathfrak{k}_i^w(r + \mathfrak{k}_i^l + \mathfrak{k}_i^w)\theta_i \bar{\pi}^S}{\phi_i^2} < 0,$$

the welfare function W_i^0 has decreasing differences across the point where $s_i = s_j$. □

Proposition 13.3. **Part 1**: This is a direct consequence of Lemma 13.6.
Part 2:
Case a: $s_i \geq s_j$. The first-order condition can be written as:

$$G_a(s_i) := \bar{\pi}^S \theta_i \left(\frac{\mathfrak{k}_i^l + \mathfrak{k}_i^w}{\phi_i^2} + \frac{\mathfrak{k}_i^l}{\phi_{ij}^2} \right) - s_i \left(\frac{1}{\phi_i} + \frac{1}{\phi_{ij}} - \frac{1}{\phi_j} \right) = 0,$$

where $\bar{\pi}^S$ stands for $\int_{s_i}^{\bar{u}} u f[u] \, du / \theta_i$. Obviously, $G_a(\bar{u}_i)$ is negative. On the other hand, $G_a(s_j)$ is positive for small values of s_j, i.e. $s_j \leq \bar{s}_j$ with

$$\bar{s}_j := \{ s_j \in [0, \bar{u}] : G_a(s_j) = (2\mathfrak{k}_i^l + \mathfrak{k}_i^w)\theta_j \bar{\pi}^S - s_j \phi_j = 0 \}.$$

Since $G_a(s_i)$ is a declining function of s_i, there exists an optimal NOS solving $G_a(s_i) = 0$ for $s_j \in [0, \bar{s}_j]$.
Case b: The first-order condition can be written as:

$$G_b(s_i) := \Delta \theta (\mathfrak{k}_i^l + \mathfrak{k}_i^w) \bar{\pi}^S + \frac{\phi_i^2}{\phi_{ij}^2} \theta_j \mathfrak{k}_i^w \bar{\pi}^S - s_i \phi_i = 0.$$

Evidently, $G_b(0)$ is positive while $G_b(s_j)$ is negative for $s_j \leq \underline{s}_j$ with

$$\underline{s}_j := \{ s_j \in [0, \bar{u}] : G_b(s_j) = \theta_j \mathfrak{k}_i^l \bar{\pi}^S - s_j \phi_j = 0 \}.$$

Again, an equilibrium exists as long as $s_j \in [\underline{s}_j, \bar{u}]$.
It is easy to verify that $\underline{s}_j < \bar{s}_j$ so that each of the cases a and b produces one candidate equilibrium in this interval. Denote the equilibrium for case a by s_i^a; and the one for case b by s_i^b. Let $\tilde{s}_j$ be defined as

$$\tilde{s}_j := \{ s_j \in [0, \bar{u}] : W_i^0(s_i^a, s_j) = W_i^0(s_i^b, s_j) \}.$$

Then, the equilibrium NOS is given by:

$$s_i^* := \begin{cases} s_i^a & \text{for } s_j \in [0, \tilde{s}_j] \\ s_i^b & \text{for } s_j \in (\tilde{s}_j, \bar{u}]. \end{cases}$$

$\square$

Proposition 13.4. The proof proceeds in three steps: (1) it is demonstrated that $s_i^*(s_j)$ is an increasing function of s_j for the cases $s_i^*(s_j) \geq s_j$ and $s_i^*(s_j) \leq s_j$; (3) it is verified that $s_i^a(\tilde{s}_j) > \tilde{s}_j$ and $s_i^b(\tilde{s}_j) < \tilde{s}_j$.
Part 1: Consider the case $s_i^* > s_j$. The sign of ds_i^*/ds_j is identical to the sign of $\partial G_a(s_i, s_j)/\partial s_j$. The latter is determined by

$$\frac{\partial G_a(\cdot)}{\partial s_j} = f[s_j] \left[2\bar{\pi}^L \theta_i \frac{\mathfrak{k}_i^l \mathfrak{k}_i^w}{\phi_j^2} + s_i \left(\frac{\mathfrak{k}_i^l + \mathfrak{k}_i^w}{\phi_j^2} - \frac{\mathfrak{k}_i^w}{\phi_{ij}^2} \right) \right]. \tag{13.13}$$

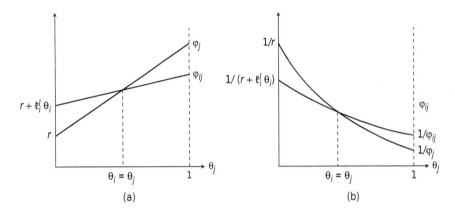

Figure 13.5 The functional form of ϕ.

To verify that the second summand within the bracket term is positive, Figure 13.5 and the notion that it is the derivative of $s_i(1/\phi_j - 1/\phi_{ij})$ with respect to s_j is useful.

For any given θ_i, functions ϕ_j and ϕ_{ij} are linear in θ_j as illustrated in Figure 13.5(a). Both functions intersect at $\theta_i = \theta_j$; and only values of θ_j to the right of the intersection point are relevant for case 2. Consequently, the functions $1/\phi_j$ and $1/\phi_{ij}$ necessarily have the functional forms as indicated in Figure 13.5(b). It is easy to see that the $|\partial\phi_j^{-1}/\partial\theta_j| > |\partial\phi_{ij}^{-1}/\partial\theta_j|$. Keeping in mind that $d\theta_j/ds_j < 0$, it follows that the derivative of $s_i(1/\phi_j - 1/\phi_{ij})$ with respect to s_j is positive. Although the optimal NOS s_i will change in response to variations in the foreign NOS s_j, the functional forms remain identical so that the sign of the derivative does not change. Hence, the first and the second summand of the bracket term in equation (13.13) are positive and the optimal NOS is an increasing function of the foreign NOS for the case of $s_i \geq s_j$.

Part 2: follows analogous steps.

Part 3: Let $\underline{s}_j$ and $\bar{s}_j$ be defined as in the proof to Proposition 13.3. According to Lemma 13.6.3, W_i^0 has decreasing differences across the point $s_i = s_j$ so that $s_i^a(s_j) > s_i^b(s_j)$ for all $s_j \in [\underline{s}_j, \bar{s}_j]$. Another consequence of Lemma 13.6.3 is that the jump point $\tilde{s}_j$ cannot attain the boundary values of $\underline{s}_j$ and $\bar{s}_j$ and the result immediately follows. □

Proposition 13.5. To prove the claim, it is demonstrated that point A_1 moves down while A_2 moves up, B_2 approaches zero and B_1 moves below A_2 as $\mathfrak{k}_j^w$ approaches zero in Figure 13.6.

Points A_1 and A_2 are defined by $\bar{s}_j := \{s_j \in [0, \bar{u}] : \overline{G}_j := \bar{\pi}^L\theta_j(2\mathfrak{k}_i^l + \mathfrak{k}_i^W) - s_j\phi_j = 0\}$ and $\underline{s}_j := \{s_j \in [0, \bar{u}] : \underline{G}_i := \bar{\pi}^L\theta_j\mathfrak{k}_i^w - s_j\phi_j = 0\}$ respectively.

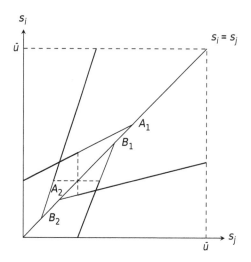

Figure 13.6 Non-obviousness standards for an industrialized and developing country.

By symmetry, B_1 and B_2 are defined by $\bar{s}_i := \{s_i \in [0, \bar{u}] : \overline{G}_i := \bar{\pi}^L \theta_i (2\mathfrak{k}_j^l + \mathfrak{k}_j^W) - s_i \phi_i = 0\}$ and $\underline{s}_i := \{s_i \in [0, \bar{u}] : \underline{G}_i := \bar{\pi}^L \theta_i \mathfrak{k}_j^w - s_i \phi_i = 0\}$. It can easily be verified that

$$\frac{\partial \overline{G}_j}{\partial \mathfrak{k}_j^w} = 2\theta_j(\bar{\pi}^S - s_j) > 0, \; \frac{\partial \underline{G}_j}{\partial \mathfrak{k}_j^w} = -s_j \theta_j < 0, \; \frac{\partial \overline{G}_i}{\partial \mathfrak{k}_j^w} = \frac{\partial \underline{G}_i}{\mathfrak{k}_j^w} = \theta(\bar{\pi}^S - s_j) > 0$$

so that　　$\dfrac{\partial \bar{s}_j}{\partial \mathfrak{k}_j^w} > 0, \; \dfrac{\partial \underline{s}_j}{\partial \mathfrak{k}_j^w} < 0, \; \dfrac{\partial \bar{s}_i}{\partial \mathfrak{k}_j^w} = \dfrac{\partial \underline{s}_i}{\mathfrak{k}_j^w} > 0.$

Consequently, as $\mathfrak{k}_j^w$ declines, the points move into the above specified directions. It remains to be demonstrated that B_2 approaches zero and that $\underline{s}_j > \bar{s}_i$ as $\mathfrak{k}_j^w$ becomes small. These fact immediately follow from the definition of $\underline{s}_i$ on the one hand and the definitions of $\underline{s}_j$ and $\bar{s}_i$ on the other. □

Notes

3 A short history of the patent system

1 One of the most important international patent treaties is not described in this chapter – the European Patent Convention. This treaty is a regional one as its membership was and is restricted to European countries. Other such regional agreements exist.
2 See e.g. Merrill *et al.* (2004) or Jaffe and Lerner (2004) for the United States.
3 Formerly, they consisted of practising a trade, buying or selling goods at pre-specified prices. Today, patents are more complex structures; they confer on the owner the exclusive right '[…] to prevent third parties not having the owner's consent from the acts of: making, using, offering for sale, selling, or importing for these purposes' (WTO 1994: Article 28) the protected products or processes.
4 At least at the beginning, these regulations served as a minimum quality standard. In addition, guild-internal (dispute) settlement processes existed. Therefore, guilds and their regulations provided at least partly informal rules that are now part of modern legal systems. As such, they were necessary prerequisites for any modern form of business.
5 Privilege systems were common all over Europe, which also experienced its perversion into a system to reward courtiers.
6 This section is mainly based on Merges and Duffy (2002: 7–13). See also Khan and Sokoloff (2001).
7 See e.g. MacGarvie and Furman (2005) for further information on the birth of industrial research laboratories.
8 See e.g. MacGarvie and Furman (2005) for an excellent description of factors that lead to formation of the private research laboratories.
9 The resentments against patents of the *big business* never quite stopped as the work of Reik (1946) and Vaughan (1948) who advocate the (limited) use of compulsory licensing shows.
10 See e.g. Hunt (1999b: 20), Lerner (2003: 2) or Menell and Scotchmer (2005: 40) for empirical evidence.
11 This section is based on Penrose (1951).
12 Most of the section is based on Drahos (2003). For detailed information see the references therein. For an alternative view, see e.g. Yu (2003).
13 According to Dutfield (2002), the Levi Strauss Corporation tried unsuccessfully to include intellectual property rights into the Tokyo Round of the GATT (1973–1979). Whereas Pfizer Inc.'s attempts were focussed on patents, Levi Strauss' interests lay with trademarks.
14 The members were: Bristol–Myers (pharma), DuPont (chemicals and health care), FMC Corporation (chemicals), General Electric, General Motors, Hewlett–Packard, IBM, Johnson & Johnson (pharma), Merck (pharma), Monsato (GM), Pfizer (pharma), Rockwell International and Warner Communications.

15 Among others, Fink and Primo Braga (2005) investigated in the effects of stronger international patent rights empirically.

16 WTO (1994), emphasis added by the author.

17 The permissible field restrictions are for: (a) diagnostic, therapeutic and surgical methods and (b) plants and animals other than microorganisms (paragraph 3). Field restrictions define certain technology fields for which patents are not to be granted. Naturally occurring plants, minerals and substances, natural laws and phenomenon as well as mathematical algorithms are still not patentable, but those exceptions are not considered to be field restrictions. They constitute a bar across all technology fields.

Paragraph 2 of Article 27 provides a *safety-hole* in that inventions may also be excluded from patentability when the public order or human, animal or plant life are threatened.

18 The US brought dispute settlement cases against Pakistan (1996), India (1996) and Argentina (1999, 2000) that dealt with the protection of pharmaceutical and agricultural and chemical produts (see Dispute Settlement Cases at the WIPO webpage).

See also Abbott (2005) on the Doha Declaration and similar declarations. They try to mitigate problems that may arise in developing countries that would be unable to pay for patented medicines.

19 As explained above, many countries revoked a patent if the owner did not work the patent in the issuing country after a certain period had elapsed. This practise was only abandoned with the TRIPs Agreement in all member countries of the WTO. In 2000, the US brought a dispute settlement case against Brazil because Brazil required the working of patents in the country.

20 Deng (2006) comes to a similar conclusion. Chadha (2009) studies the connection between the introduction of the TRIPs Agreement and the patenting activity in the Indian pharmaceutical industry.

21 The BIRPI was the international organization that administered the Paris Convention at this time and may be regarded as the predecessor of the WIPO.

22 Article 63 of the PCT provided that the Treaty enters into force three months after eight countries, four of which must be large ones, ratified the PCT. This explains why it took eight years to establish the PCT. By the end of 2006, 133 countries have signed the PCT.

4 Foundations of patent systems

1 See e.g. Merrill *et al.* (2004), Jaffe and Lerner (2004) or Bessen and Meurer (2008) for suggestions for the United States.

2 See also Bix (2000) for a modern interpretation.

3 See e.g. Demsetz (1967) for an economic view on property rights.

4 See also Claeys (2006).

5 For an overview on modern growth theory see e.g. Romer (1990), Grossman and Helpman (1991) Barro and Sala-I-Martin (1995) or Aghion and Howitt (1998, 1992). For an empirical study see e.g. Falvey *et al.* (2004).

6 See e.g. Scotchmer (2004) and Gallini and Scotchmer (2002) among others. Wright (1983) explicitly compares the performance of patents, prizes and research contracts in an environment with and without information asymmetry. Scotchmer (1996) reveals that patent protection is not necessary to encourage second-generation products under certain circumstances.

7 A more fundamental critique is put forth by Crampes and Langinier (2005) who show that the pure existence of an intellectual property rights system may be detrimental to the flow of useful innovations.

8 See Scotchmer (2004) and the references therein.

9 See Abrantes-Metz *et al.* (2006) for a study on the development phases and the subsequent success of pharmaceutical products.

10 In a recent paper, Acemoglu *et al.* (2008) show that subsidies which are in some sense similar to prizes cannot achieve the social efficient outcome; however, well-designed patent systems can.
11 See e.g. Oddi (1996) and the references therein for other utilitarian theories.
12 See e.g. Cohen *et al.* (2000), Cohen (2004), Bulut and Moschini (2006) or Hussinger (2004). Atallah (2004) models the firms' decision of using either patents or trade secrecy as a protective mechanism.
13 See e.g. Graham and Mowery (2001), Lerner (2002) or Hall (2004).
14 See Denicolò and Franzoni (2006), who studies the differences between both patent theories.
15 For an introduction to information economics see e.g. Hirshleifer and Riley (1992).
16 Creane (2006) argues that dissemination of knowledge can be excessive and thus decrease welfare.
17 The United States form an exception. Here, only inventions which are (to be the) subject of foreign patent applications are published.
18 See e.g. Bhattacharya and Guriev (2004, 2006).
19 See e.g. Grossman and Helpman (1991) or Romer (1990) on modern growth theory. See e.g. Horii and Tatsuro (2005), Futagami and Iwaisako (2007), Gould and Gruben (1996) or Grupp and Stadler (2000) on studies that directly connect intellectual property to economic growth.

5 An introduction to patent law and policy instruments

1 Guellec and van Pottelsberghe (2007) give an in-depth insight into the European patent system.
2 See e.g. the webpage of the European Patent Office (http://www.epo.org) or of the US Patent and Trademark Office (http://www.uspto.gov) for published patent applications as well as patent documents.
3 The term *prior art* is used for the entire published body of knowledge connected to the invention.
4 See Bessen and Meurer (2008) for a critique of continuation patents and how they undermine the patent system as a whole. See also Graham (2002), Graham and Mowery (2005) or Hegde *et al.* (2007) for the use of continuation patents.
5 This section largely draws from Merges and Duffy (2002) for the explanations on the provisions. See also Besen and Raskind (1991).
6 For details on the patent fees see http://www.uspto.gov/web/offices/ac/qs/fee2006may15.htm.
7 See Condon and Sinha (2005) and Beckerman-Rodau (2002) for problems that arise for the poorest countries when medicines belong to patentable subject matters.
8 Burk and Lemley (2003: 126) argue that the natural law doctrine is rather a restriction to permissible scope which affects all industries than a field restriction.
9 See e.g. Hahn (2005) or Lemley (2005b) who discusses intellectual property rights in new technology fields such as software, biotechnology or nanotechnology. Plotkin (2004), Campbell-Kelly and Valduriez (2005) or Burk and Lemley (2005) focus specifically on software patents.
10 See Merges (1995: 107) or Cohen *et al.* (2000) who both argue that only a few industries rely on patents alone to capture the returns for an invention.
11 Note that trade secrecy does not protect against independent discovery. Hence, patent protection is especially attractive for products or processes that can be re-engineered easily (cf *infra*).
12 See also Plotkin (2004) on software patents and practical utility.
13 According to the US Patent Statute, new uses for known substances are protected by the patent on the known substance. Nevertheless, the new use can be protected as a process

patent, i.e. the process of using the old substance for the new purpose is patented. However, the owner of the process patent must obtain a licence from the holder of the product patent to work his invention (cf *infra* and Chapter 9).

14 Usually, applications on new medical substances are filed long before clinical tests are carried out. However, in principle, the utility requirement could be construed so that appropriate clinical tests become a prerequisite for a patent. The fact that the courts and Congress never required such tests seems to be a conclusive proof that they always distinguished social utility from commercial value.

15 Hunt (2004) e.g. sharply criticizes this tendency since it might effectively lower the non-obviousness standard.

16 A similar development as described by Hall and Ziedonis (2001) for computer chips is observed in the pharmaceutical and biotechnological industry: small (biotechnology) firms specialize in finding new therapeutical substances which are not yet marketable products. Subsequently, they try to find a (pharmaceutical) cooperation partner that is large and experienced enough to develop a new drug, undertake the necessary (clinical) test and produce the drugs in case market approval is obtained.

17 A similar example is described in Merges and Duffy (2002: 995).

18 See e.g. Jansen (2005) on the economic effects of disclosure regulations, and Ghose (2006) or Gick (2004) on the effects on firms' incentives.

19 See e.g. Anton and Yao (2004) for a formal model describing this phenomenon.

20 See e.g. Bhattacharya and Guriev (2004, 2006) who model this problem.

21 Bessen and Meurer (2005) find that patent litigation is increasing tremendously. In relatively new patentable subject matters this might be expected since reliable databases for prior art are not existing yet and patent examiners in this field are still inexperienced. In older technology fields, such developments may indeed point to the use of patents for strategic reasons. See e.g. Lanjouw and Schankerman (1991). On broader issues see e.g. Lerner (2008) or Ménière and Parlane (2008).

22 The *experimental use doctrine* forms an exception. Everybody is allowed to use patented intellectual property for private experimentation, e.g. to test, perfect or improve the invention. See e.g. Hagelin (2005), Rowe (2005) or Mueller (2005).

23 See e.g. Lemley (2005a) on controversial aspects concerning the infringement and Margolis (2006) on possible benefits from infringements.

24 Some authors do not distinguish between the Doctrine of Equivalents and the Reverse Doctrine of Equivalents, but include both functions under the former expression.

25 See e.g. Lemley and Shapiro (2006) on the effects of a thread of a (preliminary) injunction relief on the outcome of licence negotiations.

26 On the effects of preliminary injunction relief see e.g. Lanjouw and Lerner (2001).

27 See Choi (2006) for a discussion on how to determine reasonable royalties.

28 Schankerman and Scotchmer (2001) show e.g. that lost profit damage or reasonable royalty damage may be superior to other forms of damage payments and, in fact, benefit the patent holder.

29 See e.g. Kahn (1940), Lemley (2004) or Burk and Lemley (2003).

7 The optimal patent term

1 As mentioned above many (industrialized) countries provide an extension for patents on pharmaceutical and chemical products that have to be approved by a governmental agency. The appropriate provision for the US is §155 USC 35.

2 Since a European Community patent does not exist, the renewal fees are to be paid to the national patent offices and, thus, may differ with respect to due date and amount.

3 The effective patent term measures the time period during which positive returns per period can be obtained from the invention.

4 Since renewal fees are not paid on a yearly basis in the US, the graph for the US takes a characteristic step form.
5 Indeed, a number of empirical studies use data on the maintenance of patents to estimate the value of patent rights. See e.g. Pakes (1986), Schankerman and Pakes (1986), Schankerman (1998), and for a recent study Deng (2003, 2005). See also Folkeringa *et al.* (2005), Wijen and Duysters (2005), Liu *et al.* (2008) or Serrano (2008) on related issues of patent renewals.
6 See also Deng (2005) for different renewal fees in Germany, France and the United Kingdom.
7 Machlup (1958) acknowledged patent life as a policy instrument. However, Nordhaus (1967) was the first to model the problem. See also Scherer (1972) and Nordhaus (1972) on variations and different interpretations of the original version. See also Grossman and Lai (2002) present a similar model in an international setting.
8 See also Ramello (2005).
9 See e.g. Loury (1979) or Lee and Wilde (1980) for early models on patent races and Cantner *et al.* (2005) for an experimental study on innovation races. Reinganum (1992) gives an excellent overview on the different models of patent races.
10 See e.g. Tirole (1993) or Martin (2002).
11 Under the assumption of frictionless R&D processes and perfect competition in the product market when patents have lapsed, a firm will always apply for a patent. Without patent protection, the invention can rightfully be used by every firm. When R&D processes are frictionless, it is fair to assume that the imitation process obeys the same rules so that competitors are indeed able to copy the process innovation instantly. Thus, the only way of recouping the research costs is to protect the invention by a patent.
12 This situation may arise when imitation is only to be achieved at prohibitively high costs. The level of the imitation costs may also be the result of a strong and very efficient patent system that provides for an infinite patent breadth and patent scope (cf *infra*).
13 Unless otherwise indicated, subscripts denote the appropriate partial derivatives.
14 See e.g. Goel (1996) for a model of patent length that also incorporates uncertainty.
15 One would expect that inventors have gained some kind of competitive advantages over their competitors during the patent life that does not immediately vanish once the innovation becomes publicly available. This enables inventors to earn positive profits even after the patent expired. For convenience sake we excluded this aspect, however, the analysis would follow similar lines as the one presented here.
16 Subsequently, Schankerman and Pakes (1986), Schankerman (1998) and Deng (2003, 2005) among others have refined the technique.
17 This section is based solely on the model of Cornelli and Schankerman (1999) so that the proofs are not replicated here. See e.g. Scotchmer (1999) for different formulation of optimal renewal schemes.
18 In reality, the patentee himself has often only an idea on the market potential of the patent. What really matters, however, is that the patent holder learns the value of the patent before the patent authority does.
19 See also Kreps (1990) or Mas-Colell *et al.* (1995) for alternative presentations of the mechanism design concept and its applications.

8 Patent scope

1 Lerner (1994) investigates patent scope in an empirical study.
2 See e.g. Basmann *et al.* (2007) for an empirical study linking the patent system to the pace of technological change in the United States.
3 Note that this reward need not necessarily be identical with the social value of the invention at the outset.

4 The models in the next chapter describe situations in which a subsequent technology improves upon a previous one.

5 Klemperer (1990) employs Hotelling's model of a horizontal differentiation to outline the patent scope. Gilbert and Shapiro (1990), on the other hand, simply assume that wider patents yield higher profits during the patent life.

6 As usual, it is assumed that every competitor is instantly able to use the more efficient production technology, i.e. the markets are frictionless. Note that the patentee will also earn merely the competition profit if the patent scope is very narrow, i.e. $y \to 0$.

7 See e.g. Weizsäcker (1980) on barriers to entry. Sutton (1991) writes on the closely related issue of sunk costs. Shaked and Sutton (1983) are directly formulating the idea of natural oligopolies.

8 Only if the competition profit π^c is zero, i.e. if perfect competition is resumed after the patent expired, the entire deadweight loss can be appropriated by society. Otherwise, the patentee's market power is reduced, but not eliminated after the patent lapses.

9 See e.g. Mankiw and Whinston (1986) for the business-stealing effect.

10 Note that the welfare function W is convex in the T/y-diagram even though the instantaneous welfare $w(\pi^m)$ is concave in the monopoly profit.

11 See e.g. Shaked and Sutton (1983) for a model that explains market power with the properties of the income distribution.

12 See e.g. Martin (1993) or Tirole (1993) for discussions of this standard model.

13 This interpretation is similar to the work of Mussa and Rosen (1978) where the product varieties represent different qualities of the same good. See also Cremer and Thissé (1991).

14 Actually, the disutility can be associated to monetary costs if the sub-ideal variant has to be customized at certain expenses.

15 As mentioned above, economists have used the expressions patent scope and patent breadth rather indiscriminately. Although Denicolò (1996) himself uses the term patent breadth, it fits our definition of patent scope.

16 Among numerous other authors, see e.g. Loury (1979), Lee and Wilde (1980) or Reinganum (1992) for works on patent races. Choi (1991) introduces a patent race where the participants have imperfect knowledge on the hazard rate, i.e. the pace of the patent race.

17 A prominent example is that of Pfizer's Viagra which was originally developed as a treatment for heart disease. However, the side-effects observed during the clinical test phase proved to be overwhelming so that the succeeding approval was not sought as a treatment for heart disease.

18 See also e.g. Anton and Yao (2004), Encaoua and Lefouili (2006) or Ferrando Yáñez (2003) for similar models, to mention only a few.

19 See also Denicolò and Franzoni (2006) for an alternative formulation of a firm's decision to use a patent or trade secrecy as a protection mechanism.

20 Since trade secrecy does not protect against an independent discovery (cf *supra*), this assumption implies that at least one of the firms that participated in the patent race completes its research project.

21 Note that this assumption differs from Klemperer (1990).

9 Patent breadth

1 Among others, see also Green and Scotchmer (1995), Scotchmer (1996), Matutes *et al.* (1996) or Belenzon (2006).

2 See e.g. Lemley and Shapiro (2006) on the patent hold-up problem and royalty stacking.

3 See e.g. Anton and Yao (1994) on the general problem of technology licensing and Bessen (2004) on the hold-up problem and licensing.

4 See e.g. Erkal (2005) for an alternative model.

5 Consequently, to conceive an idea, costly research is not necessary. Only the development of the invention into marketable products requires resources.

6 Direct measures to restrict competition may take the form of explicit minimum price clauses or exclusive rights for certain geographical regions.

7 Many of the patent license agreements in the biotechnology/pharmaceutical industry follow this pattern. The smaller firm that holds the intellectual property rights teams up with a large pharmaceutical firm to develop the promising new medicine to a marketable product. Typically, a large up-front payment is followed by further instalments that are contingent on passing the clinical tests and market approval. Usually, the licensee also receives royalties.

8 Among others, Green and Scotchmer (1995) demonstrate that a social optimal situation is feasible in the presence of ex-ante licensing. See also Scotchmer (1996, 2004).

9 This assumption implicitly means that the consumer price is chosen as the numéraire.

10 Firms can anticipate court rulings because the quality improvements $\{u_1, u_2\}$ become observable once the respective firm has developed the idea.

11 The possibility to sue is usually sufficient with symmetric information. Firms can indeed observe the quality improvements $\{u_1, u_2\}$ and can therefore predict the outcome of the court's investigation.

12 Alternatively, firm 2 may license its improvement to the first patentee which in turn becomes the monopoly. Firm 1 would pay $u_2/2$ as licence fees. Still another option is that firm 1 licenses its patent to firm 2 for a fee of $u_1 + u_2/2$ and only firm 2 continues production.

13 Let the licence fee be denoted by x, then the optimal net license fee is given by

$$x^* = \underset{x}{\operatorname{argmax}} \left\{ \left(\frac{1}{2}(u_1 + u_2) - u_1 + x \right) \left(\frac{1}{2}(u_1 + u_2) - x \right) \right\}.$$

14 Here, the optimal licence fee satisfies

$$x^* = \underset{x}{\operatorname{argmax}} \left\{ \left((u_1 + u_2) - u_1 - x \right) x \right\}.$$

15 Under the $NI \cap C$ regime, the optimal licence fee satisfies

$$x^* = \underset{x}{\operatorname{argmax}} \left\{ \left(\frac{1}{2}(u_1 + u_2) - x \right) \left(\frac{1}{2}(u_1 + u_2) - u_2 + x \right) \right\}.$$

16 Note that the boundaries of the subsets will depend on u_1. Furthermore, it is clear that the subsets are distinct and that their union equals $[0, \bar{u}_2]$.

17 If firms hold more than one patent that has not yet expired, the formulation of licensing activities becomes much more complex. This assumption does, however, not unduly restrict the generality of the results.

18 Alternatively, the condition can be expressed as $U_3 < U_2 + b_+$.

19 See e.g. Roth (1979) for models of axiomatic bargaining that are usually used to determine the outcome of negotiations. See also Binmore *et al.* (1986) for a connection between axiomatic bargaining and non-cooperation games.

20 Coase (1960) very carefully studied the problem. In the context of patents, it has been acknowledged also because its potential impediment to technological progress and competition. Patent pools and cross-licensing are frequently seen as one solution to the problem (Shapiro, 2001). However, both licensing forms raise anti-trust concerns.

21 See also Gabszewicz and Thissé (1980) and Mussa and Rosen (1978) for models of vertical product differentiation that are closely related.
22 Otherwise entry into the market would always be possible, although on average not strictly profitable.
23 Clearly, this result is also due to the assumption that the market is just large enough for two firms and that there are positive market entry costs. Otherwise, entry would occur and drive the expected profits to zero.

10 The non-obviousness standard

1 See also O'Donoghue (1998) for a similar approach.
2 See e.g. Loury (1979), Lee and Wilde (1980) or Reinganum (1992) for earlier works on patent races.
3 Here, inventions always become innovations so that both expressions are used interchangeably.
4 See e.g. Ross (1992) for the description of Poisson processes.
5 By assigning patent rights to inventions that make only slight contributions to the technology field, the rents of the first innovator may decline. As a consequence, inventors do not have incentives to pursue larger inventions if the NOS is weak.
6 The assumption that the improvement over the previous invention is drawn from a closed set is not crucial to the analysis.
7 Whether or not former successful innovations have a positive influence on a firm's research performance can be debated.
8 Clearly, lead time and secrecy offer protection as well. How effective those mechanisms are differs among industries (cf *supra*). By assuming that unpatentable inventions become common knowledge, attention is restricted to industries, where reverse-engineering is particularly easy.
9 This assumptions differs from the one posed in Chapter 9 where the reservation price was equal to the *quality* of the product, i.e. the cumulative improvements. In a model of an infinite sequence of cumulative patent races, this assumption makes the model economy non-stationary.
10 In the quality ladder model of Grossman and Helpman (1991) the quality leader does never undertake research.
11 This is identical to models in which only one patent race takes place and patent protection does not only statutarily last forever, but is effectively infinite.
12 Indeed, if the expected innovation size were an increasing function of the research effort making it more likely for the incumbent to come up with a large discovery, the incumbent would choose a positive effort level under certain circumstances.
13 To see this, note that $\lim_{s \to \bar{u}} \pi^I = \lim_{s \to \bar{u}} sf[s]/f[s] = \bar{u}$.
14 This is not to say that laws cannot be changed. However, changing a law is usually time consuming and the outcome often uncertain.
15 It is hard to find direct empirical evidence for this hypothesis. However, by postulating that larger inventions will eventually turn out to have a higher return, the latter can be used as a proxy for a product innovation's size. Grabowski (2002) e.g. finds that the return on drugs is highly skewed. Similarly, Duguet and Lelarge (2004) show that there is empirical evidence that there is a large number of product innovation patents that have a small value and a small number of patents that have a large value. See also Mann (2004).
16 However, even if the dynamic effect were positive, the result may still arise if the static effect is stronger.
17 It has also been argued that this result possesses limited practical relevance since (a) the demand is fixed and (b) the existence of e.g. new commodities do not contribute to the consumers' utility.

11 Introduction

1 Among the few works that allow for international relations are Helpman (1993), Grossman and Helpman (1991), Grossman and Lai (2002), and to some extent Scotchmer (2001).
2 Drahos (2003, 2005) describes how the US use bilateral trade negotiations to raise the patent standards in developing and transition countries.

12 New patentable subject matters

1 See e.g. Lerner and Zhu (2004), Vaidhyanathan (2005) or Wagner (2004) for patent protection in selected new patentable subject matters.
2 *Pure software* was long considered to be mathematical algorithms which are not patentable under the natural law doctrine. At least since the 1990s, however, pure software can be protected by a patent if it is part of an invention in a technical field in the EU.
3 According to the TRIPs Agreement, patents have to be provided in each technology field. Consequently, the underlying question in both instances is whether computer-implemented inventions and business methods are 'capable of industrial application'.
   See also Deardorff (1992) who studies welfare effects of extending patent protection.
4 As long as the majority of the shares are owned by citizens of the respective country, the effects to be demonstrated below will be weakened, but will qualitatively remain unchanged.
5 The fact that the loser of the patent race is nevertheless completing the product seems unconvincing. The firm might want to stop the development process when the winner of the patent race applies for the patent. However, exactly this action is not observable in practice. The information on the patent applications become available only much later so that the unsuccessful firm has probably finished its development process by that time. In addition, it might be unclear at first whether or not the second invention indeed infringes on the first.
6 For empirical evidence, see e.g. Levin *et al.* (1987) and Cohen *et al.* (2000) for US firms and Blind *et al.* (2003) for German information-technology-related firms.
7 Hence, it is implicitly assumed that the litigation costs are relatively low and the courts tend to approve patents.
8 To clarify the point, assume that the monopoly profit is given and firms are identical. Then, each firm earns a strictly positive profit in a homogeneous product market when the duopolists' strategic variable are quantities. In the Bertrand case, the duopolists' profits will be zero due to the higher competitive pressure.
   See also Boone (2004) on traditional and new ways to measure competition.
9 If only product innovations are considered, the pharmaceutical industry may be considered as an example for only one patent race.
10 Alternatively, it could be argued that the improvement size is always larger than the (strictly positive) NOS.
11 Scotchmer (2001) studies how international treaties can be formed. A prominent feature is reciprocity.
12 Clearly, an active industrial policy designed so that a particular sector catches up to the world leaders may veil true incentives in empirical studies.

13 Different non-obviousness standards

1 By assigning patent rights to inventions making only slight improvements upon a previous, large one, the rents of the first innovator will decline. As a consequence, inventors have no incentive to pursue larger improvements.

2 Especially when one of the countries is a developing country, this assumption may be questioned.

3 McCalman (2005) has simulated the cross-country profit flows that were induced by the TRIPs Agreement (cf Chapter 3 *supra*). They significantly affect a country's welfare in the short run. Scotchmer (2001) points out that the size and direction of expected cross-border profit flows may affect whether or not international treaties can be successfully concluded.

4 The hazard rates *and* the respective probabilities that a given invention is patentable form the transition probabilities for the underlying Markov chain.

5 Note that ϕ_v is indeed identical for domestic and foreign firms since $\mathfrak{h}_i^l + \mathfrak{h}_i^w = \mathfrak{h}_j^l + \mathfrak{h}_j^w$ per definition.

6 This interpretation presents itself since $1/\phi_\rho$ is the discount rate adjusted to account for the event that the profit stream is terminated when a small invention is made. This event arises with a modified hazard rate of $\theta_\rho(\mathfrak{h}_i^w + \mathfrak{h}_i^l)$.

7 Clearly, countries such as China or India do not belong in this category. Rather, one may picture the poorest countries as examples of this case. However, keeping the TRIPs Agreement in mind, which binds a signatory state to minimum standards of intellectual property rights protection, this special case is not without interest.

8 This does, however, not imply that a patent system is neutral from an overall perspective. If foreign firms permanently monopolize the developing country's market, there is a continuous outflow of profits that affect the country's current account and, thus, the country's economic development.

9 There are several alternative interpretations of mixed strategy equilibria: (1) The latter can be understood as the average outcome of a series of identical decision problems. (2) A player's may be uncertain about how his adversary will decide or how rational the opponent is. (3) Equilibria in Bayesian games with incomplete information approach mixed strategy equilibria (Fudenberg and Tirole, 1993: pp 230) . The latter alternative gives a convincing reinterpretation of mixed strategy equilibria.

10 Saint-Paul (2004) studies the same question.

Bibliography

Abbott, F. M. (2005) 'The WTO medicines decision: World pharmaceutical trade and the protection of public health', *The American Journal of International Law*, 99: 317–358.

Abrantes-Metz, R. M., Adams, C. P. and Metz, A. (2006) 'Pharmaceutical development phases: A duration analysis', *Journal of Pharmaceutical Finance, Economics & Policy*, 14: 19–41.

Acemoglu, D., Bimpikis, K. and Ozdeglar, A. (2008) 'Experimentation, patents, and innovation', NBER Working Paper No. 14408, Cambridge, MA.

Aghion, P. and Howitt, P. (1992) 'A model of growth through creative destruction', *Econometrica*, 60: 323–351.

—— (1998) *Endogenous Growth Theory*, Cambridge, MA: MIT Press.

Anton, J. J. and Yao, D. A. (1994) 'Expropriation and inventions: Appropriable rents in the absence of property rights', *American Economic Review*, 84: 190–209.

—— (2004) 'Little patents and big secrets: Managing intellectual property', *RAND Journal of Economics*, 35: 1–22.

Atallah, G. (2004) 'The protection of innovations', *Série Scientifique* 2004s–02, Centre Interuniversitaire de Recherche en Analyse des Organisations, Montréal.

Bainbridge, D. I. (2002) *Intellectual Property Law*, Harlow: Pearson Longman, 5th edn.

Barro, R. J. and Sala-I-Martin, X. (1995) *Economic Growth*, New York: McGraw-Hill.

Basmann, R. L., McAleer, M. and Slottje, D. (2007) 'Patent activity and technical change', *Journal of Econometrics*, 139: 355–375.

Beckerman-Rodau, A. (2002) 'Patent law – balancing profit maximization and public access to technology', Suffolk University Law School Working Paper No. 2.

Belenzon, S. (2006) 'Basic research and sequential innovation', Working Paper No. 723, Centre for Economic Performance.

Bernhardt, W. and Kraßer, R. (1986) *Lehrbuch des Patentrechts – Recht der Bundesrepublik Deutschland, Europäisches und Internationales Patentrecht*, München: C. H. Beck'sche Verlagsbuchhandlung, 4th edn.

Besen, S. M. and Raskind, L. J. (1991) 'An introduction to the law and economics of intellectual property', *Journal of Economic Perspectives*, 5: 3–27.

Bessen, J. E. (2004) 'Holdup and licensing of cumulative innovations with private infomation', *Economics Letters*, 82: 321–326.

Bessen, J. E. and Meurer, M. J. (2005) 'The patent litigation explosion', Working Paper No. 05-18, Boston University School of Law.

—— (2008) *Patent Failure: How Judges, Bureaucrats, and Lawyers Put Innovators at Risk*, Princeton, NJ: Princeton University Press.

Bhattacharya, S. and Guriev, S. (2004) 'Knowledge disclosure, patents, and optimal organization of reseach and development', Discussion Paper No. TE/04/478, Suntory and Toyota International Centers for Economics and Related Disciplines, London School of Economics and Political Sciences.

—— (2006) 'Patents vs. trade secrets: Knowledge licensing and spillover', *Journal of the European Economic Association*, 4: 1112–1147.

Binmore, K. G., Rubinstein, A. and Wolinsky, A. (1986) 'The Nash bargaining solution in economic modelling', *RAND Journal of Economics*, 17: 176–188.

Bix, B. (2000) 'Natural Law Theory: The modern tradition', in J. L. Coleman and S. Shapiro (eds) *Handbook of Jurisprudence and Legal Philosophy*, Oxford: Oxford University Press.

Blind, K., Edler, J., Nack, R. and Straus J. (2003) *Software-Patente: Eine Empirische Analyse aus Ökonomischer und Juristischer Perspektive*, Heidelberg: Physica-Verlag.

Boone, J. (2004) 'A new way to measure competition', CentER Working Paper No. 2004-31, Tilburg University.

Brodley, J. F. (1990) 'Antitrust law and innovation cooperation', *Journal of Economic Perspectives*, 4: 97–112.

Bulut, H. and Moschini, G. (2006) 'Patents, trade secrets and the correlation among R&D projects', *Economics Letters*, 91: 131–137.

Burk, D. L. and Lemley, M. A. (2003) 'Policy levers in patent law', UC Berkeley Public Law Research Paper No. 135, University of California at Berkeley, URL http://ssrn.com/abstract=431360.

—— (2005) 'Designing optimal software patents', in R. W. Hahn (ed.) *Intellectual Property Rights in Frontier Industries: Software and Biotechnology*, Washington, DC: AEI Press, 81–108.

Campbell-Kelly, M. and Valduriez, P. (2005) 'A technical critique of fifty software patents', URL http://ssrn.com/abstract=650921.

Cantner, U., Nicklisch, A. and Weiland, T. (2005) 'Innovation races: An experimental study on strategic research activities', Mimeo.

Chadha, A. (2009) 'TRIPs and patenting activity: Evidence from the Indian pharmaceutical industry', *Economic Modelling*, 26: 499–505.

Chang, H. F. (1995) 'Patent scope, antitrust policy, and cumulative innovation', *RAND Journal of Economics*, 26: 34–57.

Choi, J. P. (1991) 'Dynamic R&D competition under "hazard rate" uncertainty', *RAND Journal of Economics*, 22: 596–610.

—— (2006) 'How reasonable is the "reasonable" royalty rate? Damage rules and probabilistic intellectual property rights', CESifo Working Paper No. 1778, CESifo, URL http://ssrn.com/abstract=926037.

Claeys, E. R. (2006) 'Jefferson meets Coase: Train sparks, natural rights and law and economics', Mimeo.

Clark, J. B. (1927) *Essentials of Economic Theory As Applied to Modern Problems of Industry and Public Policy*, New York: MacMillan.

Coase, R. H. (1960) 'The problem of social costs', *Journal of Law and Economics*, 3: 1–32.

Cohen, W. N. (2004) 'Patents and appropriation: Concerns and evidence', *The Journal of Technology Transfer*, 30: 57–71.

Cohen, W. N., Nelson, R. R. and Walsh, J. P. (2000) 'Protecting their intellectual assets: Appropriability conditions and why the U.S. manufacturing firms patent (or not)', NBER Working Paper No. 7552, Cambridge, MA.

Condon, B. and Sinha, T. (2005) 'Global diseases, global patents and differential treatment in WTO law', *Northwestern Journal of International Law and Business*, 26: 1–42.

Cornelli, F. and Schankerman, M. (1999) 'Patent renewals and R&D incentives', *RAND Journal of Economics*, 30: 197–213.

Crampes, C. and Langinier, C. (2005) 'Are intellectual property rights detrimental to innovation?', Working Paper No. 05009, Iowa State University.

Creane, A. (2006) 'Socially excessive dissemination', URL http://ssrn.com/abstract=902769.

Cremer, H. and Thissé, J. F. (1991) 'Location models of horizontal differentiation: A special case of vertical differentiation models', *The Journal of Industrial Economics*, 39: 383–390.

Davis, M. H. D. (1993) *Markov Models and Optimization*, vol. 49 of *Monographs on Statistics and Applied Probability*, London: Chapman & Hall.

Deardorff, A. V. (1992) 'Welfare effects of global patent protection', *Economica*, 59: 35–51.

Demsetz, H. (1967) 'Toward a theory of property rights', *American Economic Review*, 57: 347–356.

Deng, Y. (2003) 'A dynamic stochastic analysis of international patent application and renewal processes', Mimeo.

—— (2005) 'Renewal study of European patents: A three-country comparison', Mimeo.

—— (2006) 'Trade balance of patent rights: Who gains what from international patent harmonization, and why?', Mimeo.

Denicolò, V. (1996) 'Patent races and optimal patent breadth and length', *Journal of Industrial Economics*, 44: 249–265.

Denicolò, V. and Franzoni, L. A. (2006) 'Innovation, duplication, and the contract theory of patents', URL http://ssrn.com/abstract=916094.

Drahos, P. (2003) 'Expanding intellectual property's empire: The role of FTA's', Regulatory Institutions Network, Research School of Social Sciences, Australian National University.

—— (2005) 'An alternative framework for the global regulation of intellectual property rights', Working Paper, Australian National University.

Duguet, E. and Lelarge, C. (2004) 'Does patenting increase the private incentives to innovate? A microeconomietric analysis, Mimeo'.

Dutfield, G. (2002) 'Trade, intellectual property and biogenetic resources: A guide to the international regulatory landscape', International Centre for Trade and Sustainable Development.

Eatwell, J., Milgate, M. and Newman, P. (eds) (1998) *The New Palgrave – A Dictionary of Economics*, vol. 4, London: MacMillan Press.

Ellingsen, T. and Johannesson, M. (2004) 'Is there a hold-up problem?', *Scandinavian Journal of Economics*, 106: 475–494, doi:10.1111/j.1467-9442.2004.00375.x.

Encaoua, D. and Lefouili, Y. (2006) 'Choosing intellectual protection: Imitation, patent strength and licensing', Working Paper No. 2006.39, Centre d'Economie de la Sorbonne, Université Paris 1.

Erkal, N. (2005) 'The decision to patent, cumulative innovation, and optimal policy', *International Journal of Industrial Organization*, 23: 535–562.

European Commission (2002) 'Proposal for a Directive of the European Parliament and of the Council on the patentability of computer-implemented inventions', URL http://europa.eu.int/prelex/detail_dossier_real.cfm?CL=en&DosId=172020, document: COM/2002/92/FINAL, 04.02.2004.

Falvey, R., Foster, N. and Greenaway, D. (2004) 'Intellectual property rights and economic growth', Research Paper Series: Internationalisation of Economic Policy, Research Paper 2004/12, University of Nottingham.

Ferrando Yáñez, J. A. (2003) 'Innovate AND imitate?: Dynamic innovation, patents, and costly imitation', Crest Working Papers 2003–31, Paris.

Fink, C. and Primo Braga, C. A. (2005) 'How stronger protection of intellectual property rights affect international trade flows', in C. Fink and K. E. Maskus (eds) *Intellectual Property and Development – Lessons from Recent Economic Research*, ch. 2, New York: World Bank and Oxford University Press, 19–40.

Folkeringa, M., Meijaard, J. and van Stel, A. (2005) 'Innovation, strategic renewal and its effect on small firm performance', Discussion Paper No. 3605, Max Planck Institute of Economics.

Fudenberg, D. and Tirole, J. (1993) *Game Theory*, Cambridge, MA: MIT Press.

Futagami, K. and Iwaisako, T. (2007) 'Dynamic analysis of patent policy in an endogenous growth model', *Journal of Economic Theory*, 132: 306–334.

Gabszewicz, J. J. and Thissé, J. F. (1980) 'Entry (and exit) in a differentiated industry', *Journal of Economic Theory*, 22: 327–338.

Gallini, N. T. (1992) 'Patent policy and costly imitation', *RAND Journal of Economics*, 23: 52–63.

Gallini, N. T. and Scotchmer, S. (2002) 'Intellectual property: When is the best incentive system?', in A. Jaffe, J. Lerner and S. Stern (eds) *Innovation Policy and the Economy*, vol. 2, Chicago: University of Chicago Press, 51–77.

Ghose, A. (2006) 'Information disclosure and regulatory compliance: Economic issues and research directions', URL http://ssrn.com/abstract=921770.

Gick, W. (2004) 'Little firms and big patents: The incentives to disclose competencies', Mimeo.

Gilbert, R. and Shapiro, C. (1990) 'Optimal patent length and breadth', *RAND Journal of Economics*, 21: 106–112.

Goel, R. K. (1996) 'Uncertainty, patent length and firm R&D', *Australian Economic Papers*, 35: 74–80.

Gould, D. M. and Gruben, W. C. (1996) 'The role of intellectual property rights in economic growth', *Journal of Development Economics*, 48: 323–350.

Grabowski, H. (2002) 'Patents and new product development in the pharmaceutical and biotechnology industries', Duke University, Mimeo.

Grady, M. F. and Alexander, J. I. (1992) 'Patent law and rent dissipation', *Virginia Law Review*, 78: 305–350.

Graham, S. J. H. (2002) 'Secrecy in the shadow of patenting: Firms' use of continuation patents, 1975–1994', Mimeo.

Graham, S. J. H. and Mowery, D. C. (2001) 'Intellectual property protection in the U.S. software industry', Haas School of Business Working Paper.

—— (2005) 'The use of USPTO "continuation" applications in the patenting of software: Implications for free and open source', *Law & Policy*, 27: 128–151.

Green, J. R. and Scotchmer, S. (1995) 'On the division of profit in sequential innovation', *RAND Journal of Economics*, 26: 20–33.

Grossman, G. M. and Helpman, E. (1991) *Innovation and Growth in the Global Economy*, Cambridge, MA: MIT Press.

Grossman, G. M. and Lai, E. L. C. (2002) 'International protection of intellectual property', CESifo Working Paper No. 790, CESifo, Munich.

Grupp, H. and Stadler, M. (2000) 'Technological change and market growth: An empirical assessment based on the quality ladder approach', Mimeo.

Guellec, D. and van Pottelsberghe, B. (2007) *The Economics of the European Patent System: IP Policy for Innovation and Competition*, Oxford: Oxford University Press.

Hagelin, T. (2005) 'The experimental use exemption to patent infringement: Information on ice, competition on hold', Mimeo.

Hahn, R. W. (ed.) (2005) *Intellectual Property Rights in Frontier Industries: Software and Biotechnology*, Washington, DC: AEI Press.

Hall, B. H. (2004) 'Exploring the patent explosion', Working Paper No. 291, ESRC Centre for Business Research, University of Cambridge.

Hall, B. H. and Ziedonis, R. (2001) 'The patent paradox revisited: an empirical study of patenting in the U.S. semiconductor industry, 1979–1995', *RAND Journal of Economics*, 32: 101–128.

Harhoff, D. and Reitzig, M. (2004) 'Determinants of opposition against EPO patent grants – the case of biotechnology and pharmaceuticals', *International Journal of Industrial Organization*, 22: 443–480.

Hegde, D., Movery, D. C. and Graham, S. J. (2007) 'Pionieers, submariners, or thicket-builders: Which firms use continuations in patenting?', NBER Working Paper No. 13153, Cambridge, MA.

Helpman, E. (1993) 'Innovation, imitation and intellectual property rights', *Econometrica*, 61: 1247–1280.

Hirshleifer, J. and Riley, J. G. (1992) *The Analytics of Uncertainty and Information*, Cambridge, MA: Cambridge University Press.

Horii, R. and Tatsuro, I. (2005) 'Economic growth with imperfect protection of intellectual property rights', SSRN eLibrary, URL http://ssrn.com/paper=776264.

Hotelling, H. (1929) 'Stability in competition', *Economic Journal*, 39: 41–57.

Hunt, R. M. (1999a) 'Nonobviousness and the incentive to innovate: An economic analysis of intellectual property reform', Working Paper No. 99-3, Federal Reserve Bank of Philadelphia.

—— (1999b) 'Patent reform: A mixed blessing for the U.S. economy?', Federal Reserve Bank of Philadelphia, Business Review, Philadelphia.

—— (2002) 'Patentability, industry structure, and innovation', Federal Reserve Bank of Philadelphia, Working Paper 01–13/R, Philadelphia.

—— (2004) 'Patentability, industry structure and innovation', *The Journal of Industrial Economics*, 52: 401–425.

Hussinger, K. (2004) 'Is silence golden? Patents versus secrecy at the firm level', ZEW Discussion Paper No. 04-78, Mannheim.

Jaffe, A. B. and Lerner, J. (2004) *Innovation and its Discontents*, Princeton, NJ: Princeton University Press.

Jansen, J. (2005) 'The effects of disclosure regulation of an innovative firm', CESIFO Working Paper No. 1459, CESIFO.

Kahn, A. E. (1940) 'Fundamental deficiencies of the American patent law', *American Economic Review*, 30: 475–491.

Khan, B. Z. and Sokoloff, K. L. (2001) 'History lessons: The early development of intellectual property institutions in the United States', *Journal of Economic Perspectives*, 15: 233–246.

Klemperer, P. (1990) 'How broad should the scope of patent protection be?', *RAND Journal of Economics*, 21: 113–130.

Kortum, S. and Lerner, J. (1998) 'Stronger patent protection or technological revolution: What is behind the recent surge in patenting?', *Carnegie–Rochester Conference Series on Public Policy*, 48.

Kreps, D. M. (1990) *A Course in Microeconomic Theory*, New York: Harvester Wheatsheaf.

Lanjouw, J. O. and Lerner, J. (2001) 'Tilting the table? The use of preliminary injunctions', *Journal of Law and Economics*, 44: 573–603.

Lanjouw, J. O. and Schankerman, M. (1991) 'Characteristics of patent litigation: A window on competition', *RAND Journal of Economics*, 32: 129–151.

Lee, T. and Wilde, L. L. (1980) 'Market structure and innovation: A reformulation', *Quarterly Journal of Economics*, 94: 429–436.

Lemley, M. A. (2004) 'Property, intellectual property, free riding', Working Paper No. 291, Stanford Law School, Stanford.

—— (2005a) 'Inducing patent infringement', Research Paper No. 110, Stanford Law School, Standford.

—— (2005b) 'Patenting nanotechnology', Mimeo.

Lemley, M. A. and Shapiro, C. (2006) 'Patent holdup and royalty stacking', Working Paper No. 324, Stanford Law School, Stanford, URL http://ssrn.com/abstract=923468.

Lerner, J. (1994) 'The importance of patent scope: An empirical analysis', *RAND Journal of Economics*, 25: 319–333.

—— (2002) '150 years of patent protection', *American Economic Review*, 92: 221–225.

—— (2003) 'The patent system and competition', Mimeo.

—— (2008) 'The litigation of financial innovations', NBER Working Paper No. 14324, Cambridge, MA.

Lerner, J. and Zhu, F. (2004) 'What is the impact of software patent shifts?: Evidence from Lotus v. Borland', Mimeo.

Levin, R. C., Klevorick, A. K., Nelson, R. R. *et al.* (1987) 'Appropriating the returns from industrial R&D', *Brookings Papers on Economic Activity: Microeconomics*, 3: 783–820.

Liu, K., Arthurs, J., Cullen, J. *et al.* (2008) 'Internal sequential innovations: How does interrelatedness affect patent renewal?', *Research Policy*, 37: 946–953.

Locke, J. (1824) *Two Treatises of Government*, London: C. and J. Rivington.

Loury, G. C. (1979) 'Market structure and innovation', *Quarterly Journal of Economics*, 93: 395–410.

MacGarvie, M. and Furman, J. L. (2005) 'Early academic science and the birth of industrial research laboratories in the U.S. pharmaceutical industry', NBER Working Paper No. 11470.

Machlup, F. (1958) 'An economic review of the patent system', Study of the Subcommittee on the Patents, Trademarks and Copyrights of the Committee on the Judiciary Study No. 15, United States Senate, 85th Congress, Second Session, Washington.

Mankiw, N. G. and Whinston, M. D. (1986) 'Free entry and social inefficiency', *RAND Journal of Economics*, 17: 48–58.

Mann, R. J. (2004) 'The myth of the software patent thicket: An empirical investigation of the relationship between intellectual property and innovation in software firms', Law and Economics Working Paper No. 022, The University of Texas School of Law.

Margolis, S. E. (2006) 'The profits of infringement: Richard Posner v. learned hand', URL http://ssrn.com/abstract=889342.

Martin, S. (1993) *Advanced Industrial Economics*, Oxford: Basil Blackwell, 1st edn.

—— (2002) *Advanced Industrial Economics*, Oxford: Blackwell, 2nd edn.

Mas-Colell, A., Whinston, M. D. and Green, J. R. (1995) *Microeconomic Theory*, Oxford: Oxford University Press.

Matutes, C., Regibeau, P. and Rockett, K. (1996) 'Optimal patent design and the diffusion of innovations', *RAND Journal of Economics*, 27: 60–83.

McCalman, P. (2005) 'Who enjoys "TRIPs" abroad? An empirical analysis of intellectual property rights in the Uruguay Round', *Canadian Journal of Economics*, 38: 574–603.

Menell, P. S. and Scotchmer, S. (2005) 'Intelectual property', Mimeo.

Ménière, Y. and Parlane, S. (2008) 'Innovation in the shadow of patent litigation', *Review of Industrial Organization*, 32: 95–111, doi:10.1007/s11151-008-9167-y.

Merges, R. P. (1995) 'The economic impact of intellectual property rights: An overview and guide', *Journal of Cultural Economics*, 13: 103–117.

—— (1999) 'As many as six impossible patents before breakfast: Property rights for business concepts and patent system reform', *Berkeley Technology Law Journal*, 14: 577–616.

Merges, R. P. and Nelson, R. R. (1990) 'On the complex economies of patent scope', *Columbia Law Review*, 90: 839–916.

Merges, R. P. and Duffy, J. F. (2002) *Patent Law and Policy: Cases and Materials*, Newark: LexisNexis, 3rd edn.

Merges, R. P., Menell, P. S. and Lemley, M. A. (2003) *Intellectual Property in the New Technology Age*, New York: Aspen Publishers, 3rd edn.

Merrill, S. A., Levin, R. C. and Meyers, M. B. (eds) (2004) *A Patent System for the 21st Century*, Washington, DC: The National Academies Press.

Mueller, J. M. (2005) 'The evanescent experimental use exemption from United States patent infringement liability: Implications for university and nonprofit research and development', SSRN eLibrary 691424.

Mussa, M. and Rosen, S. (1978) 'Monopoly and product quality', *Journal of Economic Theory*, 18: 301–317.

Nordhaus, W. D. (1967) 'The optimal life of a patent', Cowles Foundation Discussion Paper No. 241, Yale University.

—— (1969) *Invention, Growth, and Welfare: A Theoretical Treatment of Technical Change*, Cambridge, MA: MIT Press.

—— (1972) 'The optimal patent life: Reply', *American Economic Review*, 62: 428–431.

Oddi, S. A. (1996) 'Un-unified economic theories of patents – the not-quite-holy grail', *Notre Dame Law Review*, 71: 267–327.

O'Donoghue, T. (1998) 'A patentability requirement for sequential innovation', *RAND Journal of Economics*, 29: 654–679.

O'Donoghue, T., Scotchmer, S. and Thissé, J. F. (1998) 'Patent breadth, patent life, and the pace of technological progress', *Journal of Economics & Management Strategies*, 7: 1–32.

Pakes, A. (1986) 'Patents as options: Some estimates of the value of holding European patent stocks', *Econometrica*, 54: 755–784.

Penrose, T. E. (1951) *The Economics of the International Patent System*, vol. 30 of *John Hopkins University Studies in Historical and Political Science*, Baltimore: The John Hopkins Press.

Plant, A. (1953) *The New Commerce in Ideas and Intellectual Property*, London: Athlon Press.

Plotkin, R. (2004) 'Software patentability and practical utility: What's the use?', Mimeo.

Ramello, G. B. (2005) 'Intellectual property and the markets of ideas', *Review of Network Economics*, 4: 161–180

Regibeau, P. and Rockett, K. (2005) 'Competition, regulation, and intellectual property management in genetically modified foods: Evidence from survey data', Mimeo.

Reik, R. (1946) 'Compulsory licensing of patents', *American Economic Review*, 36: 813–832.

Reinganum, J. F. (1992) 'The timing of innovations: Research, development, and diffusion', in R. Schmalensee and R. D. Willig (eds) *Handbook of Industrial Organization*, vol. 1, ch. 14, Amsterdam: North-Holland, 849–908.

Reitzig, M. G. (2005) 'On the effectiveness of novelty and inventive step as patentability requirements – structural empirical evidence using patent indicators', Copenhagen Business School Lefic Center for Law, Economics and Financial Institutions Working Paper No. 2003-01, URL http://ssrn.com/abstract=745568.

Romer, P. M. (1990) 'Endogenous technological change', *Journal of Political Economy*, 98: S71–S103.

Ross, S. M. (1992) *Applied Probability Models with Optimization Applications*, New York: Dover Publications.

Roth, A. E. (1979) *Axiomatic Models of Bargaining*, vol. 170 of *Lecture Notes in Economics and Mathematical Systems*, Berlin: Springer-Verlag.

Rowe, E. (2005) 'The experimental use exception to patent infringement: Do universities deserve special treatment?', URL http://ssrn.com/abstract=791664.

Saint-Paul, G. (2004) 'To what extent should less developed countries enforce intellectual property?', CEPR Working Paper No. 4713.

Schankerman, M. (1998) 'How valuable is patent protection? – Estimates by technology field', *RAND Journal of Economics*, 29: 77–107.

Schankerman, M. and Pakes, A. (1986) 'Estimates of the value of patent rights in European countries during the post-1950 period', *Economic Journal*, 96: 1052–1076.

Schankerman, M. and Scotchmer, S. (2001) 'Damages and injunctions in protecting intellectual property', *RAND Journal of Economics*, 32: 199–220.

Scherer, F. M. (1972) 'Nordhaus' theory of optimal patent life: A geometric reinterpretation', *American Economic Review*, 62: 422–428.

Scotchmer, S. (1991) 'Standing on the shoulders of giants: Cumulative research and the patent law', *Journal of Political Economy*, 5: 29–41.

—— (1996) 'Protecting early innovators: Should second-generation products be patentable?', *RAND Journal of Economics*, 27: 322–331.

—— (1999) 'On the optimality of the patent renewal system', *RAND Journal of Economics*, 30: 181–196.

—— (2001) 'The political economy of intellectual property treaties', NBER Working Paper No. 9114.

—— (2004) *Innovation and Incentives*, Cambridge, MA: MIT Press, 1st edn.

Scotchmer, S. and Green, J. (1990) 'Novelty and disclosure in patent law', *RAND Journal of Economics*, 21: 131–146.

Serrano, C. J. (2008) 'The dynamics of the transfer and the renewal of patents', NBER Working Paper No. 13938, Cambridge, MA.

Shaked, A. and Sutton, J. (1983) 'Natural oligopolies', *Econometrica*, 51: 1469–1483.

Shapiro, C. (2001) 'Navigating the patent thicket: Cross licenses, patent pools, and standard setting', in A. Jaffe, J. Lerner and S. Stern (eds) *Innovation Policy and the Economy*, vol. 1, Cambridge, MA: MIT-Press, 119–150.

Siebert, R. and von Graevenitz, G. (2006) 'How licensing resolves hold-up: Evidence from a dynamic panel data model with unobserved heterogeneity', CEPR Working Paper No. 5436, URL http://www.cepr.org/pubs/dps/DP5436.asp.

Sutton, J. (1991) *Sunk Costs and Market Structure: Price Competition, Advertising, and the Evolution of Concentration*, Cambridge, MA: MIT Press.

Tirole, J. (1993) *The Theory of Industrial Organization*, Cambridge, MA: MIT Press, 6th edn.

Trajtenberg, M. (1990) 'A penny for your quotes: Patent citations and the value of innovations', *RAND Journal of Economics*, 21: 172–187.

Trilateral Patent Offices (2006) *Trilateral Statistical Report 2005*, United States Patent and Trademark Office (USPTO), European Patent Office (EPO), Japanese Patent Office (JPO).

Vaidhyanathan, S. (2005) 'Nanotechnology and law of patents: A collision course', Mimeo.

Vaughan, F. L. (1948) 'Patent policy', *American Economic Review*, 38: 215–234.

Vives, X. (2000) *Oligopoly Pricing – Old Ideas And New Tools*, Cambridge, MA: MIT Press.

Wagner, S. (2004) 'Business method patents in Europe and their strategic use – evidence from franking device manufacturers', Mimeo.

Weizsäcker, C. C. v. (1980) *Barriers to Entry: A Theoretical Treatment*, vol. 185 of *Lecture Notes in Economics and Mathematical Systems*, Berlin et al.: Springer Verlag.

Wijen, F. and Duysters, G. (2005) 'Negotiating innovation: Product renewal as the outcome of a complex bargaining process', *R&D Management*, 35: 73–87.

World Intellectual Property Organization (1972) 'Records of the Washington Diplomatic Conference on the Patent Cooperation Treaty', URL http://www.wipo.int/pct/en/texts/washington.html.

World Trade Organization (1994) 'Uruguay Round Agreements, Annex 1C: Trade-Related Aspects of Intellectual Property Rights (TRIPs)', URL http://www.wto.org/english/docs_e/legal_e/27-trips_01_e.htm.

Wright, B. D. (1983) 'The economics of invention incentives: Patents, prizes and research contracts', *American Economic Review*, 73: 691–707.

Yu, P. K. (2003) 'Trips and its discontents', Legal Studies Research Paper Series, Research Paper No. 03-03, Michigan State University.

Index